The
Epicurean
Gardener

Also by John F. Adams

Two Plus Two Equals Minus Seven
An Essay on Brewing
Beekeeping—The Gentle Craft
Backyard Poultry Raising
Guerilla Gardening

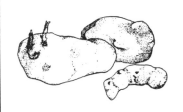

The
Epicurean
Gardener

John F. Adams

Illustrations by
Stephanie Adams

E. P. DUTTON ✺ NEW YORK

Published in the United States by E. P. Dutton,
a division of NAL Penguin Inc.,
2 Park Avenue, New York, N.Y. 10016.

Published simultaneously in Canada by
Fitzhenry and Whiteside, Limited, Toronto.

Library of Congress Cataloging-in-Publication Data
Adams, John Festus, 1930–
The epicurean gardener.
1. Vegetable gardening. 2. Fruit-culture. I. Adams,
Stephanie. II. Title.
SB321.A33   1988   635   87-9186
ISBN: 0-525-24597-9

COBE

DESIGNED BY MARK O'CONNOR

10 9 8 7 6 5 4 3 2 1

First Edition

To the testing crew
Erika, Stephanie, Susan, and Emily
A group of lovely and dedicated professionals

Contents

The
Epicurean
Gardener

The Epicurean Gardener

The fruits of epicurean gardening

My experience in reading about gardening suggests that as happy as they might have been in their backyards and fields, as soon as they sit down to write, most gardeners don a black frock coat and shovel hat and turn into frenetic Puritans. They don't instruct, they exhort; they don't tell, they preach. They begin to hate pleasure, they detest fun; they seem only to love to prohibit and to command.

Like too many instructional books, those on gardening make the subject sound difficult, laborious, and costly. Even the most well intentioned (or, perhaps, *especially* the well intentioned) become self-fulfilling prophecies of failure. Books on gardening frequently take themselves and their subject with equal seriousness, with a tone of at worst pompous, at best tiresome earnestness. In my reveries I call this

I

approach "jackboot gardening." We are never told to cut something without the astringent caution—"With a very sharp knife!" A directive like that makes me want to choose a knife I've been using to scrape rust from old bolts, or to hack the object to pieces with a screwdriver. In the privacy of my own garden I will damn well do as I please, allowing no one to intrude on my own attitudes and mind-sets. I expect everyone to do likewise, if they are worth a cup full of horse manure.

There are, by at least one estimate, some ninety million gardeners in America. An even 100 percent of these people must eat some garden truck with some degree of pleasure. And 100 percent of those who might decide to begin growing a garden are doing so at least in some measure because they anticipate eating some of their produce with some degree of pleasure. There also must be something close to 100 percent agreement that things a gardener grows are better than what he or she might buy. Therefore it should be possible to conclude that in every gardener there is a spirit at least in some degree in harmony with the spirit of the Roman philosopher Epicurus. He promoted the idea that men should adjust their lives to be guided by the pleasure principle; he was not a hedonist, he preferred pleasure but extolled moderation. Every gardener should be an Epicurean: pursuing the principles of pleasure, but enjoying pleasure in moderation.

Epicurean gardeners are distinct from gourmet gardeners in that the Epicurean enjoys all elements of the practice; the gourmet's concern is directed exclusively to gastronomic pleasures. In fact even the idea of gourmet gardening is frequently dulled and perverted. In too many things I have read on the topic, "gourmet" comes to mean garden products that are only marginally edible, items passed over—"overlooked," say the apologists—by those with uncultivated palates. We are assured that such items as pigweed and lamb's-quarter are "delicious." From childhood we know by experience when someone tells us something is delicious that we are being lied to. No one sweet-talks children by saying how delicious something is unless they are trying to sell them a bill of goods. Children know when they are being talked down to, and so should adults. When someone tells us earnestly how delicious something is, we know we are being talked down to, and we know we are being lied to. When someone tells us earnestly about how to garden, we are justified in suspecting we are also being lied to. We are also justified in suspecting that someone is trying to take the fun out of gardening.

Gardening is not difficult and is about the last thing one should be earnest about. It is not especially laborious and need not be expensive. That things grow from seeds planted in the ground is the most natural and normal thing I've ever heard of. One does not happen to "find" a flourishing vegetable garden, certainly, but then neither is it created through the application of earnest truths. When gardening, reading about gardening, or thinking about gardening, remember (to rearrange a theological platitude) that the garden was made for the gardener, not the gardener for the garden.

Consider these instructions for planting horseradish:

> In planting, make furrows 3 to 5 inches deep. Plant the cuttings with the tops all in one direction in the row, dropping a cutting every 24 inches. As the cutting is dropped, draw a little soil over the lower end of it with your foot and tamp firmly. After all cuttings are dropped, they are covered with soil to slightly above ground level (to allow for soil settling), being sure that the soil is firmly in contact with the cutting.
> *Gardening for Food and Fun. The Yearbook of Agriculture.* 1977 U.S. Department of Agriculture, p. 243.

What this means is, "Plant cuttings 3 to 5 inches deep, 24 inches apart." So awkwardly is it written with its shift in tense and vacillation in person that I had to read it several times to figure that much out. With this much information—if you need this much—you can grow horseradish until its cultivation is prohibited by some other agency of the U.S. Government. Actually this Department of Agriculture publication uses an additional three pages to discuss the proper home garden cultivation of this pungent condiment.

Clearly the expert assigned to do this segment of the *Yearbook* felt he or she had some information to pass on and a certain amount of space to use up. To use up space the author began to become a little stern and uncompromisingly exact in the information, implying a kind of superiority in the exactness and a false importance to the significance of the instruction. I have seen no recorded instance where a planting of horseradish has failed. I think if you were merely to pronounce the word *horseradish* with a clear intonation above a spot of soil, horseradish would germinate there spontaneously in a few days. What this horticultural bureaucrat should have done to fill the space, of course, was to tell a couple of interesting stories about the history of horseradish and its cultivation—magical properties attributed to it, what cultures consider it an aphrodisiac, and one or two particularly brutal murders committed with it. With that information the space would have been read gladly, with no less instruction or decreased likelihood of success.

Gardening is sometimes a kind of happy accident. Skill and experience help, but natural forces, some of them pretty mysterious, are doing the work. The gardener is a useful adjunct of nature, but ultimately the gardener is only a manipulator, and a manipulator with severe limitations. If a nice garden is a happy accident, it is an accident that seems to happen with agreeable frequency even to those who are mostly innocent of esoteric gardening skills.

Certainly gardeners improve with experience. I'm a better gardener now than when I was a small boy. I no longer plant corn rows nine inches apart as I did the first time I tried, or cabbages in a solid, unthinned row, or twenty hills of summer squash. Nor do I plant date pits, just in hope. I should admit that the most significant difference may be that I now use a string to make my rows 100 percent straight and official.

Gardening is an absorbing and fulfilling pastime, which has its practical side, but it is not an exact science, if it's a science at all. In the privacy of my own imaginings, I have separated those who garden into two classifications: those who are reflective gardeners and those who are nonreflective gardeners. These terms, if not the categories themselves, provide a limited way of isolating the attraction gardening holds for different people, as well as classifying certain things that have been written about gardening.

Reflective writers on gardening include Sir Thomas Browne, Virgil, and the authors of the Old Testament. These are people who take the essence of gardening more seriously than the substance. They are the true Epicureans of gardening. Nonreflective writers, on the other hand, often fail to consider it as a pastime significantly different from mass gymnastics, and if you're not crazy about participating in mass gymnastics, you'll never take pleasure in working their way. Such writers concentrate on gardening as a technical dedication and take for granted that any reader will approach the employment with the zeal and commitment of a member of the state gymnastic team of an Eastern Bloc nation.

The reflective gardener considers the pastime essentially an end in itself; for the nonreflective, it becomes something of a moral vocation, justified because it is good for you. Become immediately suspicious of gardening information in which use of the words *nourishing, wholesome, nutritious,* and *economical* become conspicuous. There are many kinds and degrees of both categories of gardeners. There are those nonreflectives who consider no vegetable fit to be claimed that is not so large that it must be hoisted by cables and dressed out like the carcass of a beast. And there are those reflective gardeners who become so absorbed in the employment as an end in itself that they forget what they started out to do and do nothing at all—like the cat who starts out to scratch himself, then stares contemplatively into space because he has forgotten why he has elevated his leg.

Sir Thomas Browne, who must be considered among the most reflective gardeners of all times, became totally absorbed with the aesthetics and mystical significance of the physical arrangement of the trees in his orchard. He was moved to rapture by the significance of planting in groupings of five, the mystical quincunx. Hardly less reflective, Virgil instructed his slave how and when to cultivate and reflected while the slave worked. The Scriptures tell us how the transgression of Adam, who in his unfallen state tilled Eden with pure absorbed pleasure, turned gardening into a chore. Perhaps from his fall we can date the beginnings of nonreflective gardening. If it is to be accomplished by the sweat on one's brow, some practitioners imply, one better sweat plenty.

There is certainly a large class of people to whom gardening does not appeal at all. I suspect that gardening, especially reflective gardening, mostly appeals to people who better fit on the scale of social evolution somewhere between the hunter/gatherer and the industrial/technological. This is a kind of character or personality who can handle materials very well in the form in which they are found but has no competence at all in handling materials in ways that require changing their material form. This personality can cunningly shape a bent piece of wood into a hoe, for example, but could never modify the form of metal—even with a mountain of it—to make a tractor. This is the person who carves wood or shapes words, but cannot understand what "soil pH" means.

Of the reflective gardeners in history, probably none was more a purist or more hostile to technological gardening than the seventeenth-century poet Andrew Marvell. Doggedly adhering to the purest definition of naturalism, he rejected even the sophistication of organic gardening (the only technological gardening there was in his day). In his pastoral poem, "The Mower Against Gardens," his Mower complains about modern gardeners preparing soil for their plants:

> *For them a richer earth did kneed,*
> *Which stupefied them as it fed.*

But Marvell reserved his severest censure for those breeding new varieties of plants and grafting improved strains upon native stock. In this way, he complains, modern scientific gardening has bastardized the natural world.

Perhaps Marvell overstated the case for reflective gardeners, but most who have made the comparison would concede that garden strawberries are not as sweet and luscious as the small wild strawberries. In all fairness, it must likewise be conceded that without modern genetics, tomatoes would not exist; the same is essentially true of the modern potato. But were it not for the accidental bastardizing of two wild grasses in the not too distant past, even wheat would not exist. The distinction between what is natural and what is technical can ultimately be no useful distinction at all.

This is not a book on organic gardening, and it avoids technological approaches to gardening. In my own practice I try to be as "natural" as possible, and in this way generally follow the practices advocated as "organic gardening," but I stop short of making "the natural" an end in itself, or allowing the method to become a fetish. I have been a reasonably close observer of nature all my life and think it is true that there are no fetishes in nature, and I will even postulate that "Nature abhors a fetish."

The natural world, particularly the vegetative world, proceeds by its own laws. But nothing is more pragmatic than nature. That is the whole principle behind natural selection. Nature uses what it finds, and uses it in the most efficient way possible. I have seen luxurious ferns growing deep in caves where nothing was ever intended to grow— taking advantage of the illumination provided by spotlights provided for the convenience of human visitors. Nature takes advantage of windfalls, even unnatural ones. The chance observation that in and near certain mine tailings the vegetation grew lushly led turning mine wastes into an industry manufacturing chemical fertilizers. It is hard to see a significant difference between this application of mineral fertilizer and nature's exploitation of the windfall mineral fertilizer from volcanoes.

Perhaps the most any gardener can add to horticulture is the attempt to engineer a few happy windfalls. One thing is certain: Nature uses the gardener as a fortuitous accident that widely and providently enlarges the survival and accelerates the distribution of species, as much as farmer ants are used and exploited by the fungus they cultivate.

I would not quarrel with the system of organic gardening, only with making a fetish of the practice. I concur with all but its most doctrinaire principles but stop a comfortable and safe distance away from considering the practice and those who adhere to it transcendent or favored by a higher power. Of course, a gardener should think of the soil as a crop, even as the most important crop. And, like organic gardeners, I consider indiscriminate use of pesticides and herbicides madness. But within the context of organic gardening, those writing on such subjects can be downright wrongheaded. In one such work discussing pesticides I found that the writer gave an almost audible gulp of embarrassment when conceding that in difficult cases it is permissible, but only barely, to use rotenone. This is a common vegetable-based insecticide, completely organic, harmless to mammals, and quickly biodegradable. In such a case, and this is not an exceptional one, the motivation seems to be to prohibit pesticide, not to be organic. This sort of thinking is symptomatic of fanaticism.

Therefore, I urge the use of all organic material possible in building up soil, but see no reason to scruple at using commercial fertilizer at the same time—that hated word, *chemical* fertilizer. Logic tells me that a nitrogen atom is a nitrogen atom whether it has been fixed from the air by bacteria associated with a legume, or fixed from the air by industry, or processed from stone. And phosphorus is phosphorus, and calcium is calcium, and sulfur is sulfur.

Someone starting a first garden does not need to be told that there's one way to do it, and that way a trying and often laborious way involving both spirit and body. The new gardener needs to be told some basic things about taking a piece of ground and being assured that one can actually make something grow there. When you get down to cases, for every vegetable that is practical to grow that proves to be temperamental, there must be a dozen equally practical vegetables that are not fussy at all. Remember, it is the nature of plants to want to grow if they possibly can.

When I made my first garden, at about age eight, no one told me how to do it, and I didn't think to ask. I was a farm boy, and I knew you put seed in the ground when spring felt so good you couldn't help yourself, couldn't do anything but put seeds in the ground. And that you weeded a bit, and you watered, and things grew. They did, and they will.

Looking back, I can see that the questions I should have asked would have been how far apart to have your corn rows and your cabbage plants, how many squash to plant, and could dates grow from seeds. I was not sophisticated enough to ask how to have early lettuce, and how to prolong the lettuce supply through the summer. At that age I didn't like lettuce anyway, but I did like tomatoes and melons, and I got them, and it wasn't many seasons before I figured how to get them early and good.

Basically, that's what this book is about. It assumes that you want to grow things, and at this stage you want to fuss around about it as little as possible, and want the best possible stuff for your efforts. Many duffer gardeners live a happy life, never going much beyond the expertise of an eight year old. If you asked one of these duffer gardeners if it were difficult to grow things, the reply might be, "What an odd question!"

Growing a garden does take a little time—about as much as you've a mind to give it. Fortunately, the most time-consuming period is in the spring, when the urge to work in the ground is at its highest peak, when it becomes almost a compulsion. In fact, with a small garden one is apt to feel frustrated that there is not enough to do to work off all the need to work. As the garden grows, it will take some weeding and other attentions. But, if as the season progresses, you don't feel like weeding at the rate required to keep your garden totally weed-free and immaculate, remind yourself that there's no king's law that says a garden has to be totally weed-free. In fact, I think there's a certain charm in a garden that is a little bit deshabille. If rain doesn't take care of your moisture needs, watering will be required, which can take a little time. And it takes a little time to pick what has grown, the time depending on how much you have grown and what you intend to do with it.

Here's a good time to insert a bit of moral advice. Gardeners frequently end up carrying a heavy burden of guilt about failing to use or account for absolutely everything grown in a positive way. Note carefully, for this has probably never been said: If the urge strikes you, feel perfectly free to waste; waste in good conscience; flaunt the lectures you received as a child on eating everything on your plate, being frugal with your money, thinking of those less fortunate, being temperate and moderate in all things. If you can't use it or are tired of it or don't want to fool with it, forget about it.

My wife was long uneasy about my gardens, feeling that I was tacitly saying, "I grew it, you use it—all." It took many gardens to get her over her guilt feelings and to convince her that I really meant what I said. The reason I grow dozens of tomato plants is to be sure I can select two or three a day that I consider perfect to eat while sitting in the shade. I give many away, of course, and some even end up in jars, but I do not consider it a reproach to see tomatoes unused and spoiled. This understanding has been a revelation for her and has eased our relationship where gardens are concerned considerably. If I want canned things, I can them myself; I certainly don't expect someone else to do it for me.

Whether or not a garden is of financial advantage can be debatable. If you don't get hung up on equipment, materials, and so forth, most likely it will save money. If it's large enough, and you've a mind to preserve surplus, it will save more. However, distrust people who suggest that a garden will save enough to change your life-style.

A garden will improve your eating style, however, even if you garden only in a small way. The most appealing fruits and vegetables seen in produce markets were developed and grown for the twin purposes of shipping well and looking good long after they had any right to look other than rotten. Almost categorically, anything you grow yourself and eat garden-fresh will be better; not a little better, but *much* better. A fresh-picked, "garden variety" tomato has a different taste altogether than one developed and grown exclusively for its shipping quality and appearance. Sweet corn is so perishable that it is almost a dishonesty to ship it, and the same is also true of green beans and fresh peas. Even the lowly potato, freshly dug, suddenly has a flavor, a distinct, unique, and subtle earthiness, suggestive of native mushrooms or the mysterious wild. My wife says there is something erotic in their earthiness. I always grow lots.

The majority of gardeners, even experienced ones, are limited by the tyranny of the produce markets in the varieties they grow. For the most part, plant varieties available to the gardener are the same as those used by commercial growers. This is partly a matter of convenience but also a matter of recognition and familiarity.

People tend to grow varieties that look like the varieties they see in the stores. These may be indifferent varieties, they may even be very good. But with a small-scale operation, zero transportation problems, and freedom from the imperative of heavy yields, it is possible for the gardener to grow varieties seldom or never seen in commercial outlets. Such varieties are not commonly available commercially; some because they do not ship well, some for cosmetic reasons, and some simply because they lack recognition. Most superior varieties, however, are no more difficult to grow than those picked off the seed racks.

If you are gardening for pleasure, on whatever scale, you might just as well grow varieties that give the greatest pleasure in eating. Therefore, in discussing each species, as far as I can I will indicate cultivars that are considered the best varieties for eating. I have not grown every variety of every vegetable, and never will. I have grown a lot, and as far as possible I will evaluate each from my own experience. I do mention varieties I have never grown and must rely sometimes on the experience of others, sometimes on catalogue descriptions, to characterize or evaluate these. I will occasionally offer suggestions about preparation or use of these varieties.

Many, even most of these exceptional varieties are not to be found in the seed racks or supermarkets or in commonly distributed mass market seed catalogues. Therefore, to help locate seeds or plant stock, for each discussed that is at all difficult to locate I have given the name of a seed house or nursery where it may be obtained (except for those rare few which I have heard praised but have never located). The names of these nurseries are in italic type in the text and their addresses and offerings are found in the appendix at the end of this book.

For some vegetables, such as tomatoes and corn, there are strains which are clearly superior, but acquaintance with these varieties is for the most part reasonably widespread. Also, the performance of such vegetables is often tied closely to climate and soil conditions. Even though these cultivars are not familiar to the produce markets, seed is commonly available through the popular seed catalogues. Therefore I have not emphasized varieties for these vegetables, although I do mention some.

Few things have the reputation of being as morally uplifting and physically healthy as gardening, but my advice is to do it frankly for pleasure. To paraphrase Chaucer, in every aspect approach it like you were a true son of Epicurus.

Green Things

Lobjoits Green Cos lettuce

Organized gastronomically, greens come in two kinds: those which are cooked and those which are eaten uncooked, with some overlapping. There is enough of the little boy in me still that I do not enjoy many cooked greens, but I do grow them for the palate of others, as well as because many of them are pretty. For me the royalty of greens is lettuce—freshly gathered lettuce.

Lettuce can be grown almost anywhere in the country, but is a particular joy to northern gardeners, because it likes cool weather. There are numerous varieties of lettuce, and a gardener new to local conditions might well inquire what does best in the area. Still, lettuce is so adaptable and can be used during such a large part of its life that few varieties will result in a total washout. Three main forms of lettuce are cultivated: head, semi-head, and leaf.

The most versatile and most useful over the longest period is head lettuce. There are gardeners who shun head lettuce because it "bolts," grows a seed stalk, when summer weather really turns hot, sometimes bolting without going to head at all. But head lettuce is usable continually from as soon as the leaves are big enough to pick up until the mature head is picked or the plant bolts. Even in its most immature stage, many people prefer the flavor, texture, and appearance of head lettuce to the more rapidly growing leaf lettuce. Many gardeners fail to appreciate how tolerant it is of cool weather, and do not plant it early enough. The seed will germinate in very cool soil, and contrariwise, will refuse to sprout when the soil temperature stays above 80 degrees.

In some areas of the north, and most areas of the south, lettuce may be planted in the fall or late summer and treated as a winter annual. Under a light straw mulch scattered for protection after the first frosts, fall-germinated lettuce can tolerate a fairly tough winter. Even with no protection at all the hardiest varieties can make it through a rough winter, if the plants are not too large. The little green plants will be there waiting to take off as soon as the snow melts.

Spring-seeded lettuce should be planted as early as the soil may be worked or even earlier. It prefers soil that has been newly tilled and smoothed, but really is not fussy if offered more untidy options such as doing nothing at all. Make a shallow trench (no more than an inch), and sow the seeds sparingly. Lettuce has a good track record for germination and will almost surely later need to be thinned. Cover the seeds with a sprinkling of soil, tamping it lightly on top of the trench. I regularly plant lettuce in late winter by sprinkling seed on the top of snow, with no preparation at all. If it is not used up by late spring, other lettuce should be coming along to take its place. There is no essential difference in the handling of any of the varieties. Soil moisture and rain is normally adequate to assure germination of early plantings. Remember that lettuce is succulent and likes lots of water, and should never be allowed to become even moderately dry.

Lettuce should be thinned when the plants are about an inch tall.

For head lettuce a good rule of thumb is that the plants should never be allowed to touch. Once assured that there is an adequate stand, I thin them first to about 4 inches, and later, for head lettuce, to about 14 inches. Unless they have planted an enormous amount of lettuce, most people count on using the thinnings in whatever ways lettuce is used up until the heads mature (hence thinning in two stages). But when growth becomes very rapid, it will most likely be necessary to thin them to their proper spacing even though the displaced seedlings cannot all be used. They must be sacrificed to a greater cause. Some people transplant the discards, which works well enough usually, if there is additional space to spare.

Distanced about 14 inches apart, the lettuce should begin to mature in June, although the timing varies greatly according to climate. For real prize-winning-sized heads, space the plants further apart, 18 to 20 inches. When the weather begins to become hot, the heads or forming heads will bolt—twist apart—while a coarse stalk separates itself from among the leaves. It will eventually flower and bear seeds if not removed. Varieties are offered for sale that are more tolerant of heat and which somewhat resist bolting. Lettuce from seed that has germinated in cold soil is said to bolt more quickly with the onset of hot weather than that germinated in warmer soil. Therefore lettuce grown from transplants germinated indoors might provide a marginal advantage. Since many gardeners make successive plantings of lettuce throughout the entire growing season, any advantage might be academic.

Romaine, or Cos, lettuce is characterized as a semi-heading variety. Its leaves cling tightly together, but remain upright and parallel rather than interfolded, growing in a neat bundle to a height of 12 or 14 inches, perhaps 5 or more inches in diameter. The leaves are dark green and their flavor and texture is excellent, crunchy rather than crisp. Romaine is particularly desirable in salads that need "structure," with leaves strong and resilient enough to bear the weight of crab, and so forth. Unaccountably, many gardeners overlook Romaine, or consider it too difficult or even poorer quality than other lettuces. It requires no especially different treatment from other head lettuce, actually being a bit more tolerant of crowding. Crowded together it will still head, but will not produce the produce market-style of head unless given at least 6 inches or more between plants. Like head lettuce, the young plants removed in thinning are desirable for all of the uses to which lettuce is put. Romaine is slightly more resistant to bolting than other head lettuce, but still will not tolerate really hot weather.

One use for tender young lettuce, especially the thinnings that suddenly appear in such abundance, and that deserves to be more widely used, is as wilted lettuce. This mode of preparation is more common in the Southern states and in ethnic cookery, especially German and Dutch. The preparation is quick and simple. Heat in a frying pan three tablespoons of bacon drippings. Drop in handsful of tender lettuce leaves, turning and stirring rapidly until they are dashed with the bacon drippings and wilted. They may be dressed with vinegar or lemon juice and garnished with bacon bits. Until late in the nineteenth century, lettuce was seldom eaten in America without being cooked.

Some varieties of semi-heading lettuce are particularly adaptable to hot weather. For use specifically during the summer months, they should be planted about the first of June in northern climates, earlier where the spring weather is milder. For late summer and fall use, plant in July and August. Most varieties are suitable for late planting, if it is understood that in northern areas head lettuce is unlikely to head fully, but is still of good quality used as a leaf lettuce. In warmer locations, late lettuce forms heads perfectly. The semi-heading lettuce is particularly satisfactory for late crops. Many of them may "head" quite normally in early September or even October, given tolerable weather conditions.

The limestone varieties are particularly favored for late plantings. These varieties form a kind of rosette that grows more or less closely to the ground. Varieties include Bibb and Oak Leaf. Their texture is crunchy and their flavor somewhat buttery. Most are somewhat resistant to bolting. Cultivation is identical to that for other lettuce. Bibb lettuce is widely grown in England as a winter annual, made to produce all winter in the mild southern parts of the country. Using seeds that I got in England and continue to propagate myself, I keep plants alive twelve months of the year in a USDA-designated Zone

5 area, although of course I do not get a harvest during the winter months.

Another trick for late lettuce is to broadcast seeds thinly around large leaved vining or bush cucurbits, such as squash and pumpkin, in early August. As the leaves of the cucurbits grow they provide continuous shade and help conserve moisture. The lettuce seedlings will do remarkably well under these seemingly difficult conditions and will not be troubled even by the intense heat of late summer, providing the cover plants are kept sufficiently moist. Small lettuces may be harvested from late August on. After the first frost, when the cucurbits' vines are burned down, you will discover a wealth of well-grown, well-rooted plants, which will grow happily in the mellowness of Indian summer and produce until stern weather finally withers them down. Or, as usually happens with me, deer graze them off.

Leaf lettuce has several advantages over head and semi-head lettuce. Its chief advantage is rapid growth. Like the other lettuces, it can be planted in earliest spring and will outstrip the other lettuces two to one (it is the variety I seed on top of snow). Since it matures without heading, and is at its best somewhat young, it can be in plentiful supply as early as April. It grows quickly and reaches its peak quickly, but passes it quickly as well. The leaves are thinner and less succulent than even immature head or Romaine lettuce and do not make nearly as full-bodied a salad. Its appearance is good, and there are varieties developed for scalloped and folded edges as well as blendings of color in the leaves. Even though leaf lettuce is early, it is not long before the thinnings of early-planted head or semi-head lettuce will compete with and then replace it as far as most people are concerned.

Culture of all lettuce is about the same. Leaf lettuce, however, is not as fussy about being thinned. For largest growth and the most showy bunches, thin it to 4 to 6 inches. Since many gardeners consider it to be a short-term substitute for other varieties, they never thin it at all.

European varieties of lettuce are superior enough to the commonly available commercial varieties to be worth seeking out. The best variety of Romaine I have grown is Lobjoits Green (Britain: *Urban Farmer*). The heads are longer and fuller, and the leaves are more fleshy

and crunchy than the commercially available American variety. A Cos
variety called Little Gem Sucrine (France: *The Urban Farmer*) is in
color, texture, and flavor more like a butter head than a regular Cos.
It is also much shorter (6 or 8 inches), more slender, has a head more
tightly compacted, and is pale rather than dark green in color. Its rich
buttery flavor is a nice complement to the brisk flavor of head or
Romaine. Another superior head lettuce is *Tête de Glace* (Belgium:
Epicure Seeds). Although it is classed as a butterhead, its general appearance is more similar to traditional head lettuce. It has thick "meaty"
leaves, a somewhat lighter green than standard American varieties, and
a flavor superior to any head lettuce I have had. The flavor is full and
distinctive. It also seems to retain the quality of its head better and resist
bolting better than common varieties.

The most beautiful lettuce I grow is the *Merveille des Quatre
Saisons* (France: *Urban Farmer*). The leaves are pink in the center,
with a deep edge of ruby or cranberry red. In general appearance it
resembles red leaf lettuce, but the hues are more vivid and more
striking. It forms medium-sized heads, with the leaves loose rather
than densely packed and convoluted. It is quite slow to bolt, hence,
I assume, its ironic name. When young leaves are harvested before it
begins to head, or before it has headed fully, the underside of the rib
is prickly, and the lower portion of this rib must be cut away. This
is no particular problem and does not occur within the head. It does
not have an exceptional or distinctive flavor, but its color makes a
beautiful addition to a salad, especially when contrasted with such
less colorful varieties as *Tête de Glace*. This lettuce has become more
widely recognized in this country recently, probably because it has
been featured on the popular PBS program "Victory Garden." It is
becoming generally available, usually with the name listed as *Merveille des 4 seasons*.

Corn Salad, also known as lamb's lettuce, fetticus, and rapunzel,
is popular in Europe but less well known in America. It has a flavor
sometimes described as nutty. I use it as one ingredient in salads rather
than as a solo feature, as it apparently often is in Europe. It may be
planted in early spring, like lettuce, or in late summer, to overwinter.
It is quite hardy. Harvest it a few leaves at a time rather than pulling

up the entire plant. Generic seed is fairly widely available. A named variety, Large Seeded Dutch, is offered by *Nichols Garden Nursery*. The leaves are large, and it is said to be popular in northern Europe. Blonde Shell Leaved Corn Salad is offered by the same nursery, and is said to be the most popular variety in France.

Tyfon, or Tyfon Holland Greens, is a recently developed salad green, produced as a cross between turnips and Chinese cabbage. It can be used fresh or cooked. Plant early and harvest a few leaves at a time all summer. The seed is offered fairly commonly, but I have not yet grown it.

Endive, which is sometimes known as escarole, much resembles lettuce. The leaves are tightly curled, often covering a snowy white center. A bunch of endive leaves makes a showy bed for a salad. Most varieties have a flavor that varies from slightly to distinctly bitter. Some people quite like it, some don't. Light frost makes it milder and improves its flavor. It may be grown as lettuce is, although its growing season is much longer. Plant in the early spring for a fall harvest. *Territorial Seed Company* offers a variety called Wivol, which produces a white, mild center. The same company also offers President, which is tolerant of cold and wet weather. It may be blanched, which is preferred by some to reduce the bitterness. Some people dig in the fall and reset the roots in moist sand or peat, keeping it in a dark basement until used.

However, chicory, also known as French or Belgium endive is more often grown as a forcing green. The blanching varieties are also known as Witloof, that is, white leaf—chicory—or plain Witloof. Chicory is better known in Europe than in America. For winter forcing it is dug in the late fall and planted, roots and all, in boxes of wet sand or peat. Kept in a warm, dark place and provided with adequate moisture, it will produce white shoots of tightly folded leaves. These "chicons," as they are called, are used in salads. Seed is planted in early spring, and the growing plants treated much like lettuce. Mitodo chicory, from Germany, is said to be the easiest of the forcing chicories to grow. Crystal Hat chicory is a nonforcing variety, grown and used like lettuce, which it much resembles. Both varieties are available from *Nichols Garden Nursery*.

Radicchio is a red variety of chicory. It may be grown for

forcing or, in mild climates, may be overwintered in the fields, if provided with a protective mulch. Cold weather is required to develop flavor and color. Its flavor is said to be bittersweet, although I have never grown nor eaten it. *Nichols Garden Nursery* offers an Italian variety, Red Treviso, with leaves that turn from green in summer to a brilliant red and white variegated color when cool weather sets in. The same nursery also offers a French variety, *Rouge de Verone,* which is planted in mid to late summer for fall and winter crops. If the leaves are cut back in the spring, the plant will produce several small, tight heads, which are used in salads and are reputed to be a treat for gourmets.

Sorrel is a European weed which is grown as a green. Wild Sheep sorrel is characterized by a sour flavor which some like and some don't. An improved variety, called French sorrel, is offered by *Territorial Seed Company.* Plant in May or June for fall and spring harvest. It is quite hardy, and effective as a perennial. Pick a few leaves at a time, and the plant will continue producing indefinitely.

There is a large selection of uncommon green vegetables used in Oriental cooking, most of which I have never tried. *Nichols Garden Nursery* offers such varieties as Edible Chrysanthemum—*Shungiku Mizuna*—which is said to put up a great quantity of beautiful, slender leaves with white stems; and *Namfong,* or Chinese Mustard Cabbage. The same nursery also offers the more familiar Pac Choy and Bok Choy. *Sunrise Enterprises,* which deals exclusively in Oriental varieties, offers a large selection of uncommon greens.

Whether it should be considered as a cabbage or an Oriental green, Spoon Pak Choy should interest those who experiment with Oriental cooking. It is non-heading, and it gets its name from its porcelainlike leaves, which are as thick as a spoon. It is prepared in stir fry or boiled alone like ordinary cabbage. It is a cool weather crop and should be started indoors for setting out in early spring. Seed is available from *Gleckler's Seedsman.* Chinese Celery Cabbage, also called *Michihili,* is a green used in Oriental dishes and in salads. To avoid bolting, plant the seed in early summer for fall harvest. Seed is offered by *Nichols Garden Nursery.*

A European green that is sometimes marketed as a gourmet's salad ingredient is called Garden Rocket or arugula. It has a peppery flavor, somewhat resembling the flavor of watercress. A few leaves finely cut will contribute a flavor to a salad that will puzzle one's guests. It is easy to grow, and although I have had no problems, it is said it can easily become a pest. It should be planted in early spring, sprinkling the seeds into a shallow trench and covering lightly with fine soil. Thin to about 6 inches. Commonly a few leaves are harvested as needed, without uprooting the whole plant. It will continue to provide leaves all summer. Seeds are available from *Urban Farmer*.

Among the green vegetables that are eaten either cooked or raw, probably the most universally grown are varieties of spinach. Spinach is snootily loyal to cool weather. It is tolerant of light frost and can be planted in earliest spring, but with the first touches of hot weather it bolts to seed heads. It is not just the heat that induces bolting; it has photo-periodic sensitivity, meaning that it is responsive to day length. When the season advances to where the days are becoming longer than the nights, it bolts. Therefore, plant it as soon as the ground can be worked. Scatter the seeds thinly into a trench about an inch deep, sift moist earth over them, and pack lightly. In most areas the ground will be moist in early spring when spinach is planted. If not, watering will be necessary. Spinach grows fast and bushy and consumes a great deal of moisture. It should be thinned to 2 to 4 inches when the first true leaves are about an inch long. The plants can be spaced wider than that, but crowding the plants slightly actually makes the leaves a bit more tender. The spinach can be used any time the leaves are large enough to be significant; they are at their best for eating raw in salads, sandwiches, and so on, when only 3 or 4 inches tall.

It will be necessary to allow the bunches to fill in the row pretty well and grow to a height of about 6 inches before picking if they are to be cooked. Spinach absolutely astonishes in its ability to shrink while cooking. Those who do not especially like cooked spinach as a dish in its own right may like it chopped and cooked as an ingredient in several Italian pasta dishes. If the spinach is to be enjoyed, the gardener should by all means avoid overhead watering. The expression "like sandy spinach" exists as a byword for something that sets your teeth on edge. Dirt particles are especially prone to layering on the leaves when the soil is splashed by water from a sprinkler, or by rain.

If at all possible, irrigate with small ditches or rills, or best of all use some system of drip irrigation.

As soon as the spinach bunches begin to feel the heat, they will shoot up a thick, tall, fleshy stalk from their centers, which will rapidly bloom and set seeds if permitted. As soon as this bolting begins, the leaves get coarse and tough, and for all practical purposes their usefulness is at an end. If the stalks are cut about 4 inches above the ground as soon as they begin to appear, new leaves, and ultimately more stalks, usually will appear at the remaining leaf buds. In this way you can prolong the life of a spinach planting a few days, but the new leaves are never of particularly good quality. The spinach planting is usually the first row to be cleared out in a garden, and it can be reseeded.

There are on the market varieties of spinach that have been developed for their tolerance of hot weather and their resistance to bolting. Mazurka is supposed to be especially tolerant of hot weather and will not bolt until it has produced a crop of leaves. Bloomsdale is recommended for fall planting, and is said to be especially sweet. It grows thick, crumpled (savoyed) leaves. Seed for both is offered by *Territorial Seed Company*.

New Zealand spinach and related strains are sometimes grown for their tolerance of hot weather. They are not, despite the resemblances, members of the spinach family. Although their seeds are unlike spinach seeds, they are planted about the same way. In choosing a location, remember that the plants will be permanent inhabitants of the garden for the remainder of the summer. The usual practice is to pick a few leaves at a time from each of several plants rather than harvesting an entire plant at once. Snatching up occasional trifling leaves in this way, the plants will continue to produce throughout the entire growing season. They have a flavor that is a bit stronger or, as champions of the plants express it, more "spinachy" than regular spinach. Whether or not to plant it may be influenced by that flavor hint. I prefer raw spinach in salads, but raw New Zealand spinach is a bit too much for me. It should be noted that if left unchecked to reseed themselves, these plants tend to become quite prolific. Another way to read that is pestiferous.

Collards are a favorite staple cooked green of the South but have fewer champions in the northern part of the country. They do grow in a wide variety of climates, and in spite of their Southern associations are tolerant of cool weather. They will not wilt in the intense summer heat of the South and will grow to heights of 3 to 4 feet in a long growing season. They will also tolerate some cold, down to about 15 degrees before they are damaged, which makes it possible to maintain them as a year-round crop in much of the South. Like many cool weather crops, their flavor is improved by a touch of frost.

The chief varieties of collards are semi-heading and non-heading. Both are planted and cared for in the same way. Seed them in a shallow trench, lightly covered and loosely packed, in the early spring. As they germinate, thin to about 6 inches between plants of the non-heading varieties, and up to 10 inches for the heading varieties. They should be ready for use between 75 to 80 days after planting, depending on variety and weather conditions. As with lettuce and spinach, the thinnings or young plants may be harvested and used at any time they are big enough to be worthwhile. The mature plants should be used before the stems and the veins in the leaves begin to become tough. Collards may be harvested a few leaves at a time, although usually an entire plant is taken at once. Remove the coarse part of the central rib of the larger leaves before cooking. The flavor of cooked collards resembles cabbage, and they are cooked in some of the same ways.

Kale is rather similar to collards, although it is generally less well known, except as old-fashioned slang for money. It is a member of the cabbage family, probably similar in form to the earliest varieties of the family cultivated. It is most similar to sea cabbage—also called Sea Kale and Beach Cabbage—the wild ancestor probably common to all. The name is a Scottish word adapted from the Latin *caulis* meaning "stem cabbage." It was most likely introduced by the Romans to the British Isles, where it soon became an important food crop because it grew year-round. In Scotland it became a virtually indispensable peasant food because it flourished in the harsh climate and because the harsh treatment the peasants endured for so many years afforded them nothing else. Its importance was similar to the importance of potatoes to the Irish peasants under the punitive terms of British occupation from the seventeenth through the nineteenth centuries.

Kale is one of the best food sources among the greens, not only being rich in the expected vitamins but also affording nearly as much calcium as milk. Other greens such as spinach contain oxalic acid, which combines with the calcium content and reduces its nutritional availability. Since kale is low in this substance, it provides more usable calcium than other greens. Kale is sometimes eaten raw, is often boiled, but is probably best steamed. Its "cabbagey" flavor resembles broccoli.

For best quality, kale must be grown as a cold weather plant. The surface of the leaves toughens in hot weather to retard moisture loss, which makes them leathery and the general flavor distinctly unpleasant. Because the juice has a relatively high sugar content, and the plant as a whole a relatively high fiber content, it is the most cold tolerant of the entire family. It is hardy to 10 degrees below zero, and actually is at its best only after a few sharp frosts, which turn its starches into sugar.

Kale should be summer planted to overwinter, or planted very early for harvest before hot weather. If planted in the spring for a summer crop, it will be disappointing. It can be started indoors for transplanting, but probably most people direct-seed it in the ground where it will be grown. The individual plants will take the same or slightly less space as cabbage, around 14 to 18 inches apart. Opinion varies as to how much to plant; it depends. As with so many vegetables, I find recommendations by apologists for kale almost alarming. One anticipated as a basal goal for a late planting a 100-pound yield. To me that sounds like industrial strength. Admittedly I am not much of a fan of cooked greens; half a dozen plants are fine for me. Four times a year, tops, and two heads to give to friends.

There are several varieties of kale to choose among. The commonest is Scotch kale, or Dwarf kale. It is the most familiar variety: somewhat stocky, 15 inches high, with tightly curled leaves. It is extremely hardy. A second variety is Siberian kale, which is of a different species altogether, and in spite of the name not a kale at all. In the past it has commonly been grown as fodder. I have never eaten it, but it has advocates who prefer it above all varieties. A third variety is variously called flowering kale, ornamental kale, and less accurately, flowering cabbage. It comes in a variety of colors and has leaves tightly and uniformly collected around a center in classic blossom formation, similar to an open rose blossom, but more than a foot across and 6 to

8 inches high. These are most attractive, especially when planted shoulder to shoulder to make a border or to silhouette a lower bed. Since they will last a good part of the summer, they should be planted early. They can be direct-seeded or pre-started indoors. They are edible, but to harvest them would defeat the purpose of having planted them in the first place.

A fourth variety is Chinese kale, also called Chinese broccoli, and in Oriental catalogues *Gai Lohn (Sunrise Enterprises)*. So far it is little grown in this country, but occasional notices rate it high. It little resembles the other varieties of kale, and the flowering stalk is eaten rather than the leaves. Like broccoli, the head is harvested just before the buds open, and the head, stalk, and a couple of top leaves are picked. It is prepared by steaming or stir-fry cooking. Like broccoli, when the seed stalk is cut, new stems and new buds will soon form. It is cultivated like Dwarf kale, for an early summer or early fall harvest. It is cold hardy, but not as cold hardy as Dwarf kale. My knowledge of it is strictly secondhand, but if it is as pest-free as some growers claim, it might well be an acceptable replacement for broccoli, which is so popular with insects that some people give up on it.

Chinese Savoy cabbage, which is not closely related to the cabbage family, is another cool weather green vegetable favored by lovers of cooked greens. It can also be eaten raw, shredded as a slaw, or blended with other green leafy vegetables in salads. It may be cooked by itself, like cabbage, and is especially useful coarsely chopped as an ingredient in Chinese cooking or in "American stir-fry" recipes, along with other garden vegetables.

The seeds of Chinese cabbage can be planted in the spring or in the fall. For spring harvest, plant seeds as soon as the soil can be worked. The seedlings are tolerant of a little frost. Seeds may also be started indoors like cabbage, and the seedlings transplanted after the weather has somewhat settled. For a late crop, plant seeds about ten weeks before the date of the usual first frost in your area.

The mature heads of Chinese cabbage resemble Romaine lettuce and are about the same general size, or a little larger. Spring plantings will most likely bolt quickly with the onset of the first hot weather, although they will last longer where the summer weather remains relatively cool, particularly in marine climates. Growth response seems to be to heat rather than to day length.

For those whose taste in green cooked vegetables runs to the hearty, mustard greens are a clear option. Some people, of course, especially those with rural backgrounds, look forward in the spring to collecting greens of wild mustard (a European import). Several varieties of cultivated mustard are available, which are milder than common wild varieties. It will grow in almost any climate. Seeds may be planted in the early spring, scattering them in a shallow trench and tamping them over with a light covering of soil a couple of weeks before the usual date of the last frost. For those with a real appetite for these greens, plantings may be made successively through the summer. Since they grow rapidly to the stage at which they are eaten, they are a good crop for interplantings or to replant an area from which something else has just been harvested. If not harvested when small the flavor becomes strong and bitter, although changing the water in which the greens are being boiled once or twice will help reduce undesirable flavors. Do not allow cultivated mustard to go to seed, because it reseeds itself with abandon and quickly becomes an unwelcome weed.

Swiss chard is a relative of the beet family, and the red-veined and reddish-tinged leaves clearly show this kinship. Since Swiss chard is a heat-resistant green, it is often grown in preference to or as a late supplement to spinach (although it will not replace raw spinach in salads). The cultivation is almost identical to that of beets and turnips. For early chard, plant the seeds some days before the normal period of last frosts in the spring, or at any time later up until midsummer. If a season-long crop is desired, plant successively at two-week intervals through June. Spread the seeds thinly in rows at least a foot apart (if more than one row is planted), and thin the seedlings to about 2 inches apart after the first true leaves appear. How many to plant depends entirely upon one's taste for greens and on how many other varieties of greens have been planted. Personally, except to satisfy my curiosity about an untried variety, in a given season I never plant more than one variety of greens that are eaten cooked. Chard may be harvested when the plants reach a height of 4 inches or so. Commonly gardeners will pick a few of the outside leaves of several plants rather than pulling up entire plants. So harvested, individual plants will continue producing new foliage for a considerable time. A so-called gourmet chard, *Da Taglio Verde Scure,* a ribless variety, is offered by *Epicure Seeds.* They recommend steaming it, adding no other moisture than the water the chard was rinsed in.

Varieties of chard have been developed that feature a pronounced and enlarged central rib in each leaf. This stem is cut away from the leaf and eaten raw, like a celery stalk. It is crunchy crisp with a pleasant tangy flavor, and its color makes an attractive addition to a relish tray. While I find it quite pleasant, four to six plants every couple of years does me fine. *Epicure Seeds* offers a French variety called *Ampuis Poirée,* which is reputedly superior to seed rack varieties.

Other less common, or only regionally common, greens should be considered by those who fancy cooked greens. For example, turnip greens—called salit—are simply the tops of (usually immature) turnips, or of turnips deliberately seeded densely and never thinned, which encourages all of the growth to go to the tops rather than to the roots. In fact, many people grow turnips primarily for their tops, and in some regions they are a staple green. An old song of Southern provenance extols their merits as a partner in hearty if humble cuisine:

> *Corn bread and butter milk,*
> *And good old turnip greens.*

Two varieties of turnip, Seven Top and Shogoin, have been developed exclusively for their tops; the roots are inedible.

Some extol cooked rutabaga greens and cultivate rutabagas for their greens in the same way as turnips—planted densely and left unthinned. Rutabaga is somewhat stronger flavored than turnip greens. Even pigweed, or its domestic cultivar, amaranth, is deliberately grown to be cooked or eaten raw in salads. It is nourishing, but even its fanciers recommend changing the water it is boiled in at least once. Seeds of improved varieties of dandelions are available, and some greens fanciers cultivate this otherwise weed for cooked or salad greens. The cultivated varieties are a more lush and luxuriant plant than their wild siblings, but when dandelions are grown as a garden vegetable, it should be remembered that if unchecked they can be in every way as noxious as their country cousins. Most likely dandelions originally were introduced into the New World deliberately as a food and medicinal plant, subsequently going wild from the gardens, as their parachuted seeds so easily enable them to do. Other weeds or wildings, such as lamb's-quarter and pokeweed, are sometimes collected if not actually propagated for greens. Pokeweed is acceptable, but lamb's-quarter has the most disgusting flavor of any plant I have ever deliberately put in my mouth.

Sugar Ann pea

Take the Pulse

The pulse family—peas, lentils, and all their cousins—are Old World vegetables of great antiquity. Because they are highly nutritious and, dried, keep well for long periods, they have been a staple since cultivation of the land began in the cradle of civilization. The ancients made meal or flour of dried peas for various culinary purposes, presumably including bread. And they of course made pease porridge, venerable and versatile, hot or cold.

Pease is the proper name of the vegetable we call the "pea," still usual in British usage. Like *deer* and *fish* it is a noun which is both singular and plural. But since "pease" sounds like a plural, the made-up form of *pea* came into being as a singular, by a process which linguists call "back formation." So we now have both a singular and a plural, at least in America, and the matter needn't trouble us further.

Peas are grown for both fresh, or green, consumption and are used dried. In practice, gardeners generally only grow green peas. For the most part distinct varieties are grown for use as dried peas, the principal difference being that when dried "green peas" have a shriveled appearance, while "dried peas" are almost perfectly round and smooth skinned. Immature peas of the dried pea varieties can be used in most of the ways fresh green peas are used. Sometimes commercial canneries will buy fields intended for dry harvest and can those varieties as green peas. Those dried peas I have eaten green (and have tried frozen as well) were somewhat mealy and lacking in sweetness, somewhat like field corn used as green corn.

There is no particular reason why a gardener cannot or should not grow dried peas. Most choose not to, because they require a relatively large amount of space, and homegrown dried peas have no particular virtue to recommend them over those obtained commercially. However, seeds for dried peas are relatively cheap and it might prove instructive to test some of the uncommon varieties exchanged among the seed savers, which I have not done. Freshness among dried peas has to be relative.

Freshness among green peas, however, certainly is not relative. Ideally, they should be picked as shortly before use as possible, and be shelled and cooked only just before serving (or canning or freezing). Fresh garden peas are appreciably, not merely detectably, superior to those from the produce department. Green peas are also an example of a garden product with which meaningful savings can be made by home processing—canning or freezing.

When selecting varieties to plant for processing, check the catalogue descriptions or seed packets in regard to their freezing or canning qualities. Some varieties survive processing much better than others. And by the same token, those which are superior for freezing or canning are not necessarily those which are best for use fresh. For a gardener with limited space who nevertheless intends both uses, there are respectable compromise varieties. As for most seeds when selecting varieties, consultation with extension agents, nurseries, or other local gardeners is a good idea.

The major limiting factor in growing peas is climate. Peas are a cool weather crop and do not do well when the temperature begins to edge above 70 degrees. When the instructions on the seed packet say to plant as soon as the ground may be worked—believe. They are among the very earliest seeds that may be safely planted and are not only tolerant of cool weather, they thrive on it. Planted in early March, or even late February, they should be coming into production in June, even earlier in warm climates. When hot weather comes along, blooming stops, the vines begin to look a little wheezy, the pods wither, and the green peas become pithy. Early planting is a must, except in areas that regularly experience cool, moist summers.

Green peas come in two vine types: bush or climbing. The bush peas have the advantage of compactness, and planting them eliminates the bother of providing something for the vines to climb on. Climbing peas, on the other hand, are generally more productive, and since they use vertical rather than horizontal space, provide higher yield for a given area. But the vines must be supported, and this can be a bother or inconvenience. Since I have ample space, I prefer to plant bush peas.

If the soil has been worked the previous autumn in anticipation of early planting, a quick light pass with a hoe to remove any sprouting weeds should be all the preparation necessary for planting. Bush peas do well planted in a double row. Make two parallel trenches about an inch deep and about 6 inches apart. It is helpful but not imperative to sprinkle a nitrogen inoculant, obtainable at any nursery, before dropping the seeds. This will usually improve germination, and sometimes yields.

Space the seeds about 2 inches apart, cover, and pack the soil lightly. They should germinate within two weeks unless the weather is consistently chilly, and sooner if the temperature is mild for at least part of the time. It is good for the gardener's spirit to see how the peas will flourish and grow lush and green through the gray drizzle of early spring. Even for those not partial to peas, it is worthwhile to grow them to help ease a gardener through the spring doldrums of pre-gardening time.

As with most crops, how many peas to plant depends on how well they are liked, how many are to be fed by them, and whether they are to be packed away frozen or canned. And, of course, it depends on how much space can actually be allotted to that one specific crop. I plant two 50-foot (double) rows for a family of five whose tastes for peas varies from passion to tepid tolerance, and we freeze some.

If climbing peas are planted, the same quantity can be produced in a fourth that space. Accepting that option, the possibilities for support or trellises are limited only by imagination. I have a friend, a very ambitious and industrious person, who supports his climbing peas on a 10-foot segment of woven wire attached to four 4×4's sunk in the ground with 2×6 crosspieces nailed between them; the whole system looks like a segment liberated from an elephant retaining compound. The peas never escape. On the other end of the scale, and much less ambitiously, I pounded grape stakes into the ground 10 feet apart, stretched a single wire across the stakes, tops and bottoms, and zigzagged string up and down and under and over the wires for the length of the "trellis." It was ugly and floppy, but it supported the vines and was taken down by midsummer. Probably my favorite support is a tepeelike structure consisting of three 7- or 8-foot stakes (I cut them with an electric saw from old 1×12's), with the seed planted in hills at the point where each of the legs is imbedded in the ground. The stakes, by the way, must be imbedded because the full-grown vines present a lot of surface and a heavy wind could blow the whole arrangement down.

At best, climbing peas really are something of a bother, and whatever trellising system is used the peas will have to be planted where the shade of their vertical growth will not inhibit other plants. A conventional trellis is another thing that has to be tended to in the fall—probably taken down, perhaps stored in some premeditated fashion, and put up again the next year. Those who are irritated by the fussier sort of garden chores should never grow climbing peas. If a trellis is used, the seeds are planted in the same way as bush peas, about an inch deep and 2 inches apart. But if a single horizontal trellis is used, do not plant climbing peas in a double row. The plants in a single row will branch and spread until all available space is covered. If a tepee structure is used, erect the wooden frame first, then plant 6 or 8 seeds around the spot where each leg is driven into the ground.

A "recent" innovation in pea culture is the so-called "snap pea," a cross between edible pod, or sugar pod peas, and regular green peas. Snap peas grow a mature pea within a thick, fleshy pod like a green bean, and are eaten pod and all, like green beans. These peas are exceptionally sweet and tender and are preferred raw by many people—served on relish trays or snapped into salads. They may also be snapped, or cut, into segments like green beans—however, they have a coarse string down each side that must be removed before using—and cooked for a short period of time. Many strains so far available on the market are strictly climbers, so support is required, although a few seed houses are offering bush or semi-bush varieties.

The sensation caused by the innovation in recent years of the Sugar Snap pea—some called it the vegetable marvel of the decade—is something of an anomaly. With greater or lesser visibility, these have been in existence for several centuries, enjoying such a vogue as to constitute a fad among eighteenth-century French aristocracy, and in the mid-nineteenth century were quite common in listings of American seed houses. It is impossible to know how similar those older varieties were to these developed recently, unless some of them show up among heirloom seed collections.

One parent of the contemporary Sugar Snap pea, the edible pod pea, or sugar pod, is the pea familiar in stir fry and Chinese cookery. At the stage in which they are eaten, these consist of small immature pods containing only vestigial peas. Some people are fond of eating the pods raw. Edible pod peas also should be planted in the early spring. Their habit can be described as semi-vining; they may be grown like bush peas, but with their sprawling habits will do better and be easier to pick if they are given some support. I don't like to take the trouble; they do quite well for me with no support at all, although it becomes increasingly difficult to locate the pods as the vines become tangled. Plant edible pod peas like bush peas an inch deep and 2 inches apart. Since they are so viny, there is no point in planting them in a double row. A relatively short row, perhaps 8 feet, will supply all but the most voracious appetites. If allowed to mature, the pods will grow to 4 inches long, with peas inside the pods the size of buckshot. At this stage, while they can be shelled like regular green peas, they are tough and disagreeable in flavor.

Edible pod peas are best picked when the pod is only about 2 inches long, with the pea hardly more than a swelling inside. It takes a lot of them for a mess, but the vines are prolific. They may be cooked as a dish by themselves, boiled for a short time (two to four minutes) and eaten with butter, or they may be sautéed in various ways. Often they are used in stir-fry dishes and in a wide variety of Oriental recipes. If the pods are kept picked, vines will continue to be productive until hot weather sets in, at which time the remaining pods quickly become tough and leathery. As good as they are, usually one is pretty well tired of them before their season is over, and in spite of the enthusiasm of some guides to freezing, their characteristic delicate flavor does not survive it. Sugar pods are something that should be grown, enjoyed through their brief season, and then removed. Since they are finished early, they are a good prospect for interplanting with crops that will require larger areas of space as the summer comes on, such as squash.

Usually I grow bush peas and edible pod peas in continuous rows. When their production ends—usually in mid-June—I cut the vines flush to the ground and carry the plants to my compost heap. Being legumes, the remaining roots add good quantities of nitrogen to the soil for the next crop. And with the vines removed, the rows are suddenly free for second plantings. Any crops will do—mid-season lettuce such as limestone or Oak Leaf, late root crops (in most areas it will be too late for potatoes), or late cabbage.

Among cooks a favorite variety of common green pea is the petite pois. The petite pois of commerce actually is, just as the name means, a small pea. Commercial peas are "vined" (shelled mechanically) in the field. They are trucked to the canneries, and one of the first steps of processing is to roll them across screens to separate the small from the medium, large, and so forth. The canned petite pois in the grocery store, then, are those that have been screened from the larger but otherwise identical peas (usually the mesh size of the screen will be given on the side of the can). They are indeed more tender and perhaps more flavorful because they are less mature, but basically they are the same peas found in other cans.

There are, however, cultivars of peas named properly "petite pois," which are bred to grow especially tender and flavorful tiny peas. These may be commercially available in gourmet markets, but I have never seen them. Seed for these peas is relatively uncommon, but it can be found. I obtained one such cultivar simply called Petite Pois from the *Vermont Bean Seed Company.* The dried seed is clearly much smaller than ordinary garden varieties. However, because of a pea weevil infestation my yield was not sufficient for proper testing, but at least for eating fresh—raw or cooked—they clearly outclassed any other common pea I have known.

A named petite pois variety—Waverex, from England—is obtainable from *The Urban Farmer.* The dried seed is incredibly small, being about half the size of the previously mentioned variety. These were described in the catalogue as being "heavy yielding," although my results could only be called average. Because of their size a great many more of them are required for a meal. They are exceptionally sweet eaten fresh, and marvelously tender. They have a distinctive flavor that my family characterized as "earthy"—in a favorable sense. For one gardening for the pleasure of it and not concerned with quantity, I would think either of these varieties would be irresistible. Order seeds early, for they are often in short supply. Other equally satisfactory, perhaps superior, varieties may be available through exchanges.

Kin to the pea is the lentil. It is a venerable and ancient vegetable, one of the earliest cultivated crops of the Near East. It is a small gray-green or red dried seed characterized by being shaped like a lense. In fact the word *lense* derives its name from resemblance to the shape of the seed; also the adjective *lenticular,* meaning "shaped like a lentil." And *lentigo,* meaning the condition of having freckles. The lentil seed grows on a scruffy looking little plant in about the same climate as peas. They flourish in cool weather and wither away when the weather turns hot. The seeds form in small pods, each pod containing only two kernels.

Like dried peas, lentils are relatively inexpensive to obtain commercially, and since they are eaten dried, many consider that there is little advantage to growing their own. A gardener interested in growing them will probably have to obtain them through seed exchanges (in which case there will be a considerable expansion of varieties available). Lentils may be found through such sources in a considerable range of colors and a wider range of size, from miniscule to the size of a dime. One interested in trying them but not interested in experimenting with different varieties may simply plant dried lentils bought from the shelves of the local grocery store.

Lentil cultivation is basically no different from peas, although they are not as viny as peas, so rows may be closer together and they will not need to be separated as far from interplanted crops. Where lentils are grown commercially, a field of maturing lentils in midsummer might be mistaken for an untended weed patch. Depending on the climate, the seeds should ripen in July or August. Cut the vines and lay them aside until they are thoroughly dry. They may be threshed by stomping them inside a burlap bag, or whatever might be one's favorite threshing method. The patient person with time on his hands could shell the pods individually.

Probably more people would eat lentils if they knew what to do with them. Their high protein content argues for inclusion in meal planning and, ironically, while they have been generally known in Europe and elsewhere as a subsistence food, in the United States their popularity is highest among affluent and taste-conscious people. In 1983 the Washington State Pea and Lentil Commission test-marketed lentil packages containing a leaflet of recipes. Comparing and evaluating sales in stores located in predominately high-income areas with those in predominately low-income areas, many times more packages were sold in the high-income areas. Probably this differential is easily explained by the interest in ethnic food among more affluent Americans, for whom low cost—especially ethnic—foods have often risen to gourmet status. Although thought of primarily as an ingredient in soups, lentils have a much wider range of possible uses, such as in casseroles or loafs. Many people also sprout the seeds, using them in salads.

An Old World cousin of the pulse family is the fava bean, also known as the Windsor Bean and the English broad bean. This was *the* bean of northern Europe before the discovery of the New World with its cornucopia of bean varieties. The fava bean has only recently become generally available through seed catalogues in America and a sober word of warning, which most seed companies neglect, is in order.

People of certain national origins experience a severe genetic allergic reaction to these beans, known as *favism*. A recent book on poisonous plants postulates that about one percent of those of Mediterranean origin and about 10 percent of all Blacks may be susceptible to this allergy. This inherited sensitivity has been known for centuries. It produces, among other symptoms, a severe anemia, and may result in death. As a sardonic side note, the first time I saw seed for fava beans advertised in a seed catalogue, the promotional blurb eagerly explained that they were especially valuable in Italian cooking.

To most people, however, favas are entirely harmless and are the showpiece of many English vegetable gardens. The bean itself is quite large, somewhat the diameter and shape of a lima bean, but quite chunky in its thickness, irregularly surfaced rather than smooth. In all candor, it is an ugly pulse. Because it is not widely cultivated or known among American gardeners, recipes for its preparation are rather sketchy. I inquired of a bright and cheeky English guest how it was prepared in England, and she replied that in England no one ate the English broad bean. When I pressed her answer by saying you hardly saw an English vegetable garden without them she admitted that that was certainly the case. Nevertheless, she insisted, nobody ate them; gardeners gave them all to other people. I discovered, however, that the English frequently prepare the bean when it is very young, as an edible pod bean. When the beans become filled out, or nearly so, they are shelled like lima beans and prepared in similar ways. Like a green lima, it is somewhat mealy, but has a flavor more like a pea than a lima bean. It is also prepared dried, pre-soaked, much like a dried lima or butter bean. Yet I admit neither I nor any members of my family particularly care for them.

Perhaps its chief attraction for American gardeners is that fava beans are, like peas, a cool weather crop and quite hardy. In all but the most severe climates they may be planted in the fall and treated as a winter annual. This seems to be the common way they are cultivated in England. They also may be planted in the early spring, at the same time as peas. The plants are sensitive to hot weather, but not nearly as sensitive as peas. The plant itself does not at first glance especially resemble either the pea or bean family. It grows upright, with several branchings ultimately developing from the root, and it has a sturdy *square* stem. They grow regularly about 3 feet tall, although in England I have seen them considerably taller. They are reputed to require no support (certainly mine didn't), but the English gardeners compete in ingenious support systems, usually cunning arrangements of slender sticks.

Plant the seeds in a single row, about 2 inches deep, allowing about 4 inches between seeds. These are seeds you can get your hands on, and few gardeners would be tempted to lower those monsters into the ground too close together. After germination, the plants grow rapidly and begin blooming when they are about a foot high, putting out blossoms resembling little bullets at the juncture of the leaves and stem, each spread in a little flat fan consisting of two to five individuals. The blossoms are curious, and not unattractive in themselves, a dark black contrasting with a sharp white. As the stem grows taller, blossoms will continue to open until discouraged by hot weather. New shoots that sprout from the root level will produce a number of blossoms and develop seed pods. Those beans not used green (pods and all when very small or shelled when more mature) may be allowed to ripen for use as dried beans. When most of the remaining hulls have begun to shrivel, hoe the vines off (leave the roots in the ground for their nitrogen), pile them in the sun until they are brittle-dry, then shell the beans from the hulls or thresh them in a sack and winnow away the debris.

Most catalogues simply list these beans generically as fava beans, English broad beans, or Windsor beans. A variety called *Aquadulce Claudia,* hardy to 12 degrees, is said to be superior, reaching 4 feet at maturity. Banner is recommended for Middle Eastern recipes. It is also very hardy and reaches a height of 6 feet under favorable conditions. Both are offered by *Territorial Seed Company.*

Interest in the fava bean has developed in the Western wheat-growing states for use as a green manure crop. Because of its earliness and its heavy foliage, as well as its nitrogen-rich roots, it has considerable potential in this capacity. When used as green manure, generally a small seeded variety is planted. However, the fava bean is not likely to become an important field crop in its own right, unless American taste changes drastically.

The garbanzo bean, or chick pea, is a legume native to the Far

East. It has long been associated with ethnic cooking; recent interest in it has probably been stimulated by the popularity of salad bars. It is most familiar as a cooked dried bean, although it is also used as a green shell bean. While catalogue instructions for its culture sometimes caution that it does not adapt readily to northern regions, it is currently being grown as a field crop in wheat-growing regions of the Northwest. It is also the object of research by Western universities as a rotation crop with small grains.

While a wide selection of garbanzo varieties are available through seed exchanges, they are seldom listed other than as a generic variety by commercial catalogues. *Good Seeds* offers a solid, black-seeded experimental variety called Kaboli Garbanzo, said to be tolerant of cold soils. It is a curious looking plant, not at all similar to anything else in the garden; its foliage looks like a miniature locust tree. Plant the seeds about 2 inches apart at the same time as beans are planted; their care is similar to beans. They are exceptionally tolerant of drought, but require a long hot summer.

Beans: The Poor Man's Steak

Creaseback bean

Beans must be the humblest of the New World's contributions to human nutrition. Even the New World's peanuts and okra, which were originally cultivated for slaves' food, have changed caste, or lost the relation to caste. But even though we now have "gourmet" beans, gourmet recipes for cooking beans, and latter-day Bostonian pride in calling itself "Bean Town," when someone chooses a metaphor to express economic desperation he says he's down to eating beans. With a grudging respect, it was said in the Depression that no man alive could eat a nickel's worth of beans. We dismiss something as worthless by saying it's not worth a hill of beans. There is a sniggering connotation even in the word *bean* itself, suggesting embarrassing gas. But while nutritionists might tell us that man cannot live by beans alone, many of the poor of the western world almost do.

Beans deserve better. In the first place, beans are not "just beans." They possess unexpected diversity, and a surprising number of different biological varieties. As with other fruits and vegetables, most people's range of experience with beans is controlled by the tyranny of the commercial marketplace. During any given fresh produce season, hardly more than two or three different varieties of green beans are to be found in the usual produce market. Depending on the area of the country, a slightly larger selection of dried beans will be offered, but for the most part they are labeled only generically: kidney, small red, small white, large white, pinto, black-eyed peas, large and small limas.

The gardener, however, has options unrecognized by the shopper, and should explore and exploit them. No doubt for the very reason that the bean is so humble, little is anticipated or expected of it. There is something Cinderella-like about beans. They can be, and many are, very pretty; some of the more dedicated fanciers perhaps overuse the word *beautiful* when talking about their favorites. As a food they deserve something more than merely being something that "fills the old gut." For eaters as well as gardeners there are probably more unexplored possibilities with beans than with any other class of common food. But to explore such possibilities, you must grow them yourself.

Like peas, the more familiar beans may be grown for use immature, or allowed to mature and used dried, although commonly distinct varieties are grown for each use. To be technically accurate, beans are eaten in four different stages: very immature (green, or snap beans); semi-mature but still eaten, pods and all (shelly beans); mature enough to shell but still soft (shelled, haricot, or horticultural beans); and dried and shelled beans. Few gardeners grow their own dried beans, but as awareness of their diversity becomes widespread, the number of gardeners growing their own is likely to increase, as it already has among the seed exchangers. Most gardeners do grow green beans, but here again truly exceptional varieties are most often neglected because they are unknown.

As with peas, gardeners may choose between bush and climbing varieties. It has been said that more food nourishment may be grown per unit of land with climbing beans than with any other plant (I have read the same dictum expressed about bananas and Cat Tail Tules). But, you can certainly grow a lot of beans if you plant climbers. The same considerations are operative with climbing beans as there are with climbing peas: you have to supply support. And climbing beans seem to be more upwardly mobile than climbing peas; in late August there must be gardeners all over the country who are beginning to believe literally the story of "Jack and the Bean Stalk." One June I took off for a month's work-trip to England, leaving a completely seeded garden to the care of my wife. The first telephone call we exchanged, she expressed alarm at what the "bush beans" I had planted were doing. By our second call it was clear someone had erred (I always blame a mislabeled seed packet, but would not like to take that defense to court). When I returned, bean vines were threshing around the garden like run-amok serpents, strangling everything in their path.

Any of the arrangements for supporting climbing peas will do for climbing beans. However, if allowed their preference, many climbing beans will go much higher than climbing peas. It's not necessary to completely indulge that preference, but the higher they are allowed to climb, within reason, the more productive they will be. By far the easiest arrangement for growing a relatively small number of climbing beans, and nearly as efficient as more seriously constructed systems, is to plant them with sunflowers. About a month before planting beans, plant a row of sunflower seeds and thin them to about 12 inches apart, staggered rather than in a straight line. When the soil has warmed enough to plant the beans, the sunflower seedlings should be a couple of inches high. Plant the beans on either side, about 2 inches from the sunflowers. By the time the beans are tall enough to begin to climb, the sunflowers should have started to reach for the sky. The tall, heavy stalks of the sunflowers do nicely for support, and you are provided with stakes at no labor expenditure, disposable in your compost heap in the fall, with a crop of sunflower seeds into the bargain.

The tepee-shaped trellis suggested for peas also does well for beans, but it should be quite tall—at least 7 feet. With this height, and the base fairly well spread, a hill of pumpkins or other vining members of the squash family may be planted in the center, which gives in effect a double use of space. This does not work well with peas, because their lower foliage is denser than that of beans. The squash vines should run into the clear before the bean vines are sufficiently dense to shade them.

It is much less trouble simply to grow bush beans, although many gardeners would scorn and shame me for indolence and sloth. It is certainly true that with bush beans there is not the production per unit of land as with pole beans. It is easier to harvest pole beans, but the relative difference is inconsequential. But bush or pole, they cannot be planted until all danger of frost is past. Plant them too early, and often the seed will rot in the cold earth. Bush beans may be planted either in a single row, or a double row about 6 inches apart, with the outside spacing of the rows about 18 inches apart. Space the seeds 2 inches or less from each other, and set about an inch deep. Firm the earth lightly over the seeds. If the soil is soft, sometimes I simply punch a hole in the dirt with my finger and drop a seed in each. This may seem a little too fussy for some, but it's actually faster than one might suppose.

Beans have fairly shallow roots, tending to net near the surface, so cultivate them carefully. Hand-weed close to the plants and, using a sharp hoe, shave the weeds at the top of the soil to avoid disturbing the roots. If rill or ditch irrigation is being used, draw the ditches while the plants are still quite small to avoid agitating the roots. Subsequent cultivation should be kept shallow and distant from the plants.

Most families will find a 50-foot double row of green beans ample for their needs, unless they intend to process quantities of beans for the winter. Since beans are not especially irritated by summer heat, successive plantings are practical to extend the bean harvest over a period of time. Making two or three seedings two or three weeks apart should assure a plentiful supply for the summer. I generally make successive plantings of differing varieties. Most bush beans will keep setting blossoms for a while if kept picked and should provide two or three weeks of production. If kept picked, one planting of pole beans should keep producing for the larger part of the summer.

Green beans are, in common with most vegetables, best if picked only a short time before cooking. And many people prefer them cooked a relatively brief time, although this varies with variety and maturity. Some like to allow the beans to remain on the vines until the green kernels are approaching maturity but the pods are still fleshy:

shelly beans. Most prepare them at this stage by cutting them into lengths of an inch or so, like immature snap beans. They require a longer cooking period—an hour or more—and are especially good cooked with ham. Some people like to add a few pods of sliced okra. I know people who grow a few plants of okra for this purpose alone. Small unpeeled new potatoes are also especially good added, with or without okra, toward the end of the cooking period. One almost has to grow one's own shelly beans because, except regionally, few markets stock them.

There are always green beans that are overlooked at harvest time. Perhaps there are just too many, so one grows tired of green beans, and large numbers of late beans are simply left on the vines. If allowed to dry, or if the vines are cut and laid aside until they are dried, they will do for dried beans, although they do not usually look like the familiar varieties of dried beans found in the stores. Sometimes, even perfectly dried, they are not easy to wrestle from their shells. Like most dried beans they must be soaked overnight before cooking, and most varieties are especially good after a long simmer in the company of ham.

Many gardeners have a couple of favorite varieties of green beans which they grow year after year—a variety for use fresh, another for canning, and sometimes a green and a wax or a purple for color contrast. Among the most commonly grown are varieties of stringless green pod—Kentucky Wonder, Blue Lake, or Yellow Wax. As satisfying as these varieties may have proved to be for the gardener, one might find some pleasant surprises in a sampling from the less familiar varieties. When one begins investigating, the options are almost intimidating. A single "bean collection," originally put together by a bean fancier named John Withe and now maintained by a group called the Wanigan Associates, numbers over 1,200 named varieties of beans, and this does not exhaust the possibilities. The normal seed rack or catalogue will provide the commonly grown varieties of green beans and few if any dried beans. For access to the uncommon varieties, one must resort to some of the less common catalogues—*Johnny's Select Seeds, The Vermont Bean Seed Company,* or *Good Seeds,* to name three good ones. For access to the widest range of selections, one must become affiliated with a group of seed exchangers.

A less common but excellent green bean is called the Bountiful. As a green bean it is full-flavored and fleshy and, when dried, its light brown, medium-sized bean is fine in soup or cooked as pork and beans. It is also a particularly productive bean.

A variety seldom seen except in specialty catalogues is the flageolet. This is the only bean which is invariably labeled a "gourmet" bean. Especially associated with lamb or mutton in French recipes, it is good at any stage, from green through dried. It has the odd and distinctive characteristic of slightly thickening the cooking broth, which is sometimes described as "making its own sauce." I consider it to be superlative; it is excellent green (actually it is a pale yellow, but not waxy), cans very well, and is good dried, although not as versatile dried as some others.

One variety, simply called Flageolet, I obtained from *Vermont Bean Seed*. Although described in the catalogue as requiring 100 days to mature, in my garden it was producing green beans much earlier, in about 80 days. It produces quite heavily. Cooked green it has a mild, delicate flavor, and this flavor holds up remarkably well through canning. Dried, the bean is almost perfectly cylindrical, about as long as a Great Northern white bean, but much more slender, and sort of off-white in color. When used as a dried bean it should not be pre-soaked; it is so tender it will cook to pieces.

A named variety, *Flageolet Vert,* is offered by *Nichols Garden.* As its name declares, it is of a greenish cast of color, and it is especially recommended as a shell bean. I have grown it only once, and had rather poor luck with it. For whatever reasons, germination was poor, so my sampling of it was too limited to be of value.

A variety called Vernel is offered by *The Urban Farmer.* The catalogue reports that it is described by French gardening magazines as the best of all the flageolets. The mature bean is smaller by perhaps a third than the generic variety first described, and the green pods correspondingly slimmer. Although it was reported to be good at any stage, I found the pods to be fibrous when cooked as a green or shelly bean.

An Italian variety of bean called *flageolini* is said to be very similar to the flageolet, and it is put to similar uses. Although I have heard it highly praised, I have never located its seeds. This should definitely be a variety to be sought out and examined, especially for those interested in Italian cooking.

A superb green bean is the Parfaco; the seeds I had were from Holland. Seed is difficult to locate, but is sometimes carried by *The Urban Farmer*. While individual tastes vary, of course, I rate it among the best of the green beans. It has a bright, distinctive flavor, which is particularly enhanced by cooking with bacon chunks or bacon rind. Pick when the seeds are distinctively formed, at which time the rather small pods will prominently bulge with the developing kernel. Their appearance is for this reason distinctive. This is also the proper stage at which to can them. As canned beans I rate them absolutely at the top. To a remarkable degree they retain the full flavor of fresh green beans. In fact, if I could grow only one green bean, this would be the variety I would choose.

The Creaseback is an old variety best cooked as a well-filled-out shelly bean. Even when the seeds have achieved their maximum size the pods are completely tender and fiber-free. They do require stringing. The seed I preserve was reputedly brought to the Northwest in the 1920s by strikebreakers from Tennessee who were hired during a labor dispute in the coal mines. Seed is rather generally available in specialty catalogues.

There is a specific cultivar of green beans called the Italian or Romano bean. Despite the name, these are, like regular green beans, a New World species. Most of this species are climbing or pole varieties. They have a broad, relatively flat pod, resembling a pea more than a bean, and they mature slowly. They are cooked similarly to other green beans, although they also figure in specific Italian recipes. Their flavor is excellent, but it is distinctively their own. According to my experience, they survive canning well. Grow them like any other pole beans, although more should be planted (if one develops a taste for them) since they seem to be somewhat less productive than other varieties.

The selection of varieties of dried beans is too vast to canvass; I will mention only a few. What I grow as a workhorse is a pre-Columbian variety—called variously Montezuma red, Mexican red, and Montezuma's red Mexican—a small, common-looking red bean good in chili, my favorite bean dish. They seem to be more digestible and less inclined to produce gas than the generic red beans of the marketplace. They are quite productive, requiring about 85 days to maturity. When dry, they are especially easy to shell.

The Swedish Brown bean is an attractive seed, perfectly oval and a little larger than a small navy bean. They are reputed to have been re-introduced to the New World by Swedish immigrants in the nineteenth century. They hold their consistency well in cooking and come highly recommended for use in baked bean recipes. I cook them with ham hocks and tomato sauce. They have a distinctive, slightly nutlike flavor.

The Vermont Cranberry is sometimes grown as a shell bean, but is also commonly used as a dried bean. It is a striking seed, as large or larger than a kidney bean, with bright red splashes of color on a pure white background.

The preparation of dried beans is no mystery and certainly no great chore. It is therefore somewhat surprising to see the number of "prepared" dried beans found canned on grocery shelves, or the number of times a recipe for a bean dish calls for one can of drained, cooked beans. One who grows any variety of dried beans might actually be affronted, since a problem collector-growers find is the occasion to make use of all of the beans they have harvested. Perhaps because it is a common winter evening activity, perhaps because of memory associations, I find readying beans the night before cooking distinctively calming, producing a curious sense of serenity and security. One of the earliest chores I performed as a child of about age three was shelling and cleaning dried beans. This latter operation my mother called "looking the beans." The main purpose was to identify and expel "bad beans." I believe this was my first introduction to the complexities of moral philosophy, and I felt heavily the weight of decision making in separating the chosen from the called. There is still in my memory several beans for which I'm not certain I made the correct decision.

Even store-bought beans required "looking." Aside from decisions of judgment, there was the practical necessity of removing bean-sized pieces of rock. As rural Westerners, we assumed such rock was deliberately added by Eastern gangsters to defraud us. There is a minor Western mythology surrounding ranch cooks; one story line treats of cooks careless—by suspicion deliberately so—in "looking" their beans and failing to remove all the rocks. Such legends have it that contrary to popular tradition more cowhands lost teeth to rocks in their beans than to saloon brawls. And if there is truth to these same legends, more boot hills have been populated by cooks serving rocky beans than by all the fast-draw showdowns put together.

Although the varieties of green, horticultural, and dried beans run to the thousands, all of those just mentioned are technically cultivars of the same variety, *Phaseolus vulgaris.* In addition to these there are several other distinct varieties, all likewise native to the New World. One such variety is the runner bean, properly, *Phaseolus coccineus.* The most familiar of this variety is the scarlet runner. A prolific grower, in most climates it will easily achieve a height of 12 feet in a summer and, with its many-branching habit of growth, might seem to rival kudzu in its ability to surround such support systems as fences and outbuildings. It has a most attractive red ("scarlet") blossom, and sets prodigious numbers of long pods, filled with red kidney bean–sized seeds. It is much more often grown as an ornamental rather than as a food crop. In fact, I remember people persistently asserting that the bean was poisonous. This is absolutely not true; the bean is edible both as a green bean and as a dried bean; however, it is not particularly distinguished as either. Nevertheless, it is an impressive vine; the blossoms are lovely—they attract hummingbirds—and it is worth growing for aesthetic reasons alone, if one has a suitable location. It is a long-season bean, requiring in excess of 100 days.

A more useful, if less spectacular, member of the family is called the English runner bean, although there might be some doubts about its exact family affiliation. Its appearance and growth habits certainly conform to that of *P. coccineus,* but I have not found it positively identified as a member of that family. It grows easily to a height of 10 feet, with bright blossoms, though not as brilliant as the scarlet runner. The hulls are a deep, almost black red. The seed is much smaller than the scarlet runner, only a little larger than the common navy bean, and the skin has a somewhat wrinkled appearance. Its uses are about the same as those of a navy bean, although probably most people would be inclined to grow it as an attractive novelty. It is a much shorter season bean than the scarlet runner.

Another distinct variety largely unknown outside of restricted ethnic regions is the Santa Maria Pinquito. They have been characterized as *the* gourmet bean for chili. They do not break up in cooking and are lower in starch than other beans, besides having a particularly distinctive and pleasing flavor of their own. The beans are a light dusty pink, quite small—perhaps half the size of a small navy bean—and wrinkled; they plump up and round out when soaked. Seeds are relatively difficult to locate, although they are offered by *Nichols Gardens.* In Mexico they are grown in a restricted area of the interior western valleys. *Nichols Gardens* suggests they will mature in a 90-day growing period, but in my Zone 5 they take longer. They seem to be heat lovers, and consequently do not do well for me, which is too bad because I am particularly partial to chili.

A separate species of bean that is beginning to attract attention among plant breeders is the tepary bean. This is a pre-Columbian variety that has been grown for thousands of years by Indians inhabiting the harsh desert climate of the Sonoran Desert and the Colorado Plateau. This bean not only survives but thrives in the hot desert summers. It will wait for a couple of months for a rain, then suddenly mature a crop on its moisture. The beans are thin, only two-thirds the size of a small white navy. Some varieties are flat and wrinkled, some plump. They are pretty little things. Besides their adaption to drought and intense heat, a further attraction is that they have an unusually high protein content, as much as 20 percent higher than common beans.

Tepary beans require a long growing season, from 90 to 110 days. They do not mature well where the climate is particularly moist, and their desert origin is clearly reflected in their preference for hot, dry weather. It is their growing habit to sprawl, so give them a good 2 feet on each side. Their distinctiveness can be seen with the first true leaves, which have an erect, slender, spearhead shape rather than the expected heart-shaped bean leaf. The color of the foliage inclines to something of a jade green, which is somewhat unusual.

Collectors are still accumulating cultivars of teparies, and several varieties have become commercially available. Some seed companies have temporarily withheld seed from commercial offerings because of virus infections, promising to offer them again as soon as the condition is corrected.

With little exercise in imagination or flair, I have grown three varieties—green, white, and brown speckled. My best results were with the brown speckled, perhaps because I grew the first two varieties one year, the brown speckled two years later. I had learned more about beans' habits the second time around, which should definitely have made a difference. The first year I think I planted too early, and many seeds failed to germinate because the soil was cooler than required. In their instructions, *G. Seeds* recommends soil temperature of 65 degrees or above. For my growing conditions that is unrealistically high. The second time around I planted in mid-June rather than mid-May and had a fine stand by the end of the month, although soil temperatures could not have been above 50 degrees.

Because they are so little known, recipes for the use of tepary beans are lacking. I have used them in chili and find them satisfactory, but not outstanding. They keep their texture well through cooking, and because of their small size cook completely in only about an hour and a half.

Opportunities for experimenting with teparies, horticultural as well as gastronomical, seem to be wide open, and these might well be the beans of the future. Anyone who grows them should be sure to save the seeds, because their distinctive growing preferences make it especially desirable to attempt to acclimatize them to one's own mini-climate.

Another distinct bean variety is the Adjuki—*Vigna angularis*—an Oriental adaptation of an American original, although there is uncertainty about exact origins and ancestry. The seed is quite small, about two-thirds the size of a small navy bean. The variety I have tried is called Adjuki Express, which I obtained from *Johnny's Select Seeds*. This variety is shiny and dark red. As a matter of fact, they look like lacquered Oriental beads. Adjukis require less cooking than ordinary dried beans, and are more digestible. Their flavor is distinctive but, like most flavors, defies description. Although I have not tried them in this way, they would seem to be a fine ingredient for a "seven-bean" salad. They are a long-season crop, rated by *Johnny's* at 111 days. In my Zone 5, maturity is marginal or risky, and unless the autumn is dry and warm, few ripen.

A cousin of the bean family called "black-eyed peas"—*Vigna sinensis*—is another New World addition to the human food chain. Black-eyed peas are most familiarly associated with the South and for a good reason: they require a long growing season, 125 to 140 days. Like other beans, they are eaten green in the pods (usually at about the same stage of maturity as shelly beans), shelled, and dried. To grow them to maturity requires a good bit of real summer heat. They are quite good, and worth growing along with standard green beans, if the climate permits. Plant and cultivate them almost exactly as if they were green bush beans but give them lots of room; they love to vine luxuriantly in the hot summer sun.

It has only been in this century that the Oriental soy bean has been grown in the Western world. It has assumed a dominant position in the supply of vegetable protein, first for livestock feed, more recently as a protein "stretcher" for direct human consumption. Alone it is not especially palatable to Western tastes, but varieties are emerging directed toward the home gardener, particularly a "green" soy bean to be used like a green pea or bean. It also has uses as a dried vegetable, and some home gardeners grow it for sprouting. The soy bean requires an extended growing season—120 days plus. This puts it outside the range of many American gardeners. Research is progressing in developing short-season varieties. I planted one advertised as a 100-day variety, and its performance was less than satisfactory. Their cultivation is about the same as any other bean; plant them in a warm soil after all danger of frost has passed. They will probably not be as productive as other beans.

Like peas and beans, lima beans—*Phaseolus lunatus*—are grown to be used either green or dried. This is another New World vegetable, originating in South America, hence the name Lima, after the capital of Peru. Although they require a long growing season and hot weather, they are cultivated like green beans. They are very frost-tender and will not germinate until the soil warms thoroughly. Planted too early, the seed rots. Two varieties are commonly grown, although there are numerous cultivars with more or less individual characteristics. One variety is commonly called the "baby lima" because of its relatively small bean, and the regular lima, with mature seeds the size of a nickel or larger. The baby limas mature earlier and are generally preferred in northern areas. They also seem to be a little less mealy than the larger beans. None of the limas really flourish until they get good hot summer weather. In a given region there may be wide differences in mini-climates, and only a few miles from a garden that refuses to grow an acceptable crop another garden will produce prolifically. Dried limas, regionally called "butter beans," are those that are allowed to mature and ripen in the pods.

Most of the branches of the ancient pulse family deserve a place in gardens where the climate allows, and few areas are so severe that some members cannot be grown satisfactorily. They are exceptionally good sources of the basic nutrients of proteins and carbohydrates, and, especially green, of vitamins as well. And being legumes, they are ever so nourishing to the soil.

When one begins investigating the options among bean varieties, the sheer number becomes staggering. After all, how many varieties of beans can a given gardener grow? One can envision becoming like the model railroad enthusiast, who keeps buying bigger and still bigger houses to accommodate his burgeoning trackage, until the American West itself is insufficient to provide adequate horizons. Only the tip of the iceberg, as it were, of varieties of *Phaseolus* has been mentioned. Even relatively common varieties—Jacob's Cattle Beans, Soldier's Bean, Oregon Giant—neglected by the score, and by the scores of scores, come tumbling to the tongue. Just remember, first of all, that a gardener won't do all that bad simply buying seeds off the rack, or ordering the common variety or what a catalogue is hustling as the current year's sensation. But there's something stimulating in recognizing that in something as common and homely as a bean there are options and surprises—excitements, even. There are real improvements and novelties in flavor to be investigated; for example, the little-grown flageolet. There are improvements to be discovered in "purpose-grown" beans, such as the Santa Maria Pinquito. There are distinctions in adaptability and nutrition, as in the tepary. And the varieties of color and appearance are dazzling. With a modest selection, a seven-bean salad that is absolutely stunning is within easy reach. Ultimately, any interested gardener worth a hill of beans will discover his or her own rationalizations for growing many varieties.

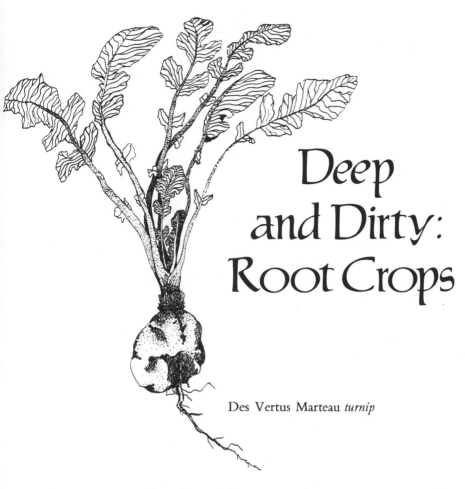

Deep and Dirty: Root Crops

Des Vertus Marteau *turnip*

It's a great pity that the radish is not a better or more versatile vegetable. It's easier to grow than mange on a stray dog. Also it is an extremely pretty little thing, and looks like it belongs in a nineteenth-century still life. If it were as useful as, for example, wheat, or potatoes, or even chick peas, there would be ships and stars named after it. It's one of the first things that germinates in the spring, or whenever it's planted, and in an astonishingly short time its little root swells, and in a few more days turns into a mature radish. As one writer observed, it is mature and ready for harvest before parsley seed has germinated.

When I was a boy and did farm labor, I once contracted to thin a seven-acre field that had just been planted to rutabaga. I moved into the farmer's tool shed, and he took off for a two-week vacation. By the time I had finished thinning the field, it was becoming clear that these were the most curious rutabagas ever; the roots were bright red and when I was finishing up they were actually beginning to swell. The farmer returned to find he had seven acres of radishes, all neatly thinned 4 inches apart rutabaga fashion, and already as big as marbles. Not happy, that man.

Even though radishes have limited use, last only a short while, and the usual varieties cannot be stored, every gardener should plant at least a small row of radishes each year. Growing them is such a quick pickup to a gardener's ego. Even the most experienced and successful gardener can use that boost early in the year. And then, they are such pretty little things.

Two varieties of radish are commonly grown—top-shaped variety and the long, usually clear-white varieties. While radishes can be planted almost anytime through the entire season, the best quality are those grown before the weather begins to turn really hot. They may be planted in the early spring, at the same time as lettuce is planted. Since they are a plant quick to mature, they are good to use in a spot that can later be reseeded with another crop. Plant the seeds in a shallow trench, cover lightly, and pack. The seeds are quick to germinate, and if they come up thickly should be lightly thinned when the first true leaf appears. The long white varieties should be thinned to about 2 inches apart for the most attractive long, straight roots.

Radishes are at their peak for only a short period, quickly becoming woody as they reach maturity. For this reason people really partial to them make a small planting every week or so during the spring, or until the weather becomes too warm to grow mellow-flavored radishes. Radishes look as if they should be a biennial, like their cousins, the turnips. However, they are most often an annual, and when the root reaches full size, it puts up a tall stalk, flowers, and produces seeds. It makes you wonder why they went to the trouble of growing such a fleshy root if they were going to go to seed in the first year anyway.

Aside from common whites and reds, radishes fall into two additional general categories—spring (fresh) and winter (storage). Spring radishes are the familiar market and garden varieties, eaten as soon after pulling as possible. Winter radishes are harvested in the fall for winter storage, or allowed to remain in the ground over winter with a heavy cover of mulch for protection, to be harvested as wanted. They are eaten raw, sliced as a salad ingredient, or cooked in Oriental recipes.

My favorite of the spring radishes is a French variety called Early French Breakfast, which is widely offered. It is quite attractive: brilliant red contrasted with a pure white, top shaped, or somewhat elongated. The flavor is mild but piquant, and it seems to me to be more digestible than the more familiar garden varieties. A quite similar variety, called Flamivil, is offered by *Epicure Seeds.* The same company also offers *Saxafire radij,* a variety from Holland which I have not tried, which they described as mild but with a bite. They also offer what is called a Munich Beer radish, *Herbstrettich Münchner Bier,* a long white radish which is sliced thin, dipped in salt or sugar, and eaten with beer. A radish used for similar purposes but as large as a turnip, called Prosit, is offered by *Le Jardin du Gourmet.*

A winter radish simply called *Winterrettich* is offered by *Epicure Seeds*—round, black-skinned, and stored to be used in salads. There are several varieties of Oriental winter radish, some very large. I have grown only one variety, Shantong Green Skin *(Sunrise Enterprises).* It is rather large, long and cylindrical, an inch or two of which is dark green in color sticking above the ground. The part beneath the ground is white. It is planted in late summer (early August for me) and thinned to about 3 inches. Roots are harvested in late autumn before the ground freezes and are kept in cool storage. This variety grew well for me, but I left it in the ground too long and the main harvest froze. To enjoy this radish one would have to have proper Oriental recipes for using it.

A winter radish that must be considered a novelty is the Mammoth White Globe from Japan *(Glecklers Seedsmen).* This variety is reputed to attain weights as great as 20 pounds, but for such size a growing season of 150 days is required. They are described as being used in relish trays and in Oriental recipes. For me to plant them in a Zone 5 was hardly a serious intent; I just wanted to get a look at them growing. Unfortunately, I had quite poor germination. Three plants grew, but never reached the size of small turnips, and I found little to recommend. I attribute all problems, however, most likely including palatability, to my climate. In a milder climate the Mammoths might truly take prizes, for flavor as well as size.

Rutabagas also have restricted, if not limited uses, but are vastly more versatile than radishes. The seeds are virtually identical, as confirmed above, and the seedlings are also identical until the first true leaves develop. Except for a general family resemblance in foliage, from this point real similarity ceases. The rutabaga, also known locally and in England, as a Swede or Swedish turnip, is close kin to the cabbage. It resembles the turnip and is even occasionally called a Purple Top turnip (a variety of turnip is also so called), but it is a rather distant relative of the turnip family. The immediate visual distinction between them is the top; the turnip has a rosette to which all the leaves are attached; clearly a top. The leaves of the rutabaga are more or less independently attached to the root itself rather than to a central crown.

American markets prefer a rutabaga about 3 inches in diameter or less, neatly top-shaped. Within limits, size is controlled by timing the planting and by thinning. Given time and space, rutabagas are capable of growing large, 10 inches and more in diameter. In the British Isles the preference is for the larger roots. I have seen them in markets weighing 3 or 4 pounds. This vegetable appears more frequently in British cookery than in American, often appearing boiled in the company of other boiled vegetables.

Rutabagas are easy to grow and are not terribly fussy about soil. They will grow in a wide spectrum of climates, but do particularly well in northern or cooler areas. They can be planted after the danger of frost is past but are more commonly planted in early summer, even up to the beginning of July, especially in commercial plantings where it is desirable to restrain the size. Planting too early in the season tends to produce very large roots. A 7-pound rutabaga may possibly be as good as a 6-ounce one, but that would be an awful lot of a single vegetable to take care of at once. A good planting time should be mid-June. Sow the seeds thinly in a shallow trench; if more than one row is desired, they should be spaced about 18 inches apart. Sprinkle a thin covering of soil and pack lightly. When the second true leaf appears, thin to 4 to 6 inches apart, depending on how large a root one can handle.

It is possible to transplant the seedlings removed in thinning, and some people do, but there's not much point in such frugality. I read an article by someone who had transplanted every seedling that germinated from a single seed packet, spacing them 6 inches apart. He harvested over 200 pounds. Good for him. As Shakespeare's clown said as he delivered a poisonous asp to Cleopatra, "May you have joy of the worm." On the farm where I grew up rutabagas were one of the diverse crops we regularly grew. As a family we would scarcely eat 10 pounds a year, although we might have as much as 40 tons stored in our root cellar. Everything in moderation, especially virtue and self-righteousness. One fall during World War II my father sold our entire crop to a processor who had a contract to dehydrate them for the U.S. Government. Together with others who grew rutabagas, we speculated on what in the world the government had in mind for all of those dried rutabagas. My father offered the definitive guess. He speculated that the plan was for the army to take the dried rutabagas to a combat zone, feed them to the fighting forces, and aim them toward the enemy. After having been fed dried rutabagas, the troops would be so insanely angry that they would attack anyone in sight. Undehydrated rutabagas are not bad, even though they come in for a disproportionate share of bad-vegetable jokes. But if you want to sustain a cheery attitude about rutabagas, don't go into the winter committed to eating 200 pounds of them.

Rutabagas are not vegetables that have to mature before eating; they can be used anytime after they are an inch or so across. They should be dug up in autumn before heavy freezing sets in, although they are capable of enduring frost with no damage, and light frost improves their flavor. When harvesting for storage, slice off the "top" very thinly, and shave away the thin line of rootlets that form a sideburn down opposing sides of the roots, taking care not to cut deeply into the skin of the root itself. The roots can be stored like potatoes, and keep well. Most people think that a rutabaga is a rutabaga, and do not think of there being different kinds, or better kinds. Although I have not tried it, a variety that comes highly recommended is called Best of All, offered by *Territorial Seed Company*.

Turnips flourish through a wide variety of climates and reach mature size quickly. For this reason they have been an important staple in impoverished rural areas. Planted early in warmer climates, they provide food in quantity before most comparably nourishing vegetables have had a chance to get going.

Turnips played an obscure but pivotal role in the development of the modern livestock industry. Because grain was too expensive and too valuable as human food in England, and hay was scarce because it was so difficult to cure, the practice up through the seventeenth century was to keep few cattle through the winter. In the land of the Beefeaters four hundred years ago it was uncommon for beef to be eaten regularly. This was a reason game in all forms was a real food item, not a luxury or novelty item, for the classes of people who had access to meat at all. In the eighteenth century the practice developed, introduced by the great English agriculturist Jethro Tull, of growing turnips for use as winter feed for livestock. Thus large numbers of cattle could be kept through the winter, making it possible for beef to become a practical item of diet. With the introduction of turnip cultivation, the scope of the livestock industry in the British Isles was transformed.

Turnips are still considered to be more a subsistence food than a vegetable of choice. Although they are cooked and eaten alone, and regionally even used as a main dish, most commonly they are prepared in combination with other vegetables or meat, typically in stews or casseroles.

Paradoxically, the objection commonly voiced by people who decline turnips is that they taste so "turnipy." They come by it naturally. There is, however, one variety advertised as lacking this flavor many do not appreciate. Called *Des Vertus Marteau* (France: *Epicure Seeds*), it is the only turnip variety I know of that is offered as a gourmet selection. I will not come on as strong in praising them as does the seed company—"An indescribably delicious turnip without the bite and strong turnipy taste of most turnips"—but these turnips are not bad. The catalogue suggests scalloping them like potatoes, parboiling and slicing them before putting them in the casserole. They are quite acceptable raw—sliced thin and included on a relish tray, or even alone like carrot sticks, which for me would be totally unacceptable with regular turnips. They are also attractive: creamy colored rather than clear white, and more cylindrical than top-shaped. All turnips are attractive to aphids, but this variety seems especially attractive to them, and aphids are a serious problem. Perhaps they, too, appreciate a non-turnipy taste. Anyway, the aphid infestation grew so rapidly in my first planting that a section of the row was severely damaged—more accurately, killed in their tracks—before I even discovered a problem was developing. I also found this variety to be infested with root maggots, which seldom trouble my garden. Except for these problems they are, like all turnips, easy to grow. I did not check them for storage qualities.

Broadly speaking, there are two kinds of turnips, winter and summer, depending on how well they keep. Preference for varieties of turnips varies locally; if they are to be stored, it would be wise to check what specific varieties are locally preferred for their keeping quality. While my experience with storing turnips is not extensive, it seems to me that even winter varieties do not keep as well as, for example, rutabagas.

When turnips bolt, the unopened seed head is especially prized for some, especially in Italian cooking. It is used in salads, or steamed like broccoli. It goes by the name of "salit raab," "rabe," and "broccoli raab." A variety developed especially for this purpose, or at least reputed to be especially suited for it, is said to be *Late Rapone.*

Other kinds of related root crops are now more commonly grown for livestock feed than turnips. Anyone with a flock of chickens or other small barnyard animals might well consider a planting for supplemental fodder. One most impressive variety which is grown exclusively for livestock feed is the mangle, or Wurtzle mangle. It is planted early and requires an extended growing season, but produces an impressively large root—perhaps 10 pounds or more. A large portion of the mangle root will be above ground, as if someone had started to pound them into the soil but given up when the job was only half done.

Sugar beets can also be grown for livestock feed. For the fanatical back-to-nature buff, it is also possible to make sugar from sugar beets, but it is hardly worth the trouble. Some kinds of preserves and conserves can be made from them. They make a quite rich livestock feed.

Until recently it was difficult to obtain seeds for sugar beets. Part of the reason was no doubt a lack of demand, but also the growing of sugar beets for commerce was a sort of monopoly controlled by beet sugar companies, which supplied seed to their contracted farmers, keeping it otherwise out of commerce. The seeds are now occasionally offered by general seed catalogues *(Henry Field Seed and Nursery Co., Olds Seed Company)*. If you want to try them, plant in well-worked soil in early spring in a shallow trench sprinkled with loose soil and lightly packed. The beet roots grow to a large size, in the 4- to 6-pound range, so must be thinned to give them room to develop. Space them about 10 inches apart, and if more than one row is grown the rows should be no less than 24 inches apart. At full growth, their foliage is thick and heavy. They like a long, hot summer, with plenty of irrigation, but they flourish under a wide range of conditions. Harvest them before severe weather sets in, although frosting won't hurt them. Since commercially it is usual to process them as soon as they are harvested, little effort has been expended on techniques of storage. If to be stored for livestock feed, their keeping quality should be about the same as turnips', or a little better.

Compared to sugar beets, regular garden beets are pygmies. Some varieties do get quite large, though most people prefer those that are no larger than 2 inches or so in diameter. The size, or sizes, grown will depend on individual preferences and uses. They are commonly planted in spring, about the time of the last frost. Since they grow rapidly, they may be planted anytime up until midsummer. People who prefer eating the very small varieties make a succession of plantings through June to be assured of having small and tender beets. Each "seed" is actually a small fruit containing 5 or 6 true seeds, each of which will likely germinate. Consequently, plant sparingly. Plant them like turnips, in a shallow trench with a sprinkling of soil, lightly tamped. They should be thinned, the distance between plants determined by the variety and the stage at which they are to be used. Small plants may be spaced as little as an inch apart, large ones up to 3 or 4 inches apart.

A number of garden beet varieties are grown, many of them old. *Epicure Seeds* offers an English and a Dutch variety. The English variety, Long Blood Red, is described as ugly but is among the best for flavor, especially notable for sweetness. The Dutch variety, *Tardel Kroten,* is slow to bolt, attractively globe-shaped, and sweet, described as the best for pickling. Some people grow beets for greens, in which case the row is seeded more heavily and the plants left unthinned. Like turnips crowded in this fashion the leaves grow quickly while the roots remain match-thin. There are also varieties developed exclusively for their tops, such as Green Top Bunching, which never develops a thick root.

Parsnips are a root crop whose value no one ever argues about. Either they are hated categorically and absolutely, or fanatically and absolutely cherished. Like most of the root crops, parsnips are easy to grow and reasonably dependable. Plant the seeds in early spring, in a shallow trench covered with about a half-inch of earth packed lightly on top. The seeds are slow to germinate, and soaking the seeds overnight in water will help push them along a little. Nothing may appear for three weeks or so, and when they do start to germinate it may be two or three weeks before there is a good stand. The early foliage resembles the leaves of young celery. If the final stand of plants is too heavy, they may be thinned to a distance of about 4 inches apart.

Gardeners tend to think of parsnips purely as generic. However, Harris Model is offered by *Territorial Seed Company* as distinctively superior. Parsnips are an exceptionally good bet to grow in cold climates. While they may be dug and stored in the fall, they are actually much better if allowed to overwinter in the ground and last longer than most overwintered root crops. They are not damaged by frost, and freezing in the ground improves their flavor considerably— as with other winter-hardy crops, it changes some of the starch to sugar. Some people mulch heavily on top of the parsnips' row, using piles of leaves, straw, or whatever is available to keep the ground from freezing solid in order to dig them out in the dead of winter. I've never been partial to digging roots in the dead of winter; they are plenty fine left until early spring.

Parsnip roots are very long. Sixteen inches is not uncommon, but they grow longer. It should be evident that one does not so much *dig* parsnips, as *excavate* them. A friend once commented that he expected more shovel handles have been broken digging parsnips than in any other activity in which shovels are used.

He was wrong. More shovel handles have been broken digging horseradish roots. Horseradish is not, properly considered, a root crop, but it's the root we use, and it grows underground. *Far* underground. It is a perennial and, once established, is a permanent fixture with tall, heavy foliage, so it must be planted where it can stay and not bother anything else. It requires little attention, and will always be there for the taking whenever the need arises.

Some seed catalogues are quite bullish on horseradish. I examined a catalogue that offered incredible savings on large purchases. The smallest package available was three cuttings at a nominal price, less than two dollars. Then proceeding in multiples of three, the savings effected were astonishing. The largest unit price quoted was for a gross, but the listing concluded enticingly, "Write for bulk prices." I can only assume that the list was aimed at a prospective customer with absolute innocence on the subject of horseradish. I can even envisage the comic possibility of a neophyte gardener, assuming some similarity between horseradish and salad radishes, who would actually order the gross package, and even plant it. Finding his entire yard by midsummer a jungle of shoulder-high leaves, attached to roots impossible to eradicate—ever—we can assume he has never attempted to garden again. Who can ever foresee the consequences of an innocent catalogue entry, or the earnest advice of the Department of Agriculture.

Before planting, make a committed decision to a permanent location. Like asparagus, a spot along a fence is a good choice. Even an otherwise marginal stretch along a roadside might do fine. The plants spread, slowly, and produce a heavy growth of tall upright leaves, each attached to the root crown. Though somewhat coarse and even rank, they are attractive and worth considering for their decorative possibilities, especially as a border planting in a difficult situation.

For actual use as a condiment, most families would be bountifully supplied by no more than three horseradish roots. An actual *row* of them, as the instructions given by the Department of Agriculture seem to conceive, is unthinkable. Plant the small root or root cutting purchased, or borrowed from a friend, bigger-end up, about 2 inches deep, 18 to 24 inches apart, and firm the soil over them. It will do the rest. The second year a root perhaps 2 inches in diameter and as much as 2-feet long will have developed and may be harvested. It may be straight (this is the ideal sought for), but may also be branched, perhaps many-branched. Enough small rootlets will be left in the ground when it is dug to make a small forest of horseradish the following year, and all years subsequently. In other words, one should not plant horseradish unless one really means it.

A given gardener may or may not grow rutabagas, parsnips, or horseradish, but almost everyone plants carrots. They are a gentle little plant, undemanding in their wants and versatile in their uses. They may be pulled from the ground, brushed against a pants' leg and eaten on the spot, with a fresh sweet tang they will never have again. Scrubbed, they appear raw on the table, slivered in salads, packed in lunches. They are steamed, creamed, cooked with peas and potatoes, stewed, cooked with roasts. Stored, they keep almost as well as potatoes. Even left in the ground over the winter, they are still usable for a short time when the ground thaws the following spring, and when the freezing has changed the starch to sugar, sweeter than they ever were during the summer. They are among the earliest seeds that can be planted in the spring, may be planted successively during a good part of the early summer, and are one of the last things from the garden to be harvested.

Carrots may be said to prefer a fertile, light soil but actually do well through a wide range of soil types; basically, they just like dirt. Because of the long roots of some varieties, it is said that the soil needs to be tilled deeply and well to accommodate their growth. It is true that a heavy soil, especially if undertilled, may tend to encourage the roots to branch under ground. If this turns out to be a problem, it is probably solvable simply by planting the short stubby varieties.

There are a bewildering range of kinds of carrots to choose from, and although most seem to flourish generally, if there is any doubt consult with nurseries or experienced gardeners respecting what does well locally. The familiar long, slender carrot is better used fresh than dug for storage. However, planted early, even in the cooler climates, they should yield plentiful quantities from mid-June until the ground freezes. Long carrots seem more prone to rot in the ground during the winter than the shorter, heavier kinds, although they are equally good fresh. There is a further choice in variety respecting the "core," or lack of it. Some carrots have a quite distinctive core, red or sometimes green, especially toward the top. The coreless varieties tend to be milder raw, and those with cores seem to retain their flavor better through cooking.

Early carrots should be planted about the same time potatoes are planted. For eating most gardeners with adequate space prefer fresh carrots which are still partially immature—"carrot points," as they are sometimes called, and for a continuous supply of them make more than one planting during the course of the growing season.

To plant, draw a shallow trench and distribute the seeds sparingly, covering with a sprinkling of earth lightly tamped. I usually plant double rows, about 6 inches apart. If more than one row or double row is planted, space them wide enough for cultivation and irrigation, certainly no closer together than 14 inches. Carrot seeds are slow to germinate, and seeds planted in the early spring will likely come up a little spotty, gradually filling in as the weather warms. Count on two or three weeks before there is a showing, unless the weather turns fair and warm. Some people (and the instructions on many seed packets) advise thinning. However, if one is sufficiently skimpy with the seeds (4 to 6 per inch), carrots should do quite nicely with no thinning at all. Grown as a commercial crop, they are seldom if ever thinned. The little roots have a way of working out space arrangements among themselves with astonishing efficiency and sometimes alarming intimacy. Since most people begin harvesting carrot points as soon as they are as big as pencils, if any thinning is necessary, this should take care of it.

Subsequent (or initial) plantings of carrots can be made as late as the end of June in most regions and still produce a worthwhile crop. Commercial plantings of carrots for storage are often made that late even in northern areas to prevent the roots from becoming overmature or woody, and to improve their keeping qualities. Except in climates where the soil regularly freezes to a depth of more than a foot and stays frozen for an extended period, some carrots should be left in the ground for spring use. Leaves, straw, or other mulch can be piled on the row—a foot or so deep, depending on climate—and even in the dead of winter it will be possible to get to them. Overwintered in the ground, these carrots are a particular treat in the late winter or early spring. It is a special pleasure then to go out and actually bring something in from the garden. As soon as they start to grow again, however, they might as well be pulled and discarded. They quickly begin to turn soft on the bottom, and as they begin to grow new foliage, the tops become woody. By that time something else may have appeared ready to use from the garden. At least a gardener will be able to dig and delve and plant, and anything seems possible again.

Carrots' nutritional values, of course, are widely appreciated. I remember a 1930s' illustration of that fact. Three very reprobate and dissolute young brothers, epitomes of the grasshoppers in the grasshopper-and-ant fable, sustained themselves in fine style as farm laborers in the summer. When winter came with its zero employment, they would move in with their widowed mother. Long-suffering only to a degree, one winter she barred the door against them. In desperation they took up abode in a decrepit old cabin. For sustenance, late one night they broke into what they thought was a potato cellar, and stole six one-hundred-pound sacks of produce. Carrots, not potatoes. They survived the winter on a diet of virtually nothing but carrots, reportedly in at least as good health as they began and, according to unreliable gossip, with eyesight so keen they could catch cats in the dark. No evidence ever surfaced that the diet improved their characters correspondingly.

The experience probably so prejudiced the palates of these three wastrels that never again could they be tempted with even the choicest varieties. With a little searching these are available to the modern gardener. One of the most highly regarded is the *Touchon* (France: *Nichols Garden*), a medium-sized carrot, rather cylindrical, with a very blunt tip. It is practically coreless, sweet, and mild flavored. The *Primenantes* (France: *Nichols Garden*) has an especially attractive bright, reddish-orange color. It is sweet and crisp, with a particularly attractive carrot flavor (unlike "turnipy," "carroty" is a term of approval). The Forto (Belgium: *Epicure Seeds*) is of medium length, and therefore especially recommended for heavy soils. It is also said to be a good storage carrot, although I have not tested this. The Nugget *(Nichols Garden)* is recommended for where soil is especially heavy. The root is almost round, like a medium-sized radish, and solid orange, with a strong flavor. While a little fibrous, these are good cooked, although I wouldn't recommend them except as being quite adaptable to heavy soil. The Nantaise Tip-Top (Holland: *The Urban Farmer*) is similar to the familiar produce market–bunching carrots. However, it seems to me to be sweeter and more flavorful than they are. The *Sucram* (France: *Nichols Garden*) is a miniature *nantes* type, said to be very popular in Europe. It is quite sweet, and is especially attractive on a relish tray—perfectly formed and tapered, but only about 3 inches long. They might be a good choice to make canned carrot points.

On the opposite extreme is the Imperial Long (Japan: *Glecklers Seedsmen*), which is said to grow to nearly 3 feet in length. For me they grew to about 14 inches, which is still a remarkably long carrot. To grow extremely long, smooth roots requires a fairly loose, preferably sandy soil. Imperial Longs are an interesting novelty to amaze and astonish your friends, as catalogues love to say, but they cannot be considered a practical choice for a gardener. Their flavor is just "all right," but except for their appearance they are hardly an epicurean item.

Of these varieties my three favorites are *Touchon, Primenantes,* and *Sucram*. All three are sufficiently superior to be sought out in preference over seed rack carrots. If I could grow only one variety it would be *Touchon*.

Sweet potatoes and yams confuse both shoppers and gardeners. By designation of the Department of Agriculture, sweet potatoes are those that feel comparatively dry in the mouth, yams those that feel comparatively moist. Dryness in this designation does not indicate actual moisture content, but the sensation of moisture in the mouth. Sweet potatoes by this designation usually are slenderish and have a light-colored skin, yams plump and yellowish. As a species, both are the same and are native to the Americas. Properly speaking, the yam is an entirely different species, a tropical perennial or shrub, having an enormous—up to several hundred pounds—tuberous root. It is mostly cultivated in the Pacific regions, and to the world at large its most familiar product is tapioca.

Typically, sweet potatoes are thought of as a Southern crop, but its possible range is much larger. They grow in a wide variety of soils, but it must be a soil that can be kept loose. It does best planted in a ridge or raised bed. For good results spread black plastic on top of the ridges or bed two or three weeks before planting to help warm the soil. Sweet potatoes are planted from sprouts grown on mature tubers. It is possible to grow one's own sprouts from tubers bought in the market, but it is preferable to order sprouts from a nursery, which is the only way to make sure you are getting varieties suitable in hardiness, habits, and quality for your area.

Sweet potato plants may be vining in habit, semi-vining, or bush. The viny varieties are space-greedy. They may be planted along a fence and trained as climbers. The foliage of all varieties is attractive, with glossy green, sometimes purple, foliage. As soon as they arrive, set the sprouts in the prepared bed—in the afternoon if the day is hot. Sometimes when the package is opened the sprouts will have an unpleasant smell, but plant them anyway, most likely they are fine. Keep the plants well watered, and hand-cultivate. As vigorous growth begins, the lush vines make them quite competitive with weeds. Dig in the fall, handling the tubers carefully; they are quite tender, especially when first dug, and if bruised at all will spoil quickly.

The Vardaman is a long vining variety with bright purple foliage that may easily be made to climb a fence or other trellis. The Centennial is the commonest American sweet potato, a variety often seen in produce markets. It will mature small tubers in 90 days. Gloria Jets and Jewell are also recommended for northern gardens. All of these varieties are available from *Steele Plant Company.*

Another all-weather root crop some gardeners might consider worth trying is the Jerusalem artichoke. It is not an artichoke, and if it has ever been to Jerusalem it was as a modern-day pilgrim. The plant is a member of the sunflower family, and its name is often explained as derived from a corruption of the Spanish *girasole,* meaning "sun plant." However, because of the date of first usage, a more likely explanation is that the name originated in Terneuzen, the place where they were first grown in Europe.

Indigenous to North America, the Jerusalem artichoke is one of the few New World food plants to originate on the northern continent. The uncultivated wild plant was eaten by Indian tribes from coast to coast, and its use in Indian diets no doubt contributed to its spread. Archeological sites of old Indian encampments have been located because thick plantings of Jerusalem artichokes reveal locations of old midden heaps. Because these plantings grew year after year at old encampments, it was an encouragement for Indians to return to the same camps, and perhaps this was a primitive first step from hunter-gatherer nomadic cultures to an agricultural society.

So the plant has a little romance and glamour in its past, always a pleasant discovery in a new acquaintance. Frequently, however, dazzling new acquaintances too soon reveal a touch of dross behind the glitter. The reality behind the romance of the Jerusalem artichokes has two flaws: some people, including myself, think they don't taste very good. Second, they are takers; once established in a garden, they are difficult to eradicate.

For those to whom Jerusalem artichokes are palatable, they are versatile. They can be eaten raw, sliced or grated into salads, sliced and used like water chestnuts, cooked in the usual ways potatoes are cooked, creamed, and so on. Sliced thin and used raw, they add an interesting texture to a salad (and this is really the only way I care for them). Cooked, some characterize their flavor as bland. More uncharitably, I'm inclined to use the word *insipid*. But they do have one commanding recommendation in that their starch is compatible with the diet of diabetics.

The edible portion is a tuber that vaguely, but only vaguely, resembles a potato. Sometimes they may be as large as a good-sized potato but are rarely as smooth. Usually they have numerous knuckle-shaped side protuberances. For the most part it is necessary to break them apart and peel the smaller pieces individually before use (although they are also used skin and all). The flesh is pure white and, when raw, pleasantly crisp.

Although they are not, properly speaking, perennials, it is best to think of them in that way when selecting a spot to plant them. Like asparagus and horseradish, Jerusalem artichokes are good candidates for the difficult to utilize areas along a fence or property line. Once a planting is established, they can be depended upon to keep coming back year after year.

Start them by planting cuttings or sets made from the tubers, in much the same way as potato seed is made. Examining the tubers, it is easy to locate the "eyes," or growth crowns. One eye per set is adequate. Many nurseries and seed catalogues offer the sets, although until recently they were an oddity not readily available. There are few named varieties, but if one's interest in growing them is serious, there are varieties which are superior, at least in size. The only named variety I have grown is Stampede, from *Johnny's Selected Seeds,* said to have been collected originally from an old Indian campsite in Ontario. At about half a pound each, tubers are at least twice the size of those seen in produce markets. The tubers offered for sale in markets are probably a cheaper source of seeds, but if one is going to grow them at all, certainly the largest varieties should be chosen. One inconvenience of Jerusalem artichokes is the small, irregular shape of the usual tubers. Produce markets seem to be trying to popularize the name "sun choke" for them, presumably to retain part of the supposed Spanish name, while distinguishing them from true artichokes. It's a silly name. Refuse to use it.

Plant the sets one to a hill, about 3 inches deep, and spaced about 12 inches apart. If more than one row is planted, allow plenty of room, at least 24 inches. They should be planted about the same time as potatoes, in the early spring. They will grow a rather tall slender stalk, 4 feet or more in height (the Stampede variety from 6 to 8), which does indeed clearly resemble other members of the sunflower family. The blossom distinctly resembles a sunflower, although on a much smaller scale. It has a distinctive smell, which some say resembles the smell of chocolate. It is a rather humble plant, putting one in mind of the many slender roadside weeds we somehow never remember the names for. In fact, in parts of the country the Jerusalem artichoke *is* a common roadside weed.

The tubers may be harvested in the fall and stored as if they were potatoes. Most people who grow artichokes dig them as they are used, anytime that the ground can be opened. It should not be necessary to replant a second year; enough small roots and tubers will have been overlooked and left in the ground to regenerate the planting. What was once a planting will soon become a clump, and then a shaggy and moderately aggressive row. If they get out of control, call them anything that comes to mind, but don't call them "sun chokes."

Potatoes: The Apples of the Earth

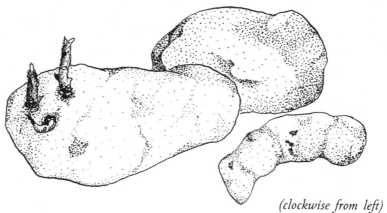

(clockwise from left)
Finnish Yellow, Russet, and German finger potatoes

Tradition has it among those who regulate their planting according to "the signs," that crops growing *under* the ground should be planted during the period in which the moon is waning. A more specific tradition says that potatoes should be planted on Good Friday. A little thought discovers that the two traditions converge. Since Easter is the first Sunday after the first full moon after the vernal equinox, almost invariably Good Friday must fall early in the period of a waning moon. And the vernal equinox is about the earliest time in temperate latitudes anyone would think of planting potatoes.

But there are many gardeners who do not plant potatoes at all, asserting that potatoes have no real place in a home garden. It is not uncommon to read or hear that since homegrown potatoes have no superiority to those commercially grown, and that potatoes are so cheap anyway, there is no advantage to the home gardener in forfeiting the necessary space for growing such a humble crop. Nonsense—on all counts. Ten hills, hardly more than 15 feet of row space, should provide a minimum of ten meals, unless they are dug very early as new potatoes (in which case there will be time to replant and double-crop with something else). Even if dug when an inch in diameter two hills should still provide a family meal. As to there being no advantage in freshness, that assertion implies either inexperience or insensitivity. A newly dug young potato is too delicately sensuous a flavor to trust to judgment by an insensitive palate.

The pleasure of digging potatoes, of rolling those compact and firm and heavy nuggets of edibility from the soil, is the epitome and summation of the private sensations and pleasures of the gardener's relationship with the soil and bringing food out of it. Retrieving those achievements of growth with bare hands is on the opposite end of the balance from "symbolic achievement," which contributes so much to the "quiet desperation" of the lives ordinary men live. One of the big attractions of gardening is finding release from the imprisonment of symbolic achievement.

Fresh homegrown potatoes are better. It is also true that, even cultivated on a small scale, homegrown potatoes are economically interesting as well. Depending on dietary habits, a hill of potatoes can compete favorably on an economic level with the produce of an equal area planted, say, to sweet corn. If one has the land to be lavish with, a gardener may be virtually self-sufficient in this useful and easily stored tuber for the major part of the year, the winter-stored produce lasting nearly until the first of the next year's crop of new potatoes.

Potatoes are no trick to grow—which may lower their caste among gardeners who cherish the temperamental. How often have we seen the word *potato* (or earth apple) prefixed with *lowly*. Unharvested potatoes left in the ground often overwinter, and sprout and grow at the appropriate time with uncanny success. I suspect some gardeners resent that show of independence from a member of the vegetable world. Likewise, seed potatoes, whenever planted, sprout and grow when things feel right to them, and seem to manage their own affairs in the early spring rather nicely. They may be the unrecognized cats of the plant world.

Preferences for the numerous cultivars vary from area to area. Inexperienced gardeners, or those gardening for the first time in an unfamiliar locale, would do well to consult extension agents or other gardeners for advice respecting varieties.

Literally hundreds, likely thousands, of different varieties of potatoes are grown throughout the world. In their native Andes, numerous pre-Columbian varieties continue to be grown, and a single farmer may grow half a dozen different cultivars. In America, collectors and breeders sustain hundreds of varieties never seen commercially, many of which are available through seed exchanges. Some unusual varieties are offered by commercial catalogues, including such novelty items as potatoes that are completely blue—skin, flesh, and all. A variety some speak highly of is a small, yellow, finger-shaped potato called, among other names, Lady Finger, German Yellow Potato, and Yellow Potato Salad potato *(Gurney's)*, a variety presumably introduced by German immigrants. It makes an extremely good potato salad. It grows more shallowly than other potatoes, and I have found it to be a spare producer.

To generalize about the varieties of potatoes, my experience has been that the "early" potatoes tend to be less flavorful—more watery and bland—than later potatoes, but I know others who would not agree with this. Although the definition certainly is not exact, a "new potato" is a tuber of *any* variety that has not yet finished growing. Usually, for gardeners at least, it is quite immature, and commercially it is one whose skin is still not completely formed and can be rubbed free of the flesh by the pressure of a thumb. Regardless of the variety—early or late—any potato is a new potato until the skin begins to firm. My preference is for immature late potatoes, which I think are superior in flavor and texture to the early varieties. The disadvantage of using them is efficiency; dug small, you get only about half to a fourth of the yield they would produce if allowed to grow to maturity. Optimally, for the best-flavored new potatoes, dig them when they are about the size of a dog's nose.

Potatoes like a light, rich—preferably enriched—soil, but grow from good to very good in a wide range of soils and climates. Although the soils are weak in organic matter, virgin western soils have produced magnificent yields of potatoes, but usually with the assistance of heavy applications of chemical fertilizer. Potatoes can quickly deplete a soil unless it is cared for by fertilization and crop rotation.

Although they frequently set seeds, potatoes are invariably planted and reproduced vegetatively. That is, a tuber is cut into pieces, and new plants grow from the "set," without any genetic exchange. The process is asexual, as is reproducing plants from stem or root cuttings. Potatoes that are to be used for planting are called "seed potatoes." Always buy good seed potatoes from a nursery. Do not try planting the tubers you find in the produce department of a market; most commercial potatoes have been treated to retard sprouting, and if you plant them, they will either never come up, or not sprout until the summer is half over. There is a variety that became commercially available rather recently that is grown from true seed. It has to be started indoors in pots, however, and at least for the present is more a novelty than a practical choice.

Potatoes you buy for seed most likely will not look very impressive—small in size, irregularly shaped, even withered. Seed potatoes are usually grown on land never planted to potatoes before, often land never cultivated before, and most likely the crop was neither fertilized nor irrigated. This kind of cultivation produces small potatoes, but the progeny, planted in fertile soil and properly watered, will yield crops of the size and quality normal to the variety. When buying seed potatoes, if there is any choice, a large number of small potatoes are more economical than a smaller number of large potatoes. Trust that, like the children of immigrants, the offspring will be larger than the parents.

The reason seed potatoes are grown in "virgin soil" is to prevent various viral infections that are transmitted through the tuber. A variety favored in England as the only acceptable raw material for crumpets, called the King Edward, became infected with a virus. For many years this cultivar disappeared from production because absolutely all tubers were infected. Recently, using modern techniques of propagation, the species was regenerated by cloning cells taken from the green vines. Since this culture bypassed the infected root, it was possible to restore a disease-free seed stock, and the British can again experience the crumpets they honored of old.

Our ancestors, of course, always by necessity grew—or saved—their own seed potatoes. Saving the seed was casual; what was planted in the spring was simply what had not been used during the winter. A story one hears is of the family who noticed that year by year the yield of their plants became slighter, and the actual size of the tubers smaller. The teller of the story will usually stop for a moment of dramatic emphasis, then explain that the family had always kept using the larger potatoes and pushing the smaller aside, until when planting time arrived only the smallest remained, and that over the course of several years they had "bred down" their crop to a race of midgets. However, since planting pieces of the tubers does not involve genetic exchange, no genetic change can take place. If such an event actually occurred and the crops became lighter and the potatoes smaller, the likely reason was depletion of the soil. There is a song from Ireland called "The Pratie [Potato] Song," which laments poor crops, saying:

The Praties they grow sma'
And we eats them skins and a'

which is probably Homering a similar domestic calamity.

There are numerous varieties of potatoes to choose from, broadly divided into two classes, early and late. Both may be planted or, if the growing season is quite restricted, only the late varieties. It is wise to check at nurseries or extension agencies for information about varieties that do particularly well, or do not do particularly well, in a given area, as well as for successful planting times.

Potatoes should be set about 15 inches apart. Each seed potato will yield about four sets, and if the potatoes are smallish, about five potatoes will make a pound. So a pound will plant about a 30-foot row; *about,* depending on the size of the potatoes. Since the seed is usually quite inexpensive, one certainly can afford to overbuy for a safety margin.

As there are more ways than one to skin a cat (although I've only been able to think of two), there are more ways than one to cut a seed potato (and again, I can only really think of two). One is simply to quarter the potato into four parts, making sure that each part has at least three eyes, the part of the potato from which the sprout emerges. Some varieties of potato have few eyes, making it necessary to third or even halve the potato in order to get the necessary number. A second method is leisurely to dissect the individual potato into as many pieces, each with three eyes, as ingenuity can supply. On examination, it is readily apparent that a potato has a head and a tail, the tail being the end that was originally attached to the plant, the head the opposite end. By far the most eyes will be found on the head, although eyes will be scattered down the sides of the potato and none or few found on the tail. Some varieties have many more eyes than others, which is another reason for selecting the smallest potatoes for seed.

There are other techniques (isn't that an absurd word to use to describe cutting up a potato?), some even amounting to schools of thought. Each potato may be peeled thickly (leaving about a quarter of an inch of flesh attached to the skin), carefully arranging the slices to avoid as much as possible cutting across eyes, and keeping the eyes more or less centered on the peel. When a potato has been worked over in this fashion, there is not much potato left, unless it was a large one to begin with. These peels are then segmented, trying to keep two or three eyes per section. Each of these sections is then planted as if it were a regular set, shallowly covered in an 8-inch trench, which is filled in as the set sprouts and grows. Adherents of this system maintain that since there is so little nourishment available from the set, it sprouts in something of a panic, and will thus sprout sooner and root more quickly than a regular set. This is folk wisdom of long standing, and the practice is widely followed, especially regionally. While many more sets per potato are obtained this way, it seems to be a lot of bother. It's difficult to believe anything that depends on understanding the psychology of a potato and what causes one to panic.

Similar to the method of making sets from peelings, others make sets by cutting out groups of eyes with a cone of flesh behind each set. Each "plug" is inserted carefully in the ground, cone down, eyes up.

Some maintain that this system gives more space for roots to form in proportion to the eye, and therefore sets will root more quickly and efficiently. Experimentation on the relative size of the potato set to the ultimate yield per hill, however, suggests that the good nourishment bank of a medium-sized set does get the plant off to a more vigorous and thus ultimately more productive start.

Potato sets can be cut several days in advance and kept in cool storage until it is time or convenient to plant. I know gardeners who store cut potato sets in dry wood ashes for two or three days before planting. Some nurseries commonly supply sets that have been pre-cut (which eliminates all the mystery and geometry out of deciding how to carve a particular potato). Potatoes are unique in having the capacity to grow skin across any exposed cut, and quite quickly, too. If sets are allowed to remain unplanted for several days, the cut will be seen forming a firm, gray, moisture-retaining surface—a new skin. This unusual ability of the potato has been the subject of considerable research in recent years, with hopes, among other things, that secrets of grafting and growing damaged human skin may be discovered.

There is no big fuss connected with planting potatoes, but it's a good idea to have the ground prepared considerably in advance. If springs in a given locale are apt to be too rainy to work the ground at the proper time, it should be prepared—spaded or tilled—the previous autumn. In a no-till garden this is no problem, and provides another example of the advantages of that system. Some people worry that unless the ground has been freshly tilled, the earth is likely to pack until the potatoes have difficulty in expanding as they grow, and thus produce small crops, small potatoes, or deformed potatoes. There may be some soils where this could be a problem, but I have gardened in a rather wide range of soil types and have never found packing soil to provide any difficulty or retard the growth of the tubers. In the first place, as the potatoes begin to set on, the plants customarily are hilled well above the original level of planting, providing plenty of loose earth for the potatoes to grow in. In the second place, one of the strongest forces to be found in nature is the hydraulic action of growing cells.

When it is time to plant, I always measure the distance between intended rows and stretch strings down the length where I intend to plant. If there is to be more than one row, they should be spaced about 18 to 24 inches apart. Inquire about the growing habits of particular varieties when buying seed, because there can be a wide range in height and ranginess of foliage. Those of large foliage—Red Pontiacs, for example—should be planted on the order of 24 inches or more apart, those with lighter foliage—such as Norbest—closer to 15 inches apart.

A good way to space the hills is to walk slowly and with measured steps the length of the row alongside the string, taking about 15-inch steps (or longer, depending on variety), putting down the heel hard each time for a marker. Retrace the steps back down the next row, paralleling the heel marks with the first row. Do the same with the remaining rows. Plots planted in this way, with the resulting hills forming a neat pattern of squares, are said to be "check rowed." With a shovel or hand trowel (or your hand, if the soil is sufficiently loose) dig a hole 3 or 4 inches deep at the point of each heel mark, drop a seed, and cover lightly. Depending on the weather, sprouts should appear in two weeks or so, but it is not unusual for sprouting to be irregular, with some straggling along two weeks or more after the first have appeared.

When the sprouts are about 5 inches tall, begin to hill by drawing dirt up from each side of the row with a hoe to make a continuous ridge the length of the row, leaving only a couple of inches of the sprout showing. Repeat when the sprout is up another 5 or 6 inches above the hill. It is the nature of potatoes to grow the new tubers above the original set. Therefore, this mound of loose dirt gives an easy and roomy place for the young tubers to grow, and helps encourage them to grow to good size. It also helps keep the growing potatoes covered to prevent sunburn. The resulting trench provides an ideal irrigation ditch, making it easy to sustain a constant level of moisture brought in at root level.

To make capital of the fact that potatoes grow their "fruit" above the set, some gardeners dig a deep (10- or 12-inch) trench, drop the seeds 15 or 18 inches apart on the bottom, and fill with straw. The seed will root itself in the earth and the sprout will grow up through the straw. In due time the crop of potatoes will be set very neatly amidst the straw. The only advantage this system offers, other than the novelty of the thing, is that it makes selecting and harvesting a few early potatoes at a time easy, without disturbing the main plant. For such purposes, a short row should suffice for most gardeners who wish to experiment.

Another novel way to grow potatoes exploiting the same growth habit is to make a "potato condo." Drive four iron posts into the ground to form a square 5 feet by 5 feet. Cut four 5-foot sections of plank (1 × 6, 1 × 12, or whatever is available or cheap), and set them against the insides of the posts. Place a potato seed a foot from each corner inside the square and cover with 5 inches of rich earth. When the sprouts are 6 inches tall, add 3 more inches of earth, and a sprinkling of general purpose garden fertilizer. When the sprout is again 6 inches above the surface, add another set of planks and another 3 inches of earth. Keep this up until the first of August, and a multiple-storied apartment for potatoes will have been erected. It is necessary that the added earth be rich in compost and/or manure, and that it be given frequent fertilizer, as well. The structure must be kept well watered. When the vines die down in the fall, remove the planks one by one, and if all has gone well the "condo" will be occupied by potato tubers from the ground level to within a few inches of the top. This arrangement makes it possible for even the most modest-sized garden plot to afford a potato patch.

When a plant begins to bloom, it is setting on potatoes below ground. The most delicate and flavorful new potatoes can be found shortly after the blooms appear. Of course, it is inefficient to dig them up when they are that small, but they are so good at this stage that it's worth it. And they are your potatoes, after all: you can be as inefficient as it pleases you.

Throughout their growing period, potatoes are heavy users of water. Some people maintain that potatoes grown on "dry land"—or never irrigated—are better flavored and keep better than those that receive a great deal of water through irrigation, but most gardeners prefer to irrigate if in a low-rainfall area.

Some of the blossoms will set on little green fruits the size of marbles, sometimes containing several wheat-sized seeds, although commonly they may be sterile. These seeds, if planted (their rate of germination is low) most likely will grow a potato quite inferior to the plant, although this is the method by which new varieties are developed. The resemblance to small green tomatoes and nightshade berries easily confirms the close relationship of the potato to this family of plants. By the time these little green fruits have matured, the period of rapid growth is over. No longer can the potatoes developing under the vines accurately be called "new potatoes." Although still somewhat fragile, the skins will be well formed, beginning to harden and darken toward whatever color characterizes the mature potato. When a piece of the skin can no longer be easily rubbed off with the thumb, growth is practically over, and if dug and stored they would keep, if of the keeping variety. Remember the potatoes' ability to grow new skin; the skin will continue to mature and harden after storage.

When potatoes reach the stage at which the skin no longer slips easily, withhold all water. Once the potato stops growing, irrigation (or untimely rain) may stimulate a spurt of growth which, since the potato itself is complete inside a skin, will form knobs and bumps as the potato attempts to start growing again. Irregular irrigation during the period of normal growth can also cause knobs to form. There are some potato varieties that are prone under even the best conditions to form knobs, and some varieties that with little attention to the watering schedule will hardly ever form knobs or irregularities of any kind.

If potatoes are to be stored for winter use, it is best to leave them in the ground until early fall, allowing the skin to become completely mature and firm. They will keep better in the ground where they have been growing (unless the ground freezes) than anyplace else. However, they must be dug before hard frost. If the ground freezes down to the potatoes, they will be ruined; rot will set in almost immediately. Potatoes are quite susceptible to sunburn, and if exposed to hot sunlight will sunburn in less than an hour. Sunburn causes patches of skin (or if severe, the whole exposed surface) to turn shades of green from pale to almost emerald, and will impart an acrid bitter flavor through most of the flesh. Sunburned potatoes are mildly poisonous, containing the alkaloid solanine which is common to the nightshade family, but the flavor is so terrible it is highly unlikely anyone would ever eat enough to be harmful.

Frost and freezing will also make potatoes taste foul. The Indians of South America who grow potatoes high in the Andes originated and still use a technique for drying them that involves a controlled and specialized use of freezing. The potatoes are left outside, spread on a hard flat surface, and allowed to freeze at night. The next morning when the potatoes thaw in the thin clear sunlight, they tramp on them and smash them. That night the pulp freezes, and is again tramped when it thaws, and so on until all the moisture is gone. The dehydrated remainder is then stored for winter use, requiring no other protection than from moisture.

An old-fashioned fad that used to amuse farm boys was to dry a potato by carrying it in their pockets. The size of the potato depended on the ambition of the boy and the capacity of his overalls. It required no brains. He would simply carry the potato in his pocket until it became nearly as hard as stone, usually flat and thin, and reduced by about a third in length. From there on it would last indefinitely. I have been shown specimens carried by ex-farm boys for thirty years and more. They develop a patina, and seem never to wear out. The only use I've known them to be put to was to bore a hole in one end and slip a key chain through it and give it to a girlfriend. They are quite ugly and totally without charm, other than the knowledge that it is a potato that someone dried by carrying it in his pocket.

Strangely, when introduced to Europe from the New World the potato was long in receiving acceptance. Sir Walter Raleigh's celebrated introduction of them into southern Ireland at the end of the sixteenth century had almost no impact. The nutritious tubers likewise generated no enthusiasm when offered elsewhere in Europe. Perhaps its cultivation was not understood, perhaps its preparation and storage; or perhaps it was nothing more than natural human resistance to the new (although Raleigh's other introduction, tobacco, even more novel, took the Old World by storm). Perhaps the New World was simply giving the Old too many foods at once to adjust properly to the revolution in diet that was taking place. At any rate, the potato did not find any degree of popularity until the eighteenth century (it seems to have been reintroduced to Ireland from Italy), and that acceptance was restricted. In fact, with a certain prescience of the danger of excessive dependence on it as a food for the poor, potatoes were called "the root of misery" and "the root of extreme unction." Consequently it is another paradox that, by the next century, so firmly dependent had the population of Ireland become on the potato that the devastating potato blight starved thousands, and helped encourage thousands more to immigrate to the New World, which had sent them the potato in the first place.

Pungent Bulbs: The Onions and Their Kin

Rocambole Garlis *("serpent garlic")*

The burning question about onions is whether to plant seeds or sets. "Sets" include both the small dormant onions, about the size of pickling onions, which are purchased in bulk or premeasured packages, or the bunches of small green onions that look like undergrown scallions. Sometimes these seedlings are available in small planters, or "ponies." The argument against starting with sets is straightforward and logical: "You plant an onion and you get an onion," so where's the gain? Otherwise, the argument implies, when one plants an onion seed, one *grows* an onion, and the gain is clear and distinct.

To plant sets achieves onions much more quickly. But part of the choice is determined by whether the intention is to produce green

82

onions, dried onions, or a little bit of both. To plant onion sets produces almost an instant garden. Whether dormant or green, they will begin to grow immediately, and within days the dry bulblets will be putting down roots and putting up green shoots. As soon as the shoots are 3 or 4 inches long, they may be pulled and used as needed for green onions. Given the full summer to grow, they will mature at the normal size for that variety. But still, you plant an onion and you get an onion.

Because the sets give such quick growth, many gardeners never bother with, or have never tried, growing onions from seed. In an experiment in late March, I planted side by side the same varieties of seeds and sets (in this case, green shoots). Obviously the sets grew more quickly. By the end of July, however, the seeds had overtaken the sets, and in the fall produced mature dry onions as large as those produced by the sets. The larger varieties of onions do require a long growing season; 120 days is not uncommon. Therefore, it is perfectly clear that seeds of these varieties planted at the end of May are going to be stretching all but the more temperate climates if they are going to mature at full size.

Like a number of other vegetables, onions have a greater tolerance for cool weather and for germinating in cool soil than many people credit them with. Frequently I plant a small row of (seed) onions in the late summer to overwinter and produce early spring green onions. If planted in mid- to late August, they will germinate and make a little growth before winter, and usually will not be harmed by anything but the coldest winter weather. They have regularly and handily survived for me through winters of minus 10 to 15 degrees, dependably providing green onions in March. Onions are a biennial and make seeds in their second year of growth, so after their period of usefulness as green onions, overwintered onions generally turn woody as they begin to put up seed stalks, and should be removed.

Whether sets or seeds, onions are little trouble to grow. Plant them as early in the spring as the ground can be worked. If beginning with seeds, plant them in a shallow trench about ¼ inch deep, packing the soil lightly over them. Plant the seeds thinly, no more than six or eight to an inch. They do not need to be thinned, although spacing them an inch, or even 2 inches, apart will make much bigger onions. Most people thin casually by pulling young onions from crowded spots for use as scallions.

Both dormant onion sets and growing sprouts can be planted close together and be thinned for green onions, or they may be spaced 3 or 4 inches apart if they are being grown for dry onions. I have found that planting them in staggered patterns two or three lines wide, a system many gardeners are using recently, works rather well. It is an efficient way to use space, and the onions seem to do well.

Although onions are commonly grown for a dual purpose— scallions and dried—there are varieties that are grown exclusively for scallions. A favorite of mine is the *Iwatsuki* from Japan *(Urban Farmer)*. This variety does not form a regular onion bulb, but it regularly overwinters and sets seeds the following spring. The flavor of the green onions is mellow, and as could be expected excels in stir-fry cooking.

In late summer when the bulbs are maturing the curing of dry onions can be improved by withholding water. Wait until growth seems to have stopped, the first dry skins begins to form around the bulb, and the neck just above the onion begins to become slender. Actually it is not necessary to do anything at all other than to wait for the end of summer, but in addition to withholding water, many people bend the tops just above the ground level. The most callous gardeners actually walk down the row, deliberately stepping on and breaking the tops. This seems to traumatize the onion into believing that the growing season is indeed over, and that it's time to biologically regroup for hard times ahead. Besides speeding up the curing, mashing down the tops is reputed to improve the keeping quality of the onions.

Like most crops, it is worthwhile to inquire about what varieties of onions do well locally. Some onions are highly regarded for their eating quality, but do not last long in storage. Many people grow a quantity of these for summer use, and to hold as long as they will keep, but plant a "main crop" consisting of a variety or varieties that store well, as well. I use the last of the "summer onions" to make chili sauce at the end of the season.

Among the rather famed mild summer onions is the Vidalia, from the town of that name in Georgia. Seed, and sometimes sets, can be obtained from Southern seed houses *(Steele Plant Company)*. I have never grown them but have eaten them, and have never had better. Another onion with regional association is the Walla Walla sweet— which sounds like the moniker of a pool hustler. I grow them every year, but they must be planted early. They reach enormous size and are, as the name attests, sweet and mild. In their native range, they are fall planted and overwintered. In recent years their seed and seedlings have become generally available.

The small, white, usually spherical onion which are sometimes pickled, or used in canning is not simply an onion that is harvested small, it is a separate kind. One variety, Crystal Wax, is offered by *Territorial Seed Company*. It is cultivated like any storage onion, although the rows may be planted closer together. It is dug when the onions become plump little spheres.

Individual taste and culinary practice, of course, play an important part in selecting varieties. People who use considerable amounts of onion raw may prefer to grow a mild onion, plus a few of the more pungent or obstreperous for cooking. Some onion fanatics will grow nothing but those famed as tearjerkers. Whatever your taste, growing your own allows you to tailor the crop to your specific preferences.

There is a family of onion loosely called "multipliers," which instead of seeds set miniature onion bulbs in their "seed heads." If allowed to, the tops will eventually twist to the ground and the sets quickly begin to grow, often in a single season growing more sets on their own tops. A regular system of leap-frogging onions may develop, which by the end of summer looks like a series of bridge arches. With most varieties of multipliers, the fully grown bulbs are so strong in flavor that only the most advanced onion eaters consort with them. The sets, however, may be planted in the spring for scallions. This is an easy and cheap way to get spring onions. While still young they are relatively placid, but soon take on the ebullience and pungency of their parents.

Leeks are a close cousin to onions, and while they are not as versatile, they are still worth cultivating. Potato leek soup, hot or cold, is so rich and good it easily supplies a main course. They may be planted from seed, and in their early growth they closely resemble seed onions, and when small are a mild substitute for green onions. Almost the entire length of the green stalk may be used. It is possible to plant leeks each year from seed, but it is easiest to establish them in a spot where they can remain permanently. A small planting of leeks will continue to renew itself indefinitely, as the mature leeks form small bulblets around the base of their roots, which come up the following spring. They are a good crop for cool weather areas; they can be dug from fall and, if mulched with straw, all through the winter and into the following spring. A quite superior variety is the Lyon Prize-taker, from England *(Urban Farmer)*. It is large, dazzling white, and very mild.

Traditionally leeks are associated with the Welch, and every Welchman is expected to eat a leek on St. David's day, March 1, honored for the patron saint of Wales. In *Henry V,* Shakespeare has a comic Welchman named Fluellen wear a leek on his cap to taunt characters who mock his accent. Eventually he makes one of his tormentors—very reluctantly—eat the leek whole.

Plant leeks exactly as onions are planted, scattered thinly in a shallow trench and covered with about ¼ inch of soil, lightly packed. As with onions, they may be thinned to about an inch apart as soon as they reach a height of 2 inches, or they may be thinned by letting them get a little larger and using the surplus as if they were green onions. Some gardeners use rather elaborate techniques of leek culture to be assured of long, thick white bulbs. I have tried several such systems, and the main result was that I felt I was being made the servant of the garden.

Leeks will grow tall and upright, with leaves that are flat rather than hollow, and a much stronger central "stem" than onions. Leeks form a long, slender bulb, in appearance much like a green onion, except larger. An inch in diameter is usual, and 2 inches not uncommon. They are strikingly handsome, with their unexpectedly large diameter and tall tops, with their stark white roots contrasting with their brilliant green tops. In fact, in older times the leek was sometimes a mocking symbol for a lecherous old man: a white head with a green tail.

Another onion cousin that should be planted where it may become permanently established is the chive. Chives may be started from a clump begged from a friend, purchased as clumps started in pots, or planted from seeds. The clump you borrow from another's chive bed will actually consist of numerous individual plants that each resemble small green onions. Separate the large clump into individual bundles about as big around as one's thumb (usually their matted roots will cause the clumps to cling tightly together) and set them out about 6 inches apart. Those purchased in pots most likely have been grown from seeds by the nursery and often will be too small to separate. Simply plant the entire clump, spacing the clumps about 6 inches apart. Plant seeds thinly in a narrow trench, covered with a sprinkling of earth packed lightly on top of them, or plant inside in late winter. Whether starting with seeds or established clumps, plant as early in the spring as the ground can be worked. A French variety advertised as appreciably superior is the *Ciboulette Civette (Epicure Seeds)*. These were also described as being slow to germinate, and those I planted—both inside in pots and direct seeded outside— failed to germinate at all.

Chives' habit of growth is most gregarious, and during the course of several years a planting will grow until it completely occupies whatever space it can. Occasionally they can become something of a pest, but are never particularly difficult to restrain. Their hollow, onionlike stems grow to the height of about a foot, and may be cut for seasoning virtually the whole year-round. Cut them freely, and they will continue to grow indefinitely. Chives are a welcome winter treat cut fresh from under the snow and chopped with sour cream on baked potatoes or sprinkled on salads. A 3-foot row of chives should provide a lifetime supply, needing to be cut back occasionally to restrain their spreading. They grow nicely against a wall and make an attractive planting against the foundation of a house. If grown against a foundation it will provide them a little heat and encourage them to maintain growth and keep them attractively green all winter in many areas. In early summer an established clump will put up numerous blossoms, each an almost spherical small pink cluster, as is typical of the onion family. If these are removed as they appear the growth of the clumps will be improved, but it is a rather tedious job to remove them all. Also they are very pretty.

Garlic, another familiar relative of the onion family, should be grown by everyone who fancies its use. It requires no pampering and once established can easily be sustained as a permanent planting. Garlic sometimes makes seed heads like onions, and usually forms bulblets alongside or even inside the stems. The most usual way of planting it, however, is to break up a bulb of garlic and plant the individual cloves. From each clove will grow a complete new plant, forming a full-sized bulb composed of more cloves. Some people contend that since a small quantity of garlic is consumed by the average kitchen, and since it is cheap, and since homegrown is not demonstrably superior to the market product, why bother. Why not? It keeps marvelously well, and takes up little space in the garden or in storage. And besides, it's fun to give to people; they are never quite sure what your intentions are.

Two general kinds of garlic are grown, those with bulbs an inch or two in diameter commonly seen in the markets, and those with uncommonly larger bulbs, the size of an apple, which is sometimes called "elephant garlic." Because the individual cloves that comprise the bulb of this variety are so large, they are easier to peel and handier to work with than smaller garlic. The larger garlic is much milder than the smaller, however, and cooks familiar with the strength of ordinary garlic will have to accommodate themselves accordingly.

Garlic bulbs for planting can be obtained from most seed catalogues and many nurseries. There is nothing wrong with simply planting garlic procured from a produce market, and it's apt to be less expensive than professionally offered "seed." Most gardeners will find a short row, 3 or 4 feet, to be ample for their needs. As with onion sets, I have found planting a multiple row—three sets across in a staggered pattern—to work well. Garlic is quite tolerant of cool weather, and the sets may be planted either in the fall or in the early spring, although fall planting makes a larger bulb at harvest time.

The shoots are slender, and remain upright until they begin to mature and die back. To plant, separate the garlic bulb into its individual cloves, placing them three across in the rows. If the soil is loose, punch a hole in the ground with a finger or stick, and place the clove blunt end down, pointy end up, with the tip about half an inch below the surface, and cover lightly.

For the size of their bulb below ground, garlic makes a singularly unimpressive growth. The slender, onionlike tops never look like they are especially thrifty, although elephant garlic is a bit more robust on top. Once planted, garlic needs no special care other than weeding and irrigating, where necessary. When the tops begin to wither in late summer, dig them and allow the bulbs to cure. The traditional way to handle the curing is to braid the long stems together (before they have become brittle) with colorful and loose-woven yarn, with the bulbs studding the central braid like an outsized necklace. The strings —from 1 to 3 feet long—can be hung in a dry place out of the sun, and with no further trouble keep nicely through the winter. A string of garlic looks very picturesque hanging decoratively in a kitchen, but eventually gets a little messy as the dried skins fall on the floor and counters. But as those who have read Bram Stoker know, those kitchens festooned with garlic are never infested with vampires!

Shallots are a less familiar garden relative of the onion family. They are often called for in French recipes, with the notation frequently appended that in their absence scallions may be substituted. Shallots are quite expensive in produce markets, but they are easy to grow and no trouble to store. Shallot sets may be purchased through the usual catalogues, or through some nurseries and seed stores. Although I have never tried them, the Italian varieties have the reputation of being superior.

Like garlic, shallots can be planted in late fall or early spring, and planting them in a staggered, multiple row works well. Unlike garlic, the individual cloves of a head of shallots are not tightly bunched into a bulb but are rather loosely attached in a rosette of roots that they share in common. Break the cloves apart and plant each separately—as with garlic, blunt end down with the pointed top about a half inch below the surface. As they begin growing, shallot tops resemble chives more than onions or garlic, although they are shorter and less dense. They come to maturity about the same time as garlic, at which time the leaves begin to wither and die. Dig or pull the bulbs and leave them to cure in the garden for a few days, or until the leaves have become dried and crumbly. Dried, they can be kept all winter hung in a "nylon" stocking or pantyhose, or even stored in paper bags. They keep exceptionally well. I once found some I had overlooked for two years, and for the sake of curiosity planted them. They came up promptly and grew as well as any. If one's garden can be planned that far in advance, next year's crop may simply be replanted at the time the harvest is dug.

Old King Cole: The Cabbage Family

Amager Green Storage cabbage

The names of many members of the diversified cole family retain vestiges of their common origin in the Latin word *caulis,* which means "stem cabbage." So we have kale, kohlrabi, cauliflower, broccoli, and cabbage, echoing in form, though modified by language or dialect, the original Latin. Sauerkraut, of course, speaks German, cole slaw speaks Dutch (from *koolsla,* meaning "cabbage salad"). The older English word for the whole family, but especially the leafy varieties, is *colewort,* meaning simply "cabbage vegetable."

The various forms in which this family displays itself is as varied, and its common forms sometimes as enigmatically concealed, as its common family names. No vegetable family, even the nightshade, comes close to the variations in form of the coleworts. It would almost seem a quirk of genetic whimsy is at work, except that the whole family seems to be the most humorless of the entire vegetable kingdom. Try to work up a smile communing with a Danish ballhead cabbage, or a stalk of Brussels sprouts. It's just not there. A tomato in a relaxed mood can crack you up, and even the stolid potatoes are fundamentally good-humored. By contrast, the inherently ridiculous kohlrabi is too earnest and takes itself too seriously ever to entertain comedy.

All members of the clan share in common a preference for cool weather and an aversion to hot weather. These habits may partially account for the general humorlessness of the group. In mild weather areas the family can be treated as a winter annual, with some cabbage, kohlrabi, and broccoli overwintering. Some varieties of most members of the family are developed for specific climatic conditions; locally successful varieties should be checked before making selections for planting.

Generally the early varieties of cabbage tend to have heads that are less dense and perhaps more watery than late cabbage, and commonly tend to split as soon as they mature, particularly if rained on or irrigated by sprinklers. Also their keeping qualities are poor. Late cabbage, of course, matures slowly. The dense heads are particularly suitable for making good quality sauerkraut and for keeping all winter. Early cabbage can be started inside and the seedlings transplanted outside when about 3 inches tall, or seedlings may be purchased. In either case they may be put in the ground quite early and are tolerant of a little frost. Set them out about 16 inches apart, and if more than one row is planted, put about 24 inches between rows. If the plants are spaced further apart, as some recommend, the heads will be larger, but it's a situation of diminishing returns. How much early cabbage do you want? And how big do you require the heads to be? Maturity of early cabbage coincides with the lettuce crop, early potatoes, green peas—one's eyes in the early spring may be larger than one's midsummer stomach. I find that a dozen heads of early cabbage is a dazzling plenty; that's one head a week for three months. I'm generous in giving to others. For planning purposes, estimate about 50 days from setting the seedlings out to having usable cabbage. The time may be crowded, since it can be picked anytime after the heads become firm, and the flavor is actually a little more delicate in heads that are slightly imma-

ture. Early Jersey Wakefield is an old variety that I find most satisfactory. The heads are cone-shaped, which gives them an odd appearance.
They are nevertheless solid and firm. Seed is widely available.

Late cabbage can be started indoors or transplanted from purchased seedlings, or the seeds may be sown directly in the ground. Since
this is an instance in which the gardener is in no particular hurry, there
seems to be no advantage in setting out transplants other than convenience. I plant the seeds in early May in a shallow trench, about half
an inch apart (the seeds are so small no one is apt to count them out
this way, but use that as a rough idea). Sprinkle about a quarter of an
inch of soil over them, and firm it gently. If the soil is not sufficiently
moist (as it should be at this time in most places) it should be dampened
before sowing the seeds. When the seedlings show their first true leaf,
thin them to about 6 inches apart. When they are 2 or 3 inches high,
the additional surplus can be transplanted to bare spots in your garden
or given away. For the ballhead varieties, end up with a spacing of
about 18 inches; large flathead varieties ought to have 24 inches. The
ultimate final spacing may be made at the first thinning, but I like to
thin them in stages to make sure enough plants get good, vigorous
starts. Reduced spacing will produce smaller heads of cabbage (but
don't space them less than a foot apart), and it is true of late cabbage
as of early that usually smaller heads are more convenient, except when
making quantities of sauerkraut. Late cabbage seeded directly into the
row will probably not look impressive until after midsummer. For
most late varieties plan about 125 days of growing season. When the
weather begins to cool, they will really begin to take off and will still
be growing, if not vigorously, after most of the rest of the garden has
been frosted down. I like Late Flat Dutch for its large, dense heads to
make sauerkraut. Custodian is recommended for its ability to stand
periods of rain without splitting. January King, with a distinctive
blue-green foliage, is recommended for hardiness, and for late fall
harvest. Both are available from *Nichols Garden Nursery.*

When harvesting early cabbage, one may cut just the head off and
allow the root and the main leaf structure to remain intact. Several
additional small heads of cabbage will form from the leaf junctures of
each plant. These small heads will not be as tight as the main head, but
they may be used in any way the larger heads are used. It is not

uncommon for heads to form from overwintered stalks the following spring that grow nearly as large as those harvested the previous fall.

Late cabbage may be stored in moist refrigeration slightly above freezing and keep for months. They may be pulled roots and all and kept for a considerable time in a cool cellar. A classic, old-fashioned way of storing them, called a "clamp," is to pull them, with the roots, and pile them upside down—roots in the air—in a heap in some sheltered corner of the garden, covering them with a heavy layer of straw. Stored this way they will last through the winter in all but the severest climates.

The ability to survive long storage accounts for one of the reasons cabbage was such a staple commodity in days before refined storage made a wider variety of commodities available throughout the year. Even the most charitable would not call cabbage a complete or perfect food. Constrained by necessity, however, cabbage could be kept through the winter under the most primitive conditions and one could survive on it alone.

There are a number of varieties of Oriental cabbage, which has a distinctive flavor, different from the common European kinds. Their cultivation is similar to that of other cabbages, although usually seed is direct-sown in the spring. Treasure Island Chinese cabbage produces a large, barrel-shaped head. *Wong Bok* has a small head, which is self-blanching. Takii's Spring is especially early, maturing in midsummer from direct seeding in the spring. Seeds for all three varieties are available from *Nichols Garden Nursery.* Those who have tried making *kim chee,* the "Oriental sauerkraut," and have been disappointed with the results might try using an Oriental cabbage variety.

As does cabbage, cauliflower likes cool weather. It should be planted in spring as early as the ground can be worked. It is best to begin with transplants, because the crop must come off before the weather turns hot. In areas where heavy freezing does not set in until the end of October, seeds may be sown directly into the ground in late August or early September. A light protective mulch of straw or other covering will help cauliflower survive the winter and have an even earlier start in the spring. In mild climates it is planted in late summer as a spring crop.

The general cultivation of cauliflower is exactly the same as cabbage. Plants should be spaced about 16 to 20 inches apart to provide room for growth. When the white, corallike growth of the blossom heads begin to form, the surrounding leaves may be drawn over and held in place by a rubber band or clothespin to protect them from direct sunlight. If this is not done, the heads will take on a dark yellow cast, and although this doesn't crucially harm the flavor, it detracts from the pleasing appearance of the snowy white heads that have been blanched and protected. The heads should be picked while still firm and compact, before the buds begin to separate, or "rice." During summer heat these heads, or "curds," immediately begin to become stringy blossom heads, which are, practically speaking, no longer edible. *Vermont Bean Seed Company* offers a variety called Violet Green that has a purple head. It requires no blanching and is described as holding well; it turns green with cooking.

Like cauliflower, broccoli is grown for its enlarged flower buds. Its requirements and cultivation is the same as that of cauliflower or cabbage, except that because of its height and branching stems it should have more space between plants, about 24 inches, or wider for the larger species. It is partial to cool weather, and if heads form during hot weather the bud, which is essentially all the head consists of, may quickly bolt and go into blossom. The heads need to be picked before any of the small yellow flowers open. Pick the heads when the individual buds are well formed and the whole head solid. If kept picked before they mature, the plant should continue to produce heads from each of the lower leaf nodes, although usually smaller ones, up until frost.

Broccoli may be planted from seeds, or set out from seedlings grown indoors or purchased from a nursery. Depending on climate, they may be planted from early April up until mid-June. In a climate that is not too severe, broccoli can also be treated like a winter annual, planting the seeds in late August, protecting the seedlings by a mulch or straw covering before the first heavy frost. In a Zone 5 climate I get them to overwinter about every other try.

In England a variety of broccoli is regularly grown as a winter annual, sometimes even as a perennial. It is planted in the summer and in the milder regions begins to put on heads at the end of February, or into March. The heads are longer and much more slender than our familiar varieties, with a purplish cast. In England the usual practice is to cut them quite long, allowing several leaves to remain to be cooked with the heads. I have had rather good luck with them in my climate and have picked tender but solidly frozen small leaves in January to add to stews. They are quite good, even considering that my palate is fussy about cooked greens. In England it is not unusual for individual plants to survive as much as five years. I have never had a plant survive a third winter, although people in Zone 4 to whom I have given seeds report longer life spans for them. Their growth is taller than our usual varieties, putting one in mind of a very leafy green shrub. I have not seen a commercial source for them in this country.

Brussels sprouts do not give a clue in their name to their kinship with the colewort family. But family relationship is obvious to even the casual glance. This member did not make its appearance until about the middle of the eighteenth century, and was, as the name suggests, associated with Belgium. It is easy to see how they might have come into existence; it is not uncommon to see numerous vestigial heads formed around the base of a head of cabbage, similar to the small heads on stalks of Brussels sprouts.

Brussels sprouts are a distinctly cool weather plant, so there is no point in hurrying their planting. Like late cabbage, they might just as well be sown from seed in the place they are intended to grow. During the summer they put on growth and set down good root systems but will not usually begin to set "sprouts" until the weather cools. They absolutely luxuriate in chilly, damp weather, and the sprouts are not at their peak of flavor until they have been through frosts. In cool climates, especially marine climates, they may remain in the garden all winter, harvested as needed. I have them at Thanksgiving—and sometimes pick them in the snow.

The care for Brussels sprouts is similar to the care for the rest of the family, whether planted from seed or transplants. A spacing of 14 to 18 inches between plants is adequate, although there are dwarf strains which can be spaced no more than a foot apart. In late summer, when the buds begin to form at the leaf unions with the main stem that will develop into the "sprouts," the leaves may be pruned to encourage the growth of the buds. Do not prune all at once; clip off (do not pull) the first two or three rows of leaves, which will probably have begun to look rather nondescript anyway. Clip another row or two every week or so, or as the buds begin to develop for the individual sprouts. If, at about the end of August, the entire crown is cut away, it will tend to make all of the buds on the stalk mature at a fairly consistent rate. I have found the irregular maturing of the buds convenient, making it possible to cut away a few large sprouts from each of several stalks over a long period. The buds are usable whenever they are firm and plump and about an inch in diameter.

The kohlrabi is a kind of vegetable freak. Although a member of the cabbage family, it puts out a bulb just above the ground. This bulb, which is actually a spherical enlargement of the stem, is crisp and turnipy and valued by many raw, in salads, or sliced for relish trays. They are somewhat winter-hardy and seeds planted in early fall frequently overwinter. Otherwise, plant the seeds in early spring about a fourth of an inch deep, tamping lightly. Thin to 4 inches apart. They grow rapidly, and may be eaten anytime the bulb is an inch or more in diameter. They are at their peak when no more than 2 inches in diameter. Like others in the family, Kohlrabi is a cool weather crop, which goes downhill in quality as the weather turns warm. Because of this, it is a good bet for interplanting, making temporary use of space other plants will grow to need, or to be replanted with a later crop. A fall variety especially resistant to turning woody is Lauko *(Territorial Seed Company)*. It is planted in summer for a fall crop. It has a purple skin.

A cabbage novelty worth trying once is called the Walking Stick cabbage. It grows wild on the Isle of Jersey, where it is used for cattle forage. Its distinctive feature is its long, hard stem, which grows to a height of 7 feet. While it is tolerant of cool weather, it cannot stand freezing. To make a hard, mature stalk takes about 150 days. When I grew it, the plants reached a height of about 4 feet, and were winter-killed. The stalk is so hard when dried that it actually is used to make walking sticks. Seeds are available from *Thompson and Morgan,* British seedsmen often franchised to American nurseries and seed stores.

Gardeners who grow any members of the cabbage family must decide whether to use or not to use insecticides. A thundering horde of bugs dearly love all members of the family. There is the cabbage flea, more destructive in warmer climates than northern, which attacks the seedlings while still very young. The insect is small and insignificant looking, yet where it is prevalent will stunt growth or totally annihilate the plants unless treated. If treated early, it is not especially difficult to control. Check local preferences for pesticides if the cabbage flea is a problem in your area.

Then there is the ubiquitous cabbage worm. When the nondescript yellow or white butterflies—cabbage moths by proper designation—begin darting among the young plants of any members of the family, there will soon be a worm problem. As they dart in and out, sometimes only brushing the leaves, they deposit eggs that quickly hatch into tiny worms. Given an early start, they will riddle the leaves of the cabbage, even destroying the developing bud in the center of the stalk so that no head forms at all. Cabbage worms love all members of the family, especially those that give them camouflage. They are particularly pernicious to broccoli; their color is so perfectly matched to the head of a maturing broccoli bud that they are virtually undetectable. The only way to control them completely is with regular use of such nonpoisonous and nonpersistent insecticides as rotenone. Other dusts or sprays may be locally preferred. If worms survive treatment the heads may be soaked in a heavy solution of salt water for an hour or so before using. This will *usually* dislodge most of them, but not infallibly. The unfastidious begin cooking by placing the heads in cold water and heating it slowly so the worms have a chance to crawl off as things begin to get uncomfortably warm; they are then skimmed off the surface of the cooking water. Several years ago my wife cooked a few well-formed heads, and when worms floated to the top of the cooking water she shrilly ordered me never to plant broccoli again. I can't resist, however, and still grow it, but always give the heads to friends of my wife.

The entire cole family is susceptible to infestations of aphids. Brussels sprouts are particularly susceptible, and because of their tight little heads, each with a couple of loose leaves around it, are especially difficult to treat with success. Aphids in Brussels sprouts also have an exasperating ability to survive late frosts, well after the cool weather should have killed them off. If not controlled, they will work their way into the leaves by way of the base of the bud, until the little sprout must be almost completely peeled away before the last vestiges of the aphids are eliminated. They may be killed by faithful, regular (once a week) applications of rotenone, nicotine spray, or whatever else is locally approved.

All cabbage pests may be controlled. The gardener must make the decision: either to use some kind of pesticide system or live with riddled or destroyed seedlings, green worms in the cabbage, broccoli, and cauliflower, and aphids in the Brussels sprouts. My wife's dictum about broccoli speaks for many. Individual gardeners should check with local preferences, and decide with their own conscience what they will or will not use. My principal insecticide is rotenone dust, and with diligence and patience I find it adequate. And safe—I also raise honey bees, so would use nothing that could harm them, and it never has. I apply dust routinely every week. Apply the dust on a still day, preferably in the morning when there is still a dampness on the leaves to help hold the powder in place. A light dusting once a week is much better than a heavy dusting every once in a while, or after it begins to look like things are getting bad. It is better to prevent an infestation from becoming a problem than controlling it once it has become a problem. A small colony of aphids, for example, can usually be stopped in its tracks, but once the infestation becomes so heavy that it is readily visible it's hard to get rid of. A dusting may cut into the population heavily, but in less than a week it may be back looking stronger than before.

The word *caulus* may be disguised in many linguistic forms, but the bugs are never fooled. If you are not morally willing to meet them in a straight attack and "fight it out on that line, if it takes all summer"—in the words of General Grant—give up on the whole cole family. Or shed all prejudice against green vermin on your supper plate.

Tomatoes:
The New World
Love Apple

Muchamiel tomato

For many gardeners, the queen of the season, and the crop by which they measure the success of their whole year, is the tomato. Gardeners gauge their success with three main units of measurement: earliness, size, and quantity, in about that order. There are even some who prize most the invisible value—flavor. There is almost no one, however, gardener or otherwise, who does not value the tomato.

In a climate with hot sunny summers and a long growing season, with anything like a reasonable soil, tomatoes will set fruit and ripen early with little trouble and produce fruit over a long period of time. More troublesome areas are those having a short growing season, summers with little sunshine and cool nights, and early frosts.

The absolute limiting factor of tomatoes is frost. They are tender and cannot stand freezing either at the beginning of the growing season, or at the end. It is possible to protect them in the spring and in the fall from occasional unseasonable frosts, and a familiar warning of the nightly weather reports in colder regions is, "Cover your tomato plants!" If the young tomato plants get hit by a spring frost, there's no alternative except replanting. And a heavy autumn frost will destroy both the vines and the fruits of unprotected tomatoes; the season's crop will be lost. Even the early weeks of summer have their own, less obvious, peril. If the soil remains cool and clammy, the plants will show little growth. If days are warm but nights are cool, they may show excellent growth and even bloom prolifically, but until the night temperature does not fall below about 50 degrees, the blossoms will set no fruit. When fruit does set, unless the days are sunny and warm it will be slow to ripen. But with all of these uncertainties, tomatoes can be grown successfully in a wide variety of climates. Since they are so popular, plant breeders have been at work to develop tomatoes for the widest possible range of climate problems.

There may be a garden crop available in more varieties than tomatoes, but I can't think of any. Many tomato varieties are tailored for particular growing conditions, as well as for resistance to strains of virus-producing wilt or blight. So multitudinous are the varieties that there is no point in treating them specifically. Among other considerations, choice should be made by discussing local growing conditions and disease problems with local gardeners or extension agents.

In general, the smaller varieties set fruit earlier and ripen more quickly than the larger varieties. Such strains usually referred to as "cherry tomatoes" or "patio tomatoes"—often with cute diminutive names—are quite small, seldom as large as a golf ball and sometimes the size of a marble, and are commonly served whole on salads. Some people, particularly those with limited space, are satisfied to grow nothing but cherry tomatoes. It is not uncommon to see a few scattered among flower beds; they make an attractive accent point.

The English, with their temperamental climate, have developed an ingenious gimmick for growing patio tomatoes. A 25-pound dark plastic sack of special potting soil is split down the middle and slightly laid open, as for abdominal surgery, and restrained by three plastic bands, like barrel hoops. Three patio tomatoes are transplanted into the soil. The plastic bags retain moisture and absorb a great deal of heat, making it possible for the casual gardener to grow a crop under the most hostile environmental conditions. The tomatoes do especially well situated on a concrete slab. Americans might find the system worth a try.

Likewise the small, yellow "pear tomato" sets fruit early, producing large quantities on rangy vines until frost. Pear tomatoes are mature when they have the color of a ripe Bartlett pear. They are pear- or bottle-shaped, and never grow large; 2 inches long and an inch in diameter can be considered optimum, and most are much smaller. Unlike the usually compact and short growing habits of most cherry tomatoes, pear tomato vines are real space hogs. The fruit is mild, low in acid, but not particularly versatile; however, they always have a place in salads and relish trays, and are good for pickles.

Many people grow the small sizes chiefly because they are dependably early. My favorite of the small tomatoes is the Sweet 100. Seed is generally available and the fruit is early, with a distinctive, sweet flavor. Fruit is an inch in diameter or larger. Earliest of all is the Tiny Tim, variously rated for 50 to 55 days growing time. Fruit is quite small and of satisfactory quality for what will likely be one's first tomatoes of the season. The compact growth habit is especially suitable for container growth. A super-early variety, which I have not tried, is the Oregon Eleven, developed by Oregon State University. It is reputed to ripen fruit 1½ to 2 inches in diameter in early July. Its production peaks quickly and is over. Seed is available from *Territorial Seed Company*.

The best varieties of tomato for canning are those with a high acid content. Not only is this a factor in retaining flavor, it is a safety feature as well. High acid content inhibits botulism. Low acid tomatoes require a longer processing time (at the cost of flavor); it is sometimes recommended that they not be used at all for canning. On the other hand, people with delicate digestive systems are sometimes constrained to eat only low acid tomatoes. The flavor of low acid fruit is generally more bland but sometimes more delicate than others, and some prefer them for their gardens on this basis. In either case, the range of varieties is large. Usually catalogue descriptions will indicate the variety's general acidity.

The Roma tomatoes are small to medium in size and generally somewhat cylindrical in shape. They have a high pulp and relatively low moisture content. While they are sometimes used in salads, their principal function is in cooking. Fresh, they are ideal for making thick sauces and stews. They are excellent for making canned tomato sauce or chili sauce. Not only does their general texture contribute to a thick final product, they also require a great deal less time to thicken than sauce made from other tomatoes. I never really seem to have all I want for these purposes. An Italian variety, *Marzano Lampadima Extra,* is top of the line. It is large and hangs on the vine a very long time after ripening, enabling one to accumulate sufficient quantity to process. It is especially good for sauce and ketchup. Seeds are available from *Epicure Seeds.* Another good paste tomato is the Napoli, which is offered by *Gleckler's Seedsmen.*

There are three varieties of regular-sized tomato that need to be singled out for the sake of curiosity. One is the Muchamiel, offered by *Gurney's,* who call it "the ugly tomato." It really isn't that ugly—except for a short, pearlike neck and deep and distinct wrinkles up the neck to the stem, it is not so different, it just isn't what one expects a tomato to look like. Its flavor, however, is first rate, very rich and mellow. A variety called Purple Calabash *(Good Seeds)* is described as producing "ugly ribbed saucer shape fruits to 12 oz; scrumptious purple skinned"—it sounds irresistible. The third variety is also somewhat of a novelty, but it needs to be taken seriously. It is called the "everlasting tomato" because it has a shelf life—unrefrigerated—of three months and more. This is no hype: it really will last. You can pick them in September and have them for Thanksgiving, literally. They ripen to a pink or dark pink color and have a tart, even astringent, flavor. I have read comments conceding their limitations, but add that they are still better than anything in the market at that season. This is a questionable judgment, but the matter is becoming almost a moot question. Increasingly the tomatoes found in produce markets in winter *are* the everlasting varieties. Perhaps everyone should grow them once, if only to know the enemy. I never thought I would ever look back to when you could buy Mexican tomatoes in winter as "the good old days."

One major distinction in the classification of tomatoes is between "determinate" and "indeterminate" vines. Determinate vines grow to a specific size and stop growing, while indeterminate vines keep growing longer and longer until stopped by frost or other calamity. The wild ancestors of the modern tomato, native to the New World, were used to a mild climate in which they could grow more or less year-round and were in effect perennials. Determinate varieties have been developed for the specific purpose of stopping vine growth after a certain size, thereafter devoting energy more or less exclusively to swelling and ripening fruit. This is a definite advantage in cooler climates. Most patio tomatoes have determinate vines; pear tomatoes do not.

Most of the super-large tomatoes, such as the beefsteak and similar cultivars, are indeterminate. In fact, where the length of the growing season is suitable, these varieties do especially fine as a climbing plant. They require support, of course, but will easily grow upward 10 feet or more if the season is long enough. My grandmother always grew beefsteaks this way, year after year on a permanent wire trellis on the west wall of her kitchen. They grew past the eaves of the house and provided shade for her kitchen window and fruit for her kitchen table. Growing on a trellis, where practical, increases leaf and fruit exposure to the sun, which improve both quantity and size, and speeds ripening. But such tomatoes will not do well without a good long growing season of 100 to 120 days, preferably with a long period of hot sunny weather, and they must be provided with plenty of water.

The vines of indeterminate varieties of tomatoes become floppy and tangled. Consequently the subject of staking or other means of support generates a great deal of interest and controversy among tomato growers. Except for the few varieties having sturdy upright stalks, vines can become quite disarranged, especially as they become loaded with fruit which is every day getting heavier and heavier.

Where they rest on the ground, fruits are prone to split or rot, and under these conditions are also slow to ripen. But supporting tomato vines is not as simple as it ought to be. The quest for the perfect stake or support among gardeners reaches the proportions of the search for the Holy Grail. The ideal would be something that is cheap, light, easy to put up and take down, requires little care and maintenance, and is easy to store. So far the ideal has proved elusive. Tomatoes are not like green beans or peas, or even cucumbers and squash. They do not have climbing tendrils that eagerly snatch any support offered them, after reaching which they take off and do the rest of the work themselves. Properly speaking, tomatoes are vining, rather than climbing. Even if provided with support, the gardener must teach them to use it.

Seemingly the simplest device is that which gives its name to the concept—a stake. This can be anything stiff enough to drive into the ground and support the weight of vines and fruit and can be wood or metal. It should be tall enough to support the growth of a particular variety of tomato. A stake that protrudes 4 feet above the ground is not a bad average. It should be put in place while the plant is small, no taller than about a foot, and positioned 4 to 6 inches from the stem of the young plant. As the vine grows, it must be trained, that is, brought to the stake and attached with one of the various brands of plastic or metal fasteners available at any nursery, or bits of old pantyhose or stockings. When attaching the fastener, leave a little slack to allow for growth of the stem. As the plant develops, additional fasteners must be attached to keep it growing erect. This probably sounds like little trouble, but with several dozen plants to attend to, it can become tedious. And in the fall the stakes have to be removed, freed of dead vines and fasteners, and stored neatly away.

A second general system of "staking" involves the use of woven wire. It is formed into individual cylinders 24 to 36 inches in diameter, one of which is set over each plant while it is small. If this system is to be used, when the individual plants are set out in the spring they should be set far enough apart to leave room for the wire, usually considerably further apart than they would otherwise be set. The tomato vines grow inside the cylinders, which supports them and forces them into erect growth. The mesh of the woven wire must be wide enough to allow a hand to reach inside and pick the ripe tomatoes. Wire mesh support cylinders are available commercially, but are not cheap. They are not handy to store away in the winter, but too expensive to discard. They are also somewhat uneconomical in terms of the amount of space required in their use. This system is, however, especially effective for use with the larger varieties of tomatoes, and is not too unwieldy if no more than half a dozen plants are grown.

Some gardeners, especially northerners with a climate problem, use 5-gallon buckets (the kind various commercial products are delivered in) with the bottoms cut out. They are pressed into the ground about 6 inches, and perhaps a foot apart. A single tomato plant is set in the center of each bucket. They provide early protection for the young plants, help absorb heat and encourage growth, and later help keep the vines sufficiently upright so that the fruit seldom touches the ground. It is possible to cover each with a piece of glass or plastic during cold and damp periods in the spring, making miniature greenhouses. The drawback of this system is getting a supply of the buckets, then cutting the bottoms out of them, and finally storing them in the winter after use. If a fairly large planting of tomatoes is to be made, they become distinctly impractical, although four or five of them gives almost a guarantee of early tomatoes.

Some people use old tires, one around each hill, as a combination support and heat retainer. The drawback is the amount of space used by the tire (unless a supply of tires from compact cars is available). A refinement on this method uses old inner tubes filled with water. The dark surface absorbs heat that warms the water and transfers heat to the ground. The warm water further heats the soil after the sun goes down. The tubes provide some support for the vines and help keep the fruit off the ground. If, at the end of the summer they have not degenerated until they will no longer hold water, they are easily stored away for the winter (emptied of their water, of course). Like tires, they use up a great deal of space, and unless one has suitable contacts with a garage, they are apt to be costly.

Another wire-mesh system places the wire, attached to stakes, flat and parallel to the ground. It is erected after the tomato plants become established and have reached a height of a foot or more. The most frequently used is the wire mesh employed in reinforcing concrete.

Sturdy stakes, usually lengths of 2 × 4's, are driven into the ground in pairs, separated by the width of the woven wire mesh to be used. They are placed at about 4-foot intervals, with about 2 feet protruding from the ground. The wire mesh is stretched and stapled to the stakes. It is possible to construct a frame on top of the stake, made of 1 × 4's, or any handy dimension of lumber (preferably scrap) upon which to spread the wire. However, this is not really necessary, since the wire gives adequate support by itself. This is an effective system; the tomatoes must be encouraged and trained up through it, but once on top they can grow and stretch as they please and never touch the ground. Proper air circulation helps keep the fruit from cracking or spoiling, and it provides excellent exposure to the sunlight to help hasten ripening. In areas where summer cloudiness makes getting fruit to ripen a problem, this "horizontal trellis" is rather common. Its drawback is obvious: it is something more than a mere bother putting up and taking down.

I have seen a similar, but more complex, system that added a 2 × 4 stake at each end, or about every 6 feet for a long row, protruding about 5 feet above the ground. A "rafter" was nailed down the center, parallel to and about 3 feet above the mesh. Over this was draped a "roof" of clear or opaque heavy plastic, attached to both edges of the wire mesh. Put on in late summer, its greenhouse effect hastens ripening, and it gives excellent protection from frost. An arrangement of this sort makes it possible to grow the largest varieties of tomatoes, even in hostile climates. The drawback to this system of combining support and protection to the vines is, unfortunately, obvious: it requires considerable effort to erect and remove, both of which must be done every year. When the plastic sheeting is on, it can be vulnerable to high winds, even when put together with care. A lesser problem is that it is difficult to weed underneath it.

Individual ingenuity will come up with multitudinous designs, based on individual circumstances and especially on materials cheaply available. Whether to stake or not ultimately may depend on how much effort and expense one is willing to go to for the earliest and the biggest tomatoes. One of the deciding factors may well be how much garden space is available to a gardener. The more space is at a premium, the more effort a given gardener will be willing to devote to tending the support of individual plants. The decision about the mode of staking, or whether or not to stake at all, needs to be made before planting, however, since it will determine the spacing and placing of the plants.

Whether to stake or not will be some influence on selecting what varieties to plant. Most gardeners begin with pre-started tomato plants, homegrown or purchased from a nursery. A major advantage to growing your own is that you will have access to a larger selection of tomato varieties from catalogues than you will find in most nurseries. There is a preseason pleasure in the armchair luxury of reading through numerous catalogues and daydreaming about possibilities. Although the seeds are cheaper than the plants, given the whole process of starting one's own plants, likely it will not be appreciably less expensive. The strongest argument for growing one's own is an extension of the pleasure of leisurely shopping in the catalogues; it is a kind of confirmation that indeed spring is going to come. Planting seeds inside is a springlike thing to do, which probably more than compensates for the practical fact that you could probably do it as cheaply if you bought from a nursery at planting time.

For pre-starting indoors, use planting trays or peat pots filled with prepared potting mixture. It's cheaper to use a rich garden soil, but the potting mixture will be more satisfactory—it is easier to keep moist, tends to promote denser root growths, and makes it easier to transplant from starting trays to larger or intermediate pots. If a tray is used, plant the seeds two or three to a spot, lightly covered, and on a grid about an inch apart. After they have sprouted and the first leaf appears, thin by clipping with scissors or knife (pulling may disturb the roots of the remaining plant) to single plants, each an inch apart. When the seedlings are about 3 inches tall they should be transplanted into individual peat pots (or, if the weather is suitable, transplanted outdoors). If the seeds are planted too early, become crowded before separating into individual pots, or if they get too much direct sunlight, they may tend to grow long, weak stems—to become "leggy," as they say. If they are nursed under the lights especially designed for indoor plants, this condition should be no particular problem, unless they are planted much too early or allowed to become crowded.

It is a good idea to begin introducing the seedlings to the real world a week or more before actually transplanting them outside. To accomplish this, give them a little daily outing by taking them to a protected spot during daylight hours, but do not expose to direct rays if the sun gets actually hot during a period of the day. This is called "hardening off" the seedlings. Their stems will thicken, their leaves will green up, and in general they will begin to look like outdoor plants rather than indoor plants. Hardening off will reduce the shock or setback of actually transplanting them and get them off to a more vigorous and energetic start. Hardening off requires a little bother, but if the individual pots are placed on trays, or even wide boards, all can be carried out with two or three trips. If plants purchased from a nursery are leggy, or lack a good deep-green color, it is advantageous to harden them off a few days before transplanting for a running start. Don't forget to bring plants in at night if there is still danger of frost.

It is possible, of course, to transplant seedlings from their individual pots into very large peat pots or other containers and keep them inside until they are practically adult size, even blooming and beginning to set tomatoes. After they are transplanted, they won't set anymore fruit until the temperature is suitably warm. Large plants seem to have difficulty overcoming the shock of transplanting. The problem does not result from the transplanting itself but because even in a large pot the root system is relatively small in relationship to the leaf surface. Until a balance is struck when the roots have spread into the garden soil, the leaves may transpire more moisture than the roots are capable of absorbing from the soil. Sometimes over a month will pass before plants that were too large begin to look "thrifty." The cherry tomatoes are an exception; these plants are naturally small and have a compact root system. They may be grown quite satisfactorily in a container for their entire life, as in the English system of "tomato sacks."

Ordinarily the tomato plants purchased at a nursery are sold in small flats or planters, sometimes referred to as "ponies," each containing six or eight plants. Some gardeners purchase these flats a week or two before transplanting time and separate them into individual peat pots to allow a little more growth and spread of the roots. The flats are subsequently transplanted pots and all, which hopefully lessens the shock of transplanting. Whether plants are started indoors or purchased as established seedlings, and whether or not they are hardened off before transplanting, they should not be set out during the heat of the day. In warm sunny weather, plant in the early evening. If a cloudy or overcast day is available, so much the better.

Having decided on the method of staking or support, or the lack of it, the row should be lined out and spaced accordingly. If the plants are not to be staked, for medium-sized tomatoes they should be spaced about 16 or 18 inches apart, up to twice that distance for varieties that produce large vines. Those plants that have been started in or transplanted to peat pots can be set out, pots and all, but buried deeply enough so that none of the pot is less than an inch below the surface of the soil. If any of the pot becomes exposed, the pot will act as a wick, drawing moisture from the roots of the seedling, almost always stunting the plant. Even though the roots will grow through the pot, I always cut several slits down the side and across the bottom of each pot before setting it into the ground to give the tender roots something to move through immediately. It may not be necessary, but it can't hurt.

If transplanting directly from a flat or pony, separate the plants carefully, distributing the planting mixture equally, disturbing the roots as little as possible. Dig the hole with a hand trowel, loosening the soil in the bottom to a depth of 6 inches or so below the bottom level the roots will occupy. This helps the young roots get a good start in their expansion. Place the plant in the hole an inch deeper than it had originally been growing. If the stem is quite long, or leggy, place it deep enough that the stem can handily support the weight of the top without it bending. The portion of the stem that is underground will quickly grow roots and actually improve the underpinnings of the plant. A very leggy plant may be placed in the ground on a slant. That is, instead of digging a hole 8 or 10 inches deep, or whatever would be required, dig one 6 inches deep and 6 inches long. Place the roots at the bottom of one end and, carefully curving the stem, fill in with dirt around the roots and stem until the top and the leaves at the opposite end of the trench are straight and sufficiently sturdy to support the weight of the top.

Tomatoes are a crop that definitely should be rotated from year to year. Do not grow them two consecutive years in the same spot. This helps cut down on possible root diseases, viruses, and funguses. Rotation also helps keep from exhausting the soil of the specific nutrients tomatoes require. They do best in a soil that was well fertilized the previous year. Newly applied manure will tend to make them grow great foliage but not very many tomatoes. Before planting the ground may be enriched with a high phosphorus fertilizer, or a specially balanced tomato fertilizer, but too much immediately available nitrogen tends to make them go all to leaves. The special tomato fertilizers are worth the trouble.

When the tomatoes begin to bloom, especially if the temperature is still cool at night, the setting of fruit can be improved by spraying each blossom cluster with a blossom-setting hormone. If used, read and follow the instructions carefully, or it may cause many of the blossoms to drop. There is a curious side effect of using a blossom set; tomatoes that have been nudged along by this means will have few, sometimes absolutely no, seeds. This makes them more fleshy, of course, and could be a boon to those people who have digestive problems and cannot eat tomatoes because of seeds. Some people think such tomatoes look strange and unnatural sliced or in salads. Some gardeners, especially very patient gardeners, encourage fruit setting during the marginally cold periods by giving each blossom a very gentle snap with the fingers. These patient old gardeners grow very nice tomatoes, and lots of them.

To hasten ripening, it is helpful to do some light to severe pruning of the vines when the fruit is beginning to turn from a deep green to a sort of lard white. Cut away leaves that shade clusters of tomatoes, and cut off those "suckers" for which there is obviously not enough time to set fruit or to ripen the small immature tomatoes that may have already set on them. Branches may be cut off above clusters of tomatoes, which both exposes them to sunshine and forces growth in the tomatoes. The shock of pruning seems to have the effect of traumatizing the plant into "desperation" ripening. Don't brutalize the plants, of course, but as the season wears on, particularly toward the frost, one can be increasingly severe with the pruning.

When tomatoes have reached full size and seem to be avoiding turning red simply as a deliberate perversity, exasperated gardeners resort to various expedients to hasten the ripening of a few. A common method is to pick tomatoes that have turned white and place them on a windowsill. They will ripen, but without optimum flavor (and they will ripen better out of the sun). A better way is to place several in a plastic bag with an apple, blow the bag up, twist and tie the open end and place away from the light. The ethylene gas exhaled by the apple skin will ripen the tomatoes quickly, and with a more nearly vine-ripened flavor.

Then comes the dreaded day when the weather prognosticator ominously intones, "Cover your tomatoes!" When this moment arrives the range of options is limited. If it is late in the season, and frosty nights can be pretty much looked for from then on, perhaps the best option is to pick all the tomatoes of a worthwhile size, ripe or not. Kept reasonably cool and out of direct sunlight, all but the most emerald green of them should ripen over the course of two or three weeks. As they ripen they may be canned or processed, eaten, cooked, or given away.

Another option at this time of the year is to pull the vines up, roots and all, and hang them upside down in a cellar or basement, hence the common name for this practice—"cellaring." This will considerably lengthen the ripening time of the tomatoes on the vines, and those ripened in this way will have a flavor superior to those simply picked and allowed to ripen. Occasionally one hears of gardeners having tomatoes still ripening as late as Christmas. On the other hand, if the storage temperature is too warm, they may suddenly all be ripe at once. It is pretty obvious that this method is messy, particularly with large and rambling vines.

A holding action against the threat of frost, especially early in the frost season, is to cover the plants with newspapers, plastic, old bed sheets, or whatever is available. Covering will protect the plants through a few degrees of frost. Most likely some leaves will be nipped, but the plants will continue to hold the fruit and allow them to ripen normally. It is only worthwhile to cover the plants in a given climate if a somewhat long spell of frost-free weather can normally be expected, or if there will be only occasional and light frosts. Frankly, covering tomatoes night after night, and uncovering them in the morning, gets to be tedious. Semipermanent arrangements made with wooden frames and plastic sheeting, as described above, gets all of the tediousness over with at one time, early in the year. With such a shelter the plants will receive better protection and for a longer time. But when the night-long temperatures begin settling into the twenties, it's time to face reality and accept that summer is over.

Limited protection can be achieved by sprinkling. The water itself will be above 32 degrees and will provide some warming. As the spray begins freezing, it will give off warmth to the air (or the plants it is on) and provide enough protection to allow the plants to make it through the period of frost. Even plants caked with ice for a short time will remain viable, although many of the leaves may turn black. A weakness limiting this system is that the autumn rains may already have begun to soak the ground. Prolonged and repeated sprinkling may turn out to be too much of a good thing. Sprinkling is best begun in the early hours, as the temperature begins sliding down to freezing, and then turned off as soon as the sun is high enough to begin warming things. This may be more of a drain on rest than a gardener is willing to allow; each person has to arrange his sleeping hours as best as possible. Sprinkling is an effective way to provide limited protection for young plants in the early spring, but with the same limitations.

The most heated question about tomatoes among nongardeners is how to pronounce their name, long *a* or short *a*. On the basis of their preference, many people assume their own social caste and identify the social standing of others. As far as etymology can determine, its ancient name in South America, *tomatl (tōmătl),* gives the nod to the short *a*.

Unlike the New World foods such as potatoes and corn, the tomato did not seem to be an especially important food plant to the Mayans. Although it was a plant early introduced to the Old World, for some time it was of interest primarily as an ornamental rather than a food. In many places it was even considered poisonous, probably because it is a member of the nightshade family, and its fruits looked like nothing so much as super nightshade berries. Even as late as the nineteenth century, it was regionally regarded to be poisonous.

It may have been the combination of the attractiveness of the fruits and the suspicion of its unwholesomeness that contributed to one of the tomato's Old World names: "love apple." Whether the name caused the fame, or vice versa, among the effects popularly attributed to the tomato was as an aphrodisiac. In this last there is at least an element of truth: nothing the gardener grows generates as much exasperation as the tomato, and exasperation has long been recognized to be the most enduring quality of love.

Corn:
A God,
a Food,
and
an Enigma

Corn zygote

As with their tomatoes, many gardeners stake a lot of emotional capital and a great deal of their reputation on corn. Earliness takes top priority in the bragging of most gardeners, possibly since quality is far better concealed by the enveloping corn husks than is true of the naked exposure of tomatoes, honestly and openly hanging among their vines. There is not much one can do by way of technique or manipulation to egg the corn into earlier maturing. The matter is pretty much decided by the genetics of the seed planted and the subsequent tender mercies of the weather.

As with the majority of vegetables, inquiry about what varieties do well in a given locality is a sound beginning for the inexperienced. Experienced gardeners moving to a new geographical area may find their old familiar favorites do not do well, even where there does not appear to be a sharp difference in climate. So-called "shoe peg" corn, for example, which is a reliable old-fashioned favorite in many eastern and midwestern regions, is not too successful in the far West. For want of a better explanation, it may miss the high humidity and hot nights found in the areas of its greatest popularity. It also requires a relatively high soil temperature to germinate. Seed catalogues list many varieties of corn, and usually give an indication of time from planting to maturing, as well as clues about areas where they are especially successful. The shortest number of days to mature sweet corn is around 65 days, although a few are listed as low as 55. From there the figures go as high as 125 or more for some varieties.

The earliest corn is mostly short-stalked and usually produces small ears. Although there have been major improvements, much early corn is inferior in flavor to full season corn. It is a normal practice for gardeners to plant more than one variety in order to blend a continuous succession of ripening corn. Some gardeners may or may not plant an early variety, but to assure a long season will plant successively, about a week or ten days apart, a variety that they prefer. This system does not guarantee that the corn will ripen exactly in the same time sequence planted, but it will help assure a longer period of yield. Others, particularly those who intend to can or freeze an appreciable quantity, will plant an early variety for immediate eating as it ripens, plus a large "main crop" that will come off more or less at once, a variety selected because it has proven qualities of freezing or canning well. In most cases it is the later corn with the longer growing season that produces the really superior crop. Some plant the same variety at two-week intervals for a continuous crop, but that works only moderately well. Ripening time is heavily influenced by day length, and although staggered planting will prolong the productive season, the same end is better achieved by planting several varieties with differing dates to maturity.

If different varieties are planted in the same vicinity, it is desirable to arrange the planting to separate those that might overlap their "blooming" periods. Corn is fertilized by pollen that falls or blows from the tassels to the silks of the ears, which are each in effect tubes to the individual kernels. If pollen from one variety falls on silks of another variety, the strain of the second variety will be upset and not "throw" true to type. In this case a few kernels might be affected, or perhaps the whole ear. The ears will form normally, but desirable qualities of flavor, tenderness, sweetness, and so forth, for which the variety was selected to begin with will be lost. The pattern is that white corn is recessive, yellow dominant. Therefore, white kernels will always cross to yellow, never the other way around.

To assure pollination and to prevent cross-pollination corn is best "block planted"—that is, in several short (or long, as the size of the garden allows) rows consisting exclusively of the same varieties. This will concentrate the pollen within its own variety. Plant blocks of early corn between crops of mid-season and late corn to prevent overlapping of pollen during blooming periods. If possible, arrange corn rows to run more or less heading into the line of the prevailing winds, rather than across the wind. This will not only be a help in keeping errant pollen from running astray, it will also help assure that pollen does indeed reach the silks, and that the ears will completely fill out, since each kernel will have been pollenized.

Modern geneticists have thrown a wild card into the already complicated game of choosing corn varieties. Through gene splicing, genetic engineers have provided an extra "sweetness gene" to several varieties of corn. So far four classes are being marketed, called Extra Sweet, Ultra-sweet, E.H. (for Everlasting Heritage), and Sugar Extender. The seed of the first two forms is extremely shriveled; the latter two are normal sized. Because of the emaciated seed of the first two varieties, they germinate poorly in cool soil. The first two types require isolation from other corn to maintain sweetness; the latter two do not. Not only are these strains distinctly sweeter when harvested, they maintain their sweetness much longer. Common varieties may lose as much as half of their sweetness hours after picking. Those varieties with the E.H. gene are said to hold their sweetness up to two weeks after picking. I have grown two varieties of E.H.—Early Extra Sweet *(Pony Creek Nursery)* and Miracle *(Nichols Garden Nursery)*. Both were extremely good—noticeably sweeter but not masking the corn flavor with the sweetness.

Corn appreciates and responds to a rich, well-tilled soil. It also responds to a rich, mellow no-till garden soil. Sow corn only after the soil begins to warm. A piece of old folk wisdom says to plant corn when the leaves on oak trees are as big as a squirrel's ears. If it is planted too early in cold, clammy soil, even if there is no frost, the seed may rot rather than sprout. Plant corn in hills about 8 inches apart, with three or four seeds to the hill. Place the seeds about an inch deep, with the soil lightly tamped over the top, and in rows about 24 inches apart. To improve pollination, plant at least two rows of each variety, preferably four. The seeds should germinate in a week or ten days, depending on the temperature. During this period before germination, the soil should not be allowed to dry below the level the seeds were placed, but should not be overwatered either.

In climates where rainfall is undependable and irrigation necessary, there are advantages to irrigating with rills or little ditches between each row, drawn with a ditching tool or the corner of a hoe. These ditches should be made before the corn gets more than an inch or two tall to avoid disturbing the roots. Watering with these small ditches puts the water directly in the root zone and encourages the roots to go deeper and more firmly anchor the corn to the ground. Watering with a sprinkler results in shallower root depths, and once the corn reaches 3 or 4 feet, the weight of the water on the leaves, especially when a good stiff wind stirs up, can knock the corn flat to the ground.

When the corn is about 3 feet tall (sooner or later, depending on the variety), offshoots or "suckers" will begin to grow from just above the roots on many of the corn stalks. Removing these helps to keep the growth and strength directed into the main stalk. If allowed to grow, most of these suckers will tassle and many will set small ears. In the main, however, most of these ears would be small, some having few if any kernels, and the ears on the main stalk may be correspondingly smaller. These suckers can be removed by twisting them off as close to the main stalk as possible, or they may be cut away with a knife. There are gardeners who prefer to leave the suckers, insisting a higher yield results. I believe it depends on how suitable, or ideal, one's conditions for growing corn are. My situation is not ideal, and production is improved by "suckering."

When there is insufficient natural moisture the corn must be irrigated. Water often enough that the plants never suffer from a lack of moisture, but not so often as to keep the soil actually wet in the top 2 inches. Overwatering tends to make the roots shallow and weak and the stalks susceptible to falling or being blown over. Also, too shallow roots tend to make the plants susceptible to damage by extremely hot dry weather. By spacing waterings until the top surface of the soil becomes dry—timing will depend entirely on local climate conditions and the water-retaining quality of individual soils—the roots are encouraged to penetrate deeply as they seek the retreating moisture supply.

A few gardeners pride themselves on growing gardens that make their families virtually self-sufficient. They therefore like to try their hands at growing dry corn and grinding their own meal, or perhaps, having sufficient space, grow corn for chickens or other livestock. Such corn, which is grown to be harvested dry, is called field corn, as opposed to sweet corn, which is eaten green. When sweet corn matures, the kernels become wizened; mature corn kernels are large, plump, smooth, and very hard. The ears of field corn are long, at least 8 inches and often a great deal longer, and may be up to 2 inches in diameter. The rows of kernels are evenly filled, each seed being erect and firm. The stalks of field corn are correspondingly tall, at least 6 feet, and often much taller. The immature ears of field corn may be eaten while the kernels are still milky in all the ways sweet corn is prepared, but at their best are tough and lack the delicate flavor of the better varieties of sweet corn.

Field corn is planted and cultivated in the same way as sweet corn. However, since the stalks are so much taller, it grows best with a wider spacing of the rows—28 to 30 inches for the home garden, a little wider if mechanized cultivation is to be used. Most field corn requires a full growing season of 125 days. That can be a rather long stretch for some northern climates. The old saying is that if it's "going to make," field corn must be "knee high by the Fourth of July." All corn flourishes best during hot, humid summer weather, which is why the South and Midwest are justly famous for the quality of their corn, whether field or green. During optimum growing conditions, on a still evening it is actually possible to hear corn growing in a large field; a strange unlocalized rustling, moaning sound is clearly audible, which is eerie and sobering. When conditions are just right, it is not at all difficult to work up belief in a corn god inhabiting your very field.

And corn was a god among many of the Americas' aboriginal inhabitants. Exactly what would be considered the New World's major contribution to the world's diet is probably impossible to decide, but corn must be one of the top contenders. For the majority of the early dwellers of the American Southwest, Mexico, and South America corn was not only the staple of the diet, but what made civilization possible. It could have been the inability of the Indians of much of North America to grow corn that prevented them from establishing a farming culture and establishing cities, as did their neighbors to the south. In a notebook, a clerk accompanying the explorer De Soto notes that Indians informed him no corn would be found growing west of the great rivers because of the herds of buffalo. As much as we may decry the shameful waste in the slaughter of the buffalo, coolly considered, the agricultural Midwest could not coexist with roving millions of the handsome beasts. We can imagine the afternoon scene of Chicago's Loop as the buffalo came down at five o'clock to drink at their age-old watering hole, from which presumably the city of Chicago ("stinking water") derived its name.

So it was corn, giving the stable capital of a dependable and long-range food supply, which made the cities and civilizations of the Indians of the Americas possible. But there is a genetic mystery of how corn came into existence. Most food crops can be traced to a wild ancestor or combinations of ancestors. Corn cannot. It is, in fact, an evolutionary paradox. Although kernels compactly arranged around a central core, and protected by a thick wrapping of leaves, could hardly be more ideally suited for human needs, corn could hardly be more badly engineered for natural propagation and, therefore, natural selection. No corn that is known in modern times, or even archeologically, would be capable of sustaining itself in a wild state more than a few generations at most. Nature has provided no competitive way to distribute the seeds. It must be propagated by deliberate cultivation, or it ceases to exist.

Which brings in a second evolutionary paradox. Since no certain natural ancestral form of modern corn can be determined, a logical deduction is that corn as we know it, as well as corn as the ancients knew it, was developed by selective breeding directed by human intention. But this in turn presupposes that these early geneticists had in mind a model or ideal they were striving to achieve. No form exists in nature, however, that would suggest this model or ideal to be worked toward. To have developed corn, in other words, supposes the thinking of the unthinkable.

Teosinte, a wild plant of Mexico, has long been considered as a possible ancestor of corn, but the common plant has the wrong number of chromosomes. Recently a wild plant of the teosinte family has been discovered that has the necessary number of chromosomes. The plant is so rare that the single wild colony known to exist in a remote and forbidding part of southern Mexico measures about a quarter of an acre. While this teosinte promises a clue to the origin of corn, the mystery is far from solved.

Almost every summer most gardeners will find at least one corn plant that has produced an odd or deformed tassel. Along the stamens will develop small kernels that look very much like corn. This anomaly might suggest a throwback to an ancestor of domestic corn. This is not, however, the case. These are examples of a rather common biological occurrence called a zygote, resulting from the union of two similar gametes, or sexual cells. In this case the gametes are both male cells from the tassel.

Twentieth-century geneticists have continued what has been the work of a millennia of plant breeders and produced the various hybrid corns that are grown almost everywhere where large-scale agriculture is practiced. In fact, so universally has hybridization progressed that there is the possibility the strains from which these hybrids were developed would disappear, which would make it difficult to start over, should a blight or disease prohibit the growing of present strains. It is theoretically possible that through hybridization corn could become extinct. To forestall such a potential calamity, "seed banks" have been established where a large number of strains of seeds are kept, regrowing them sufficiently often to keep on hand a source of viable seeds.

Some gardeners, just for fun, because of flavor, and for nutritional considerations have been cultivating varieties of "mazo" corn, the source of mazo meal, the corn meal of Mexican and South American cookery. Meal ground from standard American hybrid field corn is quite different in quality, and reputedly inferior nutritionally. Mazo comes in different cultivars, but is related to one or more of the literally innumerable cultivars of "antique" corn grown from the American Southwest to the full length of South America. In Peru, for example, corn grown at sea level will be quite different than that grown at high elevations; sometimes in a given region cultivars may change with just a few hundred feet of elevation, all adapted by those superb plant breeders who began growing corn there some fifteen hundred years ago. A gardener who is picky enough to grow his own dried corn for food should probably seriously think about growing mazo. The seed is not generally available, but can be obtained from specialty seed houses *(Good Seeds; Johnny's Select Seed)* and is occasionally advertised in gardening magazines.

So-called "Indian corn," or ornamental corn, is more closely related to the mazo strains than to modern field corn. It is grown for the bright and often variegated colors of the kernels. The ears are long and usually tapering, and with the dried husks pulled back it makes a picturesque fall and winter arrangement. Most is, like field corn, tall, and requires a long growing season. It is cultivated in the same way as field corn, although usually gardeners will only want to plant a few hills unless they plan to be decorative indeed. If it is planted near enough to sweet corn for cross-pollination to occur, it will virtually ruin the corns it crosses with. One summer I planted a few hills at what I thought was a sufficient distance from my sweet corn but failed to take into account the prevailing wind direction. The end rows of sweet corn that received the foreign pollen were tough and mealy, and many of the kernels had variegated colors.

A simple, old-fashioned way of getting "corn meal" involves using fresh sweet corn. Make a grater by punching numerous holes in a shallow tin can (or a tall one, if you have a long enough tool to reach to the bottom conveniently). Take sweet corn that is over the hill for optimum eating and, using this perforated can, grate the kernels from the cob into a bowl. Use this pulp as a substitute for part, or all, of the corn meal in various corn meal recipes. It makes a rather heavy bread, extremely moist and crumbly. It retains a surprisingly good bit of the sweet corn flavor. The pulp can be used in the same way in making corn pudding. With or without adding corn meal on flour, it can also be fried in flatcakes or corn fritters.

Most gardeners with any particular sense of curiosity will eventually want to try growing popcorn. There are many varieties, including tiny "strawberry" ears that are grown mostly as an ornamental. Probably the best results will always be obtained with the various hybrids that are advertised in the seed catalogues. It is possible, of course, simply to plant seed from the popcorn canister in the kitchen. Most likely it will grow fine, but will not turn out to be especially cooperative in the popper because hybrids do not throw true from first generation seed. Hybrids have been developed to deliver maximum expansion of kernels and to produce the highest possible ratio of kernels that actually pop. If you want to grow popcorn, buy good seed.

The limiting factor in growing popcorn is climate. It takes a long—in the range of at least 125 days—growing season. It also likes hot weather in the peak of its growing and ripening season. Like ornamental corn, popcorn should be segregated from the other varieties of corn in the garden. It will ruin sweet corn if it cross-pollinates with it.

Several years ago I grew a small row of popcorn in my Zone 5 garden; although I started with proper seed, production was light. In other respects it was an altogether satisfactory crop, except it wouldn't pop. I decided to conduct a scientific test to determine the degree to which it would not pop. One-half cup of corn expanded to a total volume of one and a quarter cups. It was something to be shunned by anyone with expensive denture work. In other words, growing popcorn is a little like growing artichokes; the plants grow well in a wide variety of places, but if the climate isn't right, the product may be lovely but worthless.

Big Fat Fruits
that Grow
on Vines

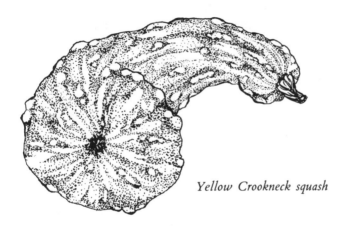

Yellow Crookneck squash

Some of the larger members of the winter squashes are of staggering size, and in the fall as the vines are bent down with age these enormous hulks seem to be hoisting themselves from the earth itself. When the vines have frosted down, a farm hillside planted to acres of marblehead squash looks as if it had been seeded to boulders by a retreating glacier.

Most of the larger varieties, and many of the smaller, are terribly glutinous of space. A modest-sized garden spot can be overwhelmed by a single hill of such standard field varieties as marblehead or banana squash planted in the middle. There are even super varieties of squash and pumpkins, largely ornamental, common in weights above a hundred pounds, with records above five hundred, that are even more wolfish of space. Except for astonishing the eyes of the beholders, the fruits of these varieties are almost worthless. Despite their seductive attractions, most gardeners simply cannot sacrifice the space some of the large varieties of the squash family require. Alas.

The problem is not, however, hopeless, although getting to a solution may require a little backing off and retrenching. Bush varieties have been developed for many of the cucurbits, which have much more modest space requirements than the sprawling vines of the common varieties. Although they are not as prolific, hill by hill, as the large varieties, and although their fruit will likely not be as large, their production as fully answers the average gardener's need as the more space-greedy vines. Think it over: How many 15-pound pumpkins, for example, do you really need? Some varieties have not been brought under the disciplined breeding of bush configuration, but probably the time is not distant when practically all will have been.

Except for the fact that they do not like an acid soil, most members of this large family are not fussy. Although they are tropical in origin, with a few exceptions they adapt to a wide range of climatic conditions. They appreciate rich soil and will respond enthusiastically to fertilization, organic or chemical. Most of them grow handily in a range of soil types from sandy to heavy, with a modest preference for light soil structures. As would be expected from their tropical origins, all are frost-sensitive, and all refuse to germinate in cold soil. Therefore they must be planted not only after danger of frost has passed, but after the soil begins to become languidly warm. With a few exceptions, there is no major difference in the ways in which the various members of this family are treated.

Of course, the ubiquitous squash of the modern garden is zucchini, although that has not always been the case in America. Every garden should have zucchini, and since most common varieties are bush rather than vining, they can be grown without too great a commitment of space. Two hills of hybrid bush will supply the needs of an average family, and then some. Zucchini are *very* prolific, usually quite early, and within my experience totally dependable. The most expensive pack of hybrid seeds, niggardly in content, will plant at least two hills, and the common packets bought off the rack might plant eight to ten, which of course would be madness.

American cooks have made almost a game out of collecting

ingenious recipes for using zucchini. European cooks seem to take it more seriously, and traditional European recipes are better prepared from traditional European varieties of zucchini. The only European specimen I have grown is the Italian *Lunghissimo Bianco Di Palermo (Epicure Seeds)*. The skin is of a paler green than familiar varieties, with pale or white longitudinal stripes. The flesh is much less watery than common zucchini, which is for me a sufficient plus to prefer it. It is clearly the choice ingredient for Italian dishes. *Epicure Seeds* recommends it crisp-fried and tossed with pasta. Those which are allowed to mature, and by necessity some are bound to, make a surprisingly satisfactory winter squash. The meat is thick, an attractive bright orange color, and free of fiber. They also keep well. A French zucchini, which I have not grown, is *Abondance (Epicure Seeds)*. Picked very small, it is recommended raw in salads or used with dip, as well as thin sliced and deep fried. At this stage of growth the skin is white.

Zucchini are the easiest of all squash to grow. Although a handful of compost or humus spaded into the earth at the time of planting helps them to get off to a good start, and probably promotes earlier production, they require no special attention. To sow, place the seeds, about five of them per hill, in a circle about 8 inches in diameter, and about an inch deep. Press the earth firmly over the seeds, and mark each hill with a stake. After the first true leaf appears, thin each hill to the three most vigorous seedlings, cutting or pinching the excess plants off rather than pulling them to avoid disturbing the soil around the roots of the remaining seedlings. However, explaining how to grow zucchini is a little embarrassing, like presuming to teach a toad to cause warts. They grow so well and so vigorously that we might almost suppose that zucchini is a weed for which we have found a use.

The best varieties of zucchini are quite early, from 45 to 50 days; they begin producing fruits when the bushes seem to be hardly more than infant rosettes of leaves. Like all of the family, they bloom in two sexes, male and female. The male blossom will open first, followed by the opening of female blossoms. The difference between them is easily noticed. The stem below the blossom of the male is slender, while the female stem will show a bulbousness, containing the ovum which will swell after pollination into the eventual fruit. Upon opening, the male blossoms will show only the pollen-bearing stamens, while in the female blossom the single pistil is prominently displayed. The fruit develops from the ovum at the base of the blossom.

Zucchini are ordinarily eaten very young, almost as soon as the blossom withers, at which time the fruit may already be 3 or 4 inches long. They grow rapidly, and in a matter of days each fruit may be more than a foot long. If the fruit is kept picked, the vine will continue to bloom and set fruit in most areas up until frost. Even the most diligent gardener is apt to overlook an occasional fruit, with its dark green color the same as the dark foliage serving as a very efficient camouflage. Often the gardener will literally stumble over such fruit, which seems suddenly to have achieved gargantuan size.

Because of the zucchini's amazing productivity, after the first week or so gardeners are constantly trying to find people to give their surplus. On one occasion, knocking on a friend's door, and having several zucchini visible on the top of a sack of produce I intended to give him, I had the door slammed in my face, and heard from the interior of the house an urgent voice cry: "Zucchini alert! Zucchini alert!" Thus I learned surplus zucchini should always be disguised under clearly visible carrots, onions, corn, or other garden truck that might not be in such conspicuous plenty. I sometimes forego planting zucchini at all, simply for the pleasure it affords other gardeners when I accept their offer to give me zucchini.

There are, of course, many other summer squash besides zucchini. All of them, by the way, correspond to the generic term used by the English of "vegetable marrow," or often just plain "marrow." Most of us were bewildered by this term when we first encountered in Beatrix Potter's *Peter Rabbit* the fact that Mr. McGregor was cultivating marrow. Nearly as popular among the varieties of summer squash as zucchini is the Yellow Crookneck. It grows almost as prolifically as zucchini, although it does not grow as large, and is also picked young when the attached blossom is still withering. Its culture is identical with zucchini. They are decidedly at their best while still young enough that the rind may be easily cut through with a fingernail. They are frequently used without removing the rind. The meat is somewhat firmer than that of zucchini, and for freezing they are superior.

An old-fashioned variety of vegetable marrow is the Pancake or

Scalloped Summer squash. They are mostly white, although some recent adaptations are green. The original white is a quite attractive fruit, flattened, circular as a dish, and fluted regularly around the edge like a well-made apple pie. They may grow to 10 or more inches in diameter, although they are usually picked much smaller. If allowed to mature they may be used as a winter squash, although there are other varieties of much better quality to be used in that way. Their cultivation is identical with the cultivation of zucchini, although the old-fashioned Scalloped Summer squash is usually found in vining rather than bush varieties.

Many or most of the summer squashes, if allowed to mature, will develop a typically tough squash rind and will actually keep into the winter. It may sound like a depressing thought after a summertime of zucchini dishes, but I have had large zucchini perfectly sound well into the following January. To cook they may be treated much as the usual winter squash, although their flavor is bland and, I suspect, their nutritional value much inferior.

For winter squash a good compromise with size and convenience is the acorn or Danish squash. Although commonly grown as a vining squash, seeds are available for bush varieties, which require much less space. The bush varieties are not as productive as the vining, but these hybrid fruits are superior in flavor and in thickness of meat, in addition to being larger and more attractive. Acorn squash may be picked immature and used in the same way other summer squash are used. Commonly they are allowed to mature, and picked after the first frosts kill the vines. They should not be allowed to remain long after frost, as they may be damaged by freezing. They keep well and are often halved and baked until tender, with a little butter and syrup or brown sugar in the cavity. Very small ones are sometimes cooked whole and served one to a plate, with the diner performing the necessary surgery at the table. This method has a certain appearance of elegance, but frankly is a little awkward and messy.

Even though the squash family originated in tropical America, traditionally we think that nothing is more Yankee than the pumpkin. This association is reflected in a couplet of a song from the time of the American Revolution:

Every Yankee will have a sack,
With a great big pumpkin across his back.

It came to me as a disappointment to learn that there is no single species that is the *true* pumpkin. The most commonly grown "pumpkins" are actually cultivars of two distinct and separate species of cucurbit; in fact, most commercial canned pumpkin is actually hubbard squash. It is sort of like learning that the bald eagle can be either an English sparrow or a cockatoo, and the one figured on the American Seal is actually a vulture.

Given the fact that there is no pumpkin, in the practical world of gardening, seeds are offered for orange spheroids with thick flesh which merchants call pumpkins. Under the circumstances, however, to designate any variety as a "gourmet pumpkin" would do violence to the language. Generally speaking, whatever they are, the smaller varieties have thicker flesh, less fiber, and are generally superior for pies. A large variety called the Connecticut field pumpkin is quite ancient, and might even have been the pumpkin the Yankee carried in his sack. It is large, handsome, and makes a perfect jack-o'-lantern.

It is almost irresistible to grow pumpkins occasionally, but they are terrible space thieves. To save space they are sometimes interplanted with corn, a practice probably originated by the American Indians. Traditional interplanting presupposes the corn to be a variety with sturdy stalks. Many modern varieties of sweet corn have stalks that are much weaker than those of the older field corns and may be bent and mangled by the weight of the vines and fruit. I have not found interplanting to be at all satisfactory. Aside from problems of breaking down the corn stalks, when the vines really start reaching for distance you must for practical purposes abandon all efforts of cultivation.

Fortunately pumpkins are available now in bush varieties, which take up about the same amount of space as a bush of zucchini. One bush probably will produce only one or two pumpkins, but they are of quite respectable size. Of those I have grown, the color seems a little paler than the field varieties, but they are well formed and attractive. A couple of hills of bush variety should be adequate for most home needs and take up considerably less space than a single hill of the vining types.

Few things are as tempting to grow as the giant pumpkins (and squash) advertised every year by the seed companies. These strains require a great deal of space and a long growing season. Without assurance of 125 frost-free days, including warm weather at the beginning of the growing season, they are a chancy prospect. If one has the space and the growing season to produce the truly extravagant-sized fruits, thin each hill to a single plant, and after the first few true leaves appear, side dress weekly with a dash of liquid fish fertilizer. When blossoms begin setting, thin each vine and allow no more than two fruit to grow. When the selected fruits have reached a diameter of about a foot, it is a good idea to place each on a square of cardboard or plywood to protect the bottom side and improve the appearance. For most practical purposes, however, these large varieties are finally good only for ornamentation and bragging; the flesh is inferior and recommended for nothing but stock feed.

Members of the large squash family keep well through the winter, or a good part of it, and some better than others. They survive well under cool, dark storage such as a basement or cellar, where they should be kept from contact with the damp. Some of the most durable can be kept clear through the winter and for little effort with a few squash one can store away a great deal of nutrition.

A bonus from the cultivation of pumpkins and the larger squash is their edible seeds. There is reason to believe that the early Indians may have cultivated squash more for their seeds than their flesh. As primitive art and artifacts confirm, the seeds were certainly considered an important product. So when dressing out a squash, always save the seeds. Separate them from the surrounding pulp and fiber, then allow them to dry exposed to freely circulating air. Then, as needed, blanch briefly in boiling water and toast them on a cookie sheet in a hot oven. If desired the seeds may be lightly dusted with salt. They are then eaten, cracked between the teeth. Pumpkin and squash seeds are especially good in the fall with freshly fermented cider.

This is a gardening book, not a recipe or processing book, but one unusual use for pumpkins must be noted. Take a medium-sized pumpkin (a foot or so across) and cut the top out as if to make a jack-o'-lantern. Remove the seeds and scrape away the clinging tissue from the inside flesh and from the top. Now pack the pumpkin completely full with brown sugar, leaving only enough space to allow the cap to be tightly refitted back into place. Set the pumpkin (on a mat of newspapers) in a cool, dark corner of a basement for about two months. If all has gone well, when you lift the lid the pumpkin shell should be nearly full with a rich, dark liquid. The flesh will have disappeared, and the liquid will be contained only by the hard rind. The shell will be too fragile to support the weight of the liquid, so it should be removed by dipping. Strain, and serve it as a nonalcoholic after-dinner liqueur. Or, better, fortify it with brandy, neutral spirits, or vodka, and serve it as an alcoholic liqueur. Stored in a closed container it will keep a long time. Anyone who grows a quantity of pumpkins would surely find it irresistible to try this novelty. Call it "pumpkin shrub."

Although they may have vestigial or semipractical uses, most people grow gourds strictly for fun. There are innumerable different gourd forms, mostly developed for their unusual shapes and forms and varied colors. All require a relatively long growing season—about 100 days—and the larger gourds, the so-called Calabash, Bird House, and Drinking gourd varieties, even longer. All are also space hogs. Gourds have a natural preference for climbing rather than creeping, however, and with no assistance or encouragement at all will shinny up a fence, trellis, or even tree. The fruit looks pretty hanging above the ground from the climbing vines. It is possible to buy seeds according to the individual specimens, but I usually simply buy a packet of mixed seeds. The seed packet contains more seeds than the average gardener can afford space to use, unless he has a long fence for them to climb. By the way, livestock seem uninterested in eating the foliage of gourds, so they may be planted on a pasture fence. If you have an asparagus row growing along a fence, plant the gourds near the fence and they will soon grow out of the way of the asparagus as it goes to seed.

The Lufa gourd is frequently advertised as the dishrag plant or the vegetable sponge. Although often identified as an Oriental exotic, it seems to be New World in origin. It requires a long growing season, from 125 days and up. It is a prodigious climber and is said to take well to climbing trees. Plant at the same time as ornamental gourds, and allow plenty of climbing room. Pick the fruits when the skin has hardened, just before frost, and allow them to dry completely. Then soak to soften the skin. Peel it away, and use the fibrous interior as a bath sponge.

Returning to the edibles, cucumbers are a useful and versatile member of the cucurbit family. Happily most cucumbers are a little less greedy in their space requirements than squash or pumpkins. And like gourds, they like to grow on trellises and fences. They prefer warm weather, but since they are prolific and the fruit is eaten immature, even a chilly northern garden can have an ample supply by late summer. They are not terribly fussy about soil, but will show their gratitude for a shovel full of compost or well-rotted manure dug deeply into each hill before planting. They also respond well to a modest application of a general fertilizer, particularly applied as a side dressing about the time the plants begin to vine, or spread out.

Some gardeners try to get a jump on the season by setting out plants that have been started indoors (or purchased from a nursery). There seems to be almost inescapable shock and setback in transplanting, and since the plants will not begin to grow strongly until the weather turns warm, to gain any real advantage they should be protected with plastic cloches or other coverings. In planting seeds, place eight or ten to the hill, spread over an area about the size of a luncheon plate, and cover with half an inch of soil, packed lightly. When the first true leaf appears, thin each hill to three or four of the strongest plants, cutting or pinching rather than pulling to avoid disturbing the roots of the remaining plants.

There are numerous varieties of cucumbers. The differences, except for local preference, is determined chiefly by whether they are grown for processing or grown to be used fresh. There are the "burpless" varieties, grown for their mildness and ease in digestability. Practically, the various pickling varieties are also good for fresh use, although they may not be as large or as attractive as the table varieties. The smallest of the pickling varieties are often grown for sweet pickles, the larger for other varieties of pickles and for relish. In general the table varieties are not satisfactory for pickling, having a somewhat less firm texture than those grown specifically for pickling and tending to soften or develop hollow centers when processed. A more or less novelty variety, grown exclusively for pickling, is the small Thorny Gherkin. They are no more difficult to grow than the other varieties but are prolific only when treated to hot weather. The small yellow "lemon" cucumbers are an old variety, grown like any other variety. They actually do have a flavor reminiscent of citrus.

There are a number of varieties of cucumber that are uncommon, mostly European or Oriental in origin, which have superior qualities to recommend them. The most serious contender for the designation "gourmet" is the *Cornichon de Bourbonne,* the tiny fruit of which is used to make French "bitter pickles." Seed is offered by *Nichols Garden,* and they include with the packet a recipe for the pickles. A French variety called *Le Genereaux (Epicure Seeds)* is basically a slicing cucumber, similar in appearance to standard American varieties. It is superior in flavor to those varieties, however, with a flavor that is almost melonlike. If kept picked, it has a long productive period. Another French variety, *Vert De Massy (Epicure Seeds),* produces a cucumber flavored with a distinct and piquant snap. They are excellent in salads and should be picked while still small, soon after the blossom drops off. There is an Indian variety, *Poona Kheera (Gleckler's Seedsmen),* which sounds promising, although I have not yet grown it. It is said to have small fruits with greenish-white smooth skins and to be fine flavored in all stages of development. Several varieties of bush cucumbers have recently become available, the chief attraction of which so far seems to be their saving of space rather than the quality of their fruit.

All varieties of cucumber require a great deal of water. It is estimated that each plant consumes one gallon of water per day. If allowed to become dry, even for a short while, the vine may experience shock and suffer a setback in vigor and ultimately in productivity. Most varieties produce more or less continuously all summer, if the fruit is kept picked. Some pickling varieties show a sharp decline in productivity after their first heavy set, and some varieties are deliberately bred to produce one big crop, which can be harvested in a relatively short time for ease in processing.

People in urban areas frequently experience problems with a light setting of fruit although the vines seem otherwise completely healthy. While the vines blossom normally, only a few prove fertile. Almost always the problem is a lack of insects, particularly bees, for pollination. Commercial growers who cultivate cucumbers in greenhouses for winter sale sometimes resort to hand-pollinating the blossoms with camel's hair artist's brushes, and in the largest of these houses they actually maintain hives of bees. If there is a problem with fertility in your area, and cucumbers mean that much to you, try scattering pollen from the male blossoms to the female blossoms with a small brush. It's tedious, but is supposed to help.

Beyond question the real glamour set of the cucurbit population consists of the melon family. Melons originated under hot, dry desert conditions and still show a distinct preference for a habitat as similar to their homelands as can be arranged. However, early varieties of watermelon and cantaloupes have been developed that will mature melons in the coldest regions of this country, although exotic melons can only be grown in the more temperate areas of the northern states.

All members of the family prefer a light, or even sandy, soil and put down roots to impressive depths in search of moisture. In spite of this preference, respectable melons can be grown in a wide variety of soils. Soil that is too dense or packed, however, inhibits the development of deep root systems, and the results will probably be disappointing.

Like the other cucurbits, melons occupy a great deal of territory. Plant their seed in hills, allowing six or eight seeds per hill, providing 6 or 8 feet of space in all directions between hills. Do not plant the seeds before the soil has thoroughly warmed (from early to late May in northern areas, April further south). The seeds require distinct warmth to germinate and may rot if they remain long in the ground without sprouting. A soil temperature of about 70 degrees is optimum, although early varieties may sprout at a cooler temperature. When the first true leaf develops, thin each hill to three or four plants.

Some people try to get a jump on the season by starting melons indoors. There is at least a psychological advantage to this practice, for gardeners if not for the melons: it makes them feel that they are really doing something about their problems with climate. But melons do not transplant very well. For those sprouted indoors, do not set them out into a soil cooler than 70 degrees. For seeds planted outside a good trick that really helps is to place a collar of black plastic or tar paper some 3 feet in diameter around each hill, firmly attached to the ground, and with the center cut out. The black surface absorbs heat from the sun and makes the soil underneath considerably warmer. It also helps the soil to retain heat at night. This method will not protect from frost, but it will make the plant grow with greater vigor and produce more prolifically during the regular growing season than otherwise.

Any gardener with a good, long growing season that includes at least two months of good, hot summer days and nights will have little trouble finding varieties of watermelon that will ripen with excellent flavor. Several varieties, mostly bearing smallish fruits, have been developed for colder climates and are commonly available.

There are also less common varieties that are worth experimenting with. The Kodama Yellow (Japan: *Urban Farmer*) is an early melon with yellow flesh, a high sugar content, and a spicy flavor. It is also exceptionally early at 70 days; I had ripe melons in mid-August. Earliness aside, they are the best of the small watermelons I have grown. A very recent introduction from Japan is called the Lucky Sweet Hybrid *(Vermont Bean Seed Company)*. It is also listed as a 70-day melon, able to set fruit under low temperatures. It is an attractive, dark green–striped color, perfectly round. A longer season—100 days—Epicurean watermelon from Italy is the *Di Brindisi (Epicure Seeds)*, described as an antipasto melon; it is yellow fleshed. From Belgium is the Jivaro *(Epicure Seeds)*, 82 days. It is described as an exceptionally flavored melon with a fine aroma, and lavishly productive. An old-fashioned variety of limited use is the Citron *(Urban Farmer)*. It is usually dark green, round, and medium-sized, although all of these qualities vary. I remember them from childhood as enormous, but we all know what time does to the memory of size. Old yarns abound concerning farmers who planted a row of citrons at the edge of their watermelon patches to bait thieving boys, since they are so attractive they would be taken in preference for watermelons. They are, however, inedible raw, and are used principally for pickles, relishes, and to be candied, especially as an ingredient in fruitcake.

There are two Oriental varieties of watermelon which are of limited use. One is the Chinese Bitter Melon *(Sunrise Enterprises)*, which is an ingredient in several Oriental recipes, including a cold soup. Every schoolboy at some time hears that in China people eat the seeds of watermelons and throw the rest away. Partly true. There is a Chinese watermelon grown especially for its seeds, the flesh of which is inedible, called here Kily Edible Seeds *(Gleckner's Seedsmen)*. The melons are absolutely crammed with seeds, which are dark colored, large, and somewhat rough. I found them unpalatable; as used in the Orient they require elaborate treatment to make them a delicacy; simple roasting doesn't do it.

Cultivars developed for size and hardiness aside, there are two main types of cantaloupe. The most common is that with the familiar golden yellow flesh, firm but tender, and the only variety seen in produce stores in most parts of the country. The second variety has a firm, usually lime-green flesh. It is a bit smaller than the common variety, and shows a greenish cast of skin under a cream ribbing, which is less distinctly defined. If fully ripe they are quite sweet, with a flavor that most people find altogether agreeable once they overcome the immediate surprise of texture and color. Another strain of this variety has peach-colored flesh, but with much the same texture and flavor of the green-fleshed variety. There is no consistency in terminology, but often the name muskmelon is applied to the green-fleshed cultivar (presumably for the distinctive aroma), and the name cantaloupe (literally, "wolf song," from the name of an Italian villa where they were grown at an early time) to the familiar yellow-fleshed cultivar. The name muskmelon, however, is often indiscriminately applied to both.

None but the gardeners who grow their own (or buy directly from a farmer) will ever have the chance to appreciate the flavor of cantaloupes at their best. Only a melon that ripens on the vine has the opportunity to fulfill its true destiny, since unlike some fruits a cantaloupe ceases to add to its sweetness the moment it is removed from the vine. A cantaloupe is ripe and ready to be picked when the stem easily detaches itself from the fruit when the melon is lifted or lightly rotated. If the stem does not fall away easily, the fruit is not ready to be picked. The stem itself turns from bright, slick green to a paler, softer color, and the edges where it bells out and attaches to the fruit begin to separate and pull away from the rind. By contrast, melons in produce markets usually have the broken stem still firmly attached, bright green and with no separation from the rind apparent. Cantaloupes allowed to ripen properly would be impossible to ship for any appreciable distance or remain in the stores for any length of time, because they are quite fragile and perishable.

As with watermelons, anyone with a long, hot summer will have no trouble finding excellent varieties of cantaloupes to grow. There are also varieties of cantaloupes with shorter season requirements developed for shorter seasons. Increasingly foreign varieties, especially Oriental, are becoming available, offered as epicurean melons, although many of them are not yet widely known. One of the most promising I have found is the Swan (China: *Urban Farmer*). It is small, with white skin and white flesh. It has a melony flavor of its own, not especially similar to the flavor of cantaloupe, and is exceptionally sweet. It is advertised as being as easy to grow as a cucumber. For me they began to ripen in early August and are quite prolific. Watch them closely, because the stem does not fall away from the fruit when ripe, and they go from ripe to overripe in a couple of days. The Golden Crispy from Japan *(Gleckler's Seedsmen)* is a small, yellow melon that is eaten skin and all, like a pear. The Hybrid Red Queen (China: *Gleckler's Seedsmen*) is medium to large, with a smooth golden skin and pink flesh. It is said to have a unique flavor and to be a vigorous producer. When one hears of cantaloupes that sell in Japan for twenty-five dollars each, it is probably varieties such as these that are involved (whether or not there is any accuracy in the reported price). Two French gourmet varieties are offered by *Nichols Garden.* The *Charantais* is a large, long-season melon, described as *the* French gourmet variety. At 68 days, the Chaca Hybrid is an early cultivar of the same variety. It is sweet and aromatic, with a salmon-colored flesh, and is stunningly good. Another cantaloupe deserving consideration as an epicurean variety is an uncommon heirloom cantaloupe with white flesh which is called a "cob melon," because the seeds cling together in the center like corn around a cob. They are offered by *Gleckler's Seedsmen,* who also offer an epicurean variety from Italy which they call "Mr. Ugly Muskmelon," which they describe as rough and warty but most sweet. They do not indicate earliness. Of all the melons which I have grown, if I could only grow one it would be the Chaca or the Swan.

No other fruit has the mystique connected with determining its ripeness as the watermelon. Practically any judgment made after the fruit has been picked is really nothing more than an educated guess, although this could give rise to quarreling. If you buy a watermelon from a farmer's roadside stand, ask him to select a good one. If he's a proper showman he will handle, rub, thump, fondle, scratch, and turn it over several times to examine the light patch on its belly, the ribbing, the bumps, the resistance. Then, after administering the same scrutiny to three or four, with a grand flourish he will say, "This one!" And it will be excellent, because they all are: the farmer wouldn't have picked them otherwise.

If you are so lucky as to have the occasion to pick your own, look closely at the stem of the melon. Just below where the stem attaches to the melon, "up-vine," as it were, usually at the first leaf joint there will be a single, curling tendril. When the melon ripens, this tendril withers and turns brown. But don't tell anyone else. Always thump, fondle, caress, commune with, and examine a melon's belly to impress onlookers with your command of the arcane science of determining melon ripeness. They can never know you already made your decision when you saw the brown and withered tendril when you first pulled aside the leaves.

Asparagus: The Gilded Lily

D'Argenteuil Hative *asparagus*

Asparagus is a touchy or temperamental vegetable only if you are trying to grow it commercially and make money. Then a late spring, unseasonable freezes, chilly weather, and spells of wind, may cost a whole year's profit, and the farmers can be heard cursing, "That temperamental damned grass!" The home gardener who wants a few meals and perhaps a bit left over for friends, or to can or freeze, will wonder what all the fuss is about. For those not trying to grow it for a living, once established it turns out to be a perennial doing quite well with little care, and to be a generally modest and unassuming member of the permanent planting.

Mostly modest and unassuming. The asparagus spear, which is steamed, sauced, boiled, or eaten raw, is actually only the bud of the asparagus plant, usually cut within two days of its first appearance above the ground. If allowed to mature, this tender shoot will grow into a tough, many-branched body resembling in shape and color a healthy young Christmas tree 3 or 4 feet tall. This is a normal mature asparagus plant, which few people other than farmers and gardeners actually ever see, or at least notice. In the fall it turns a golden brown, the female plants heavy with colorful reddish or yellowish berries about the size of peas, each containing several small black seeds, which are eaten with relish by winter birds. A full-grown plant which has not yet begun to turn color will make one see the logic of the name "asparagus fern."

It is absolutely necessary to allow the asparagus plants to make these large rank growths, because that *is* the mature plant, the asparagus machine, and it is how the root receives and stores energy for the crop of green tender shoots the following spring. While these rank tops are not unattractive in themselves, they can become an annoyance if the plant has been placed in an unhandy spot in the garden, or if the gardener decides to change the arrangement and order of the garden. A good locale to select is along a border or a fence, which might be only semi-usable anyway. Otherwise asparagus is best located along an edge of the garden where it will not interfere with cultivation or tilling, and where its size can be taken into account when planning adjacent plantings. Probably a row aligned east-west will less interfere with the tall fronds shading other plants.

Although neither roots, foliage, nor flowers seem similar, the asparagus is closely related to the lily family. Instead of a bulb, it has a dense spreading root, something like a vegetative octopus with pencil-sized roots radiating from a center, or crown, and spreading out as much as 2 feet in all directions. The mature crown, which may be the size of a soup bowl, contains numerous buds from which the asparagus shoots grow; the older and larger the crown, the more shoots, and the bigger and healthier the crown and root system, the more prolific and more succulent the crop. When the ground begins to warm in the spring, the buds on the crown begin to swell, and one by one, or two or three at a time, shoots quickly form, maturing overnight as the familiar spear. In warm weather the shoot may grow 4 or more inches a day once it surfaces. If not cut, probably a dozen or more shoots would ultimately grow from the same crown, each developing into deep fronds as they mature, forming a dense floppy thicket.

During the spring harvest period, for two months or so depending on the region, plants will continue to send up shoots almost daily if they are kept cut. In harvesting, each spear should always be cut an inch or inch and a half below the surface of the soil. The reason for this is that if the spear were to be broken off above the ground, or not cut deeply enough below the surface, the crown would not be stimulated to put up new growth. I have read a surprising number of otherwise respectable authorities, including seed catalogues, instructing to break or cut the stalks at the surface of the soil. That is absolutely wrong.

To keep the crown putting up new growth the asparagus should be harvested regularly, every day, during the peak of the season. When the weather becomes warm, with the delay of even a day the tips may begin to "rice," or open into individual buds, spoiling the superior quality. On commercial asparagus farms, picking asparagus is a grueling, backbreaking exercise, beginning at daybreak and ending when it's done. In home gardens, however, it is merely the pleasant employment of a few minutes, and there should be no problem in keeping the plants properly picked.

The part of the spear that was growing beneath the ground when cut—the "butt"—is white and tough and inedible. I have never seen an animal, from pigs and cattle to rabbits and wharf rats, that would eat them. But its fibrous vascular system will help keep the grass fresh and crisp in storage for some days, longer if kept submerged in water or in contact with a damp, absorbent pad. Removing the butts prematurely will cause the spears quickly to wilt, which is why asparagus bought at a produce market invariably shows an inch or so of white. Remove the butts just before cooking.

Practically speaking, most people plant far too much asparagus, or even reject planting it at all because they feel their space is too limited for the size plantings recommended by catalogues or books and articles. The only reasons I could offer for planting more than six or eight hills is to have larger harvests during the first two or three years after they come into production, when the yield per plant is low, and to have more spears during the first week or two of spring while the weather is still cold.

Asparagus is not only a spring crop, it is a crop of spring; even palates pampered by "produce market magic," which blurs the seasons, respond with keenness to the first green tastes of spring. When spring is over, so is much of the enthusiasm that attaches to asparagus in March and April. It is possible to harvest asparagus all summer, or at least both in the spring and in the fall. It doesn't matter dramatically if asparagus is allowed to frond out in the spring or in the summer, as long as it has about three months in which to store food in its roots. For late asparagus, a portion of the planting is allowed to go to fronds immediately in the spring. About midsummer, the maturing fronds are cut down, and the roots will soon send up fresh spears, which may be cut as in a spring harvest. The quality may or may not be as high as a spring cutting. Asparagus is a spring treat, however, and in late summer it is competing for grace with virtually the entire harvest of the prime garden season.

Every year I find we let our patch go to seed much before we would have to. For the same reason I find we use little frozen asparagus in the off-season. Realistically, unless one is especially partial to it and plans to give a great deal away, in the long run a small planting will suit a gardener much better than a large one; knowing this is true may make an undecided gardener choose to plant. If you intend to cut the spears off level with the surface of the ground, which is wrong, you should plant several times more. My guess is that so doing would reduce production by about 80 percent. That may be why those who direct that harvesting be done that way recommend such Bunyonesque plantings.

I spent over ten springs harvesting asparagus in commercial operations in my grade school and high school years and can promise I know how it's done. Of course it is possible to damage the crown by cutting too deeply; that's why the roots are planted so deeply in the first place. Nevertheless, asparagus cutters have to be careful in their work. If asparagus spears have bits of crown attached to the bottom, the cutter will be fired.

Not to become polemical, but a reason for growing one's own

asparagus is to avoid being party to child labor. I was about seven years old when I began regular work cutting asparagus in the spring, which was about average for that place and that time. Probably at least half of my classmates through grade school and high school cut asparagus every morning in late March through early June before going to school, and on Saturday and Sunday. Teachers saw, as a matter of course, students lethargic from lack of sleep, with four or five hours of work behind them before coming to school and no breakfast. You can't do that kind of stoop labor with a full stomach, and there was no time to eat afterwards, if you could.

As the saying goes, I guess it never hurt me none; but if it did me any good, I'll be glad to pay someone for it. It has been many years since I have been near a commercial field of asparagus that early in the morning, but I have no reason to suppose that things have changed since I was a child. Anyone who has eaten produce market asparagus can be reasonably certain he has eaten asparagus cut by a ten-year-old kid at 3:30 in the morning before school. To ease your conscience, grow your own, and cut it in the afternoon, deep below the surface.

Comparatively speaking, there are not too many varieties of asparagus. By far the most widely grown variety in America is Mary (or Martha) Washington and improved strains developed from it. Although other strains were sometimes grown in the past most commercial plantings today are cultivars of Mary Washington, and many seed companies offer it exclusively. A few nurseries offer it in improved varieties. Since it takes asparagus a relatively long time to come into bearing, I have not experimented with them. Introduced by the New Jersey Asparagus Council, a strain called Beacon is being recommended for the size of its stalks and because it comes into bearing a year sooner than other strains *(Nourse Farms)*. Another large variety, said to produce 30 percent more poundage, is the Faribo Hybrid F-1 *(Farmer Seed and Nursery)*. Another large variety called California 711 would probably not be suited for northern climates, but should do well in the southern regions *(Dean Foster Nurseries)*.

There are European varieties that are completely white, or white with a purplish-violet tip. The colorlessness comes from blanching the spears (although it is also a different variety from those commonly grown in America). This asparagus is sometimes found in American stores canned, or in specialty markets. Apparently it is becoming increasingly less common in European markets, where the farmers seem to be turning to American varieties, which are less labor intensive.

For those who wish to try the European varieties, which have the reputation of being the gourmet asparagus, starts are difficult but not impossible to find. There may be sources for roots, but I have found none. The standard French variety is the *D'Argenteuil Hative (Urban Farmer)*. The redoubtable Epicurean gardener Eleanor Perenyi extols the Italian Genoa as the preeminent gourmet variety, but I have found no American source for it.

In their instructions for growing *D'Argenteuil Hative,* the company advises that the ground should be more enriched with compost and manure, than for American varieties. When the plants have sufficiently matured to allow a harvest, they instruct placing a one-foot mound of soil over each plant, removing it periodically to harvest the spears, then replacing it. When the harvest is over, the mound is removed completely and the plant allowed to mature its fronds in the usual way.

Although I have not tried that system, on appearance it seems unnecessarily labor intensive. French market gardeners frequently use various forms of cloches to cover the crown to keep out the light and blanch the spears. The favorite French method of cultivation uses relatively small raised beds. Pictures I have seen of the French method show cloches consisting essentially of wooden planks, most usually a pair leaned together to form a long, inverted trough. Any system that would exclude the light would seem suitable, the more convenient the better. I use inverted five-gallon plastic buckets.

Since I had to begin with seed, I have proceeded somewhat differently from the instructions for beginning with roots. There seemed to be no perceptible advantage to following the instructions that came with the seeds—to start them indoors in peat pots. Instead, I planted directly into the garden where the plants will remain, right next to a pasture fence. The soil was already heavily enriched with manure and humus, so after tilling moderately, I drew a trench as deeply as was practical with the corner of my hoe. I planted the seeds sparingly (they cost about one cent apiece!) and covered them with a light sprinkling of soil. Late in the first summer, when the Christmas-treelike sprouts were about 3 inches high, I filled what was left of the planting trench with composted manure. In late fall I erected a plank retaining wall, consisting of lengths of salvaged 2 × 6's, on the garden side, about 18 inches from the fence, securing it with stakes driven in on alternate sides. On top of the soil I placed about 2 inches of compost. In the following spring, when the shoots appeared and began branching, I once again added a couple of inches of compost. Eventually the surface of the bed was level with the top of the plank, contained on the opposite side by the woven wire fence, with the crowns of the asparagus roots some 6 or 8 inches below the surface of a rich and mellow growing medium. Essentially this imitates the French raised-bed system.

Planting American varieties, most gardeners begin with roots. There is nothing complicated about setting out asparagus roots, but a little care will pay handsomely in future production, especially in quality and quantity in the initial years of harvest. Timing is not crucial, but they should be planted between mid-March and early May in Zones 5 and 6. Dig a trench about a foot deep and a foot wide, placing the soil a little to one side for backfilling later. On the bottom of the trench place several inches of manure or rich compost. If the soil is reasonably productive this enrichment is not imperative. Level the surface of the trench bottom evenly about 6 inches from the surface. Place the roots 12 to 16 inches apart, spreading the roots flat and even, and cover with 2 or 3 inches of soil. As the season progresses and the plants begin to make sturdy top growth, gradually return soil into trench until by fall there is a slight mound the full length of the row. This mound will help shed water that might otherwise collect and perhaps encourage root rot.

Some recommend planting year-old roots, maintaining that there is no real advantage accrued by planting two- or three-year-old roots. However, I once planted what were described in a catalogue advertisement as year-old roots, and they turned out to be miniscule, hardly more than an inch long. Less than 10 percent of them grew. Admittedly I was taken in by a sucker advertisement, one that continues to appear almost annually in mass-distributed catalogues every spring. If a purchaser can physically examine roots at the nursery, and year-old roots are no less than 3 inches long, it would be safe to use them. Ordering sight unseen, unless the catalogue is specific about size, it is best to order two-year-old roots. When investing in a lifetime planting like asparagus, be instructed by my error and avoid false economizing.

Once established, the crown will get larger year by year, and the number of stalks a given hill produces will also increase. Given minimal care, a planting of asparagus will continue to produce indefinitely. There are patches that are known to have been in production over a hundred years.

Increasingly even commercial growers are starting their fields with asparagus seed rather than roots; it is said that by the fourth or fifth year the seedlings will probably outstrip the production of those started by roots. Some recommend placing the seeds in the pattern of the five spots on a domino, rather than in line as I described for planting the French asparagus, with each block being about 6 inches long. The theory behind this is that within the five or six years to full maturity the patch will produce twice the number of usable spears as it otherwise would, and after that the plants will thin themselves, with the superior plants surviving and the weaker dying. There is also an opinion that the male plants produce more and better quality spears, so as soon as it is possible to identify the female plants by their berries they should be eradicated, which would further thin the row by about half.

Asparagus is a heavy feeder and thrives on yearly applications of manure or compost, as well as applications of standard garden fertilizers. It does best in regions having dry, sunny springs, but it does pretty well in a wide range of conditions. In the absence of rain it should be irrigated periodically during the period of harvest. It should be kept weeded, but after harvest is over and it is allowed to head out, further weeding becomes difficult, and largely unnecessary. Its toughest competitors are such pernicious perennials as quack grass and wild morning glory. The modern herbicides designed to be effective against such weeds may be applied carefully by hand before the plants are allowed to head out. An established asparagus plant can be very competitive, however, and anyone who has collected "wild" asparagus has surely found it growing through thick grass and tough weeds and holding its own very well. But it will appreciate and repay a modest care.

A frost or freeze will damage the spears that are above ground but will not damage the roots. In fact, the roots are capable of withstanding intense cold. Whether it is typical or not, I had a bed survive a winter in which the temperature dropped to a whacking 40 degrees below zero, and the crop the following spring was quite normal. Stalks that have been frosted are useless, but nevertheless each must be cut off below the ground as if it were being harvested. Otherwise, if it is merely damaged it will continue to grow slowly and the deformed stalks will head out; or, if completely frozen to the soil level, if that portion below the ground is not cut, the crown will not be stimulated to send up a new shoot, and it may be days before normal production is resumed. One of the most onerous chores when harvesting for a commercial farm was cutting back the frozen stalks for a day or two after a frost. Although there were not the spears to pick and carry, there were many more stoops and jabs to get the field covered.

A wind will cause the spears to bend, sometimes to the extent that they will make complete circles, like the tusks of a wild boar. Except for toughening the skin, this is harmless to everything but the temper of the cook. The stalks are not bent by the pressure of the wind against them, but by drying of the surface by the wind. For the commercial trade stalks having any appreciable bend are worthless except for some processing purposes.

Occasionally an asparagus stalk will grow flat instead of round, exactly like a green yardstick. When this occurs, there is nothing wrong with the plant—it's just something that happens. For curiosity's sake such stalks may be eaten, but they will be found to be fibrous.

There is some uncertainty among those who buy asparagus in markets about what the proper indicator of quality is. Some consistently choose the most slender spears they can find, assuming that as with certain other vegetables smaller means more tender or more delicate. Actually with asparagus the reverse is true. The plumpest stalks, certainly no smaller than the circumference of one's index finger, are superior in every way. They are the stalks that have made the most rapid growth and therefore are most crisp and contain less fiber. Cutting in a field daily, one can see the slender stalks taking at least twice as long to reach harvest length, during which time they are beginning to develop the fiber that will hold them erect as they begin to go to head. Only rich soil and optimum growing conditions will produce the premium plump stalks.

A man for whom I once worked prided himself on the size and plumpness of his asparagus. A dealer who bought from him asked him his secret. As he was fond of telling, he replied, "I use only genuine baby manure." Such pains are not necessary; he did, however, use enormous amounts of cow manure, and his soil was deep and rich and had the tilth of greenhouse soil. Rich and consistently renewed soil is necessary to grow premium, plump tender stalks of asparagus, but to maintain such conditions requires hardly more than common care.

Asparagus seems to be relatively disease resistant. There is an asparagus rust that is soilborne; before planting inquire if that is a problem in your locality. If so, the best strategy is to plant a rust-resistant strain (such as Faribo Hybrid F-1). There is a virus that infects the roots, resulting in premature senility, and that means an infected bed could run out in as little as ten years. At present there does not seem to be any treatment for this condition, although it seems that plants grown from seeds rather than transplanted as roots are less susceptible to it. This is another factor encouraging commercial growers to begin with seeds rather than roots.

The principal insect pests asparagus is susceptible to are the asparagus beetle and the cutworm. The asparagus beetle makes small nips and bites, particularly in the head, which damages the spear cosmetically more than materially. Likewise the cutworm will make incisions at ground level or a little above, with small spears sometimes completely severing the stalk. If one sifts through the top half-inch of dust near where cutworm damage appears, usually the culprit can be found and executed. Except where a stalk has been completely sliced off, cutworm damage, too, is mostly cosmetic. Since the spear grows so rapidly and is harvested usually within two days after its first appearance above ground, the gardener is fortunate in having a minimal exposure of his crop to insects. Most likely the gardener can live with the damage that is likely to occur, and except for occasionally tracking down a cutworm, will not need to worry about control.

For those who like asparagus, it is a plant that definitely deserves a place in the garden. Even though asparagus is never grown commercially anywhere nearby, even severe climates can allow a gardener to grow all he or she really wants and without too much fuss. While it has a certain greediness for space, it is a seasonal greediness, and may actually enable a gardener to use a slender parcel of ground that otherwise might be restricted, or even wasted.

Herbs
and Savories

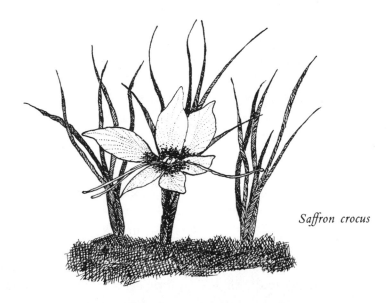

Saffron crocus

A large number of garden products are grown not for their own value as food, but to flavor or garnish other foods. A few of these herbs and savories are eaten alone, but most are used by themselves or in combinations to complement or accent other foods. Some herbs are hard to find commercially, many if found are merely generic, and at best few can be found fresh. To have genuine French tarragon, it is almost a necessity to grow it yourself. In large produce markets or in ethnic neighborhoods it may be possible to find fresh basil, but even there it may be hard to find the best kinds, or the kind preferred for making pesto. Under the force of necessity, most people never use fresh herbs, or have never tried the choicest varieties if they do have access to them.

Most herbs and savories are not difficult to grow; some are the easiest crops in the garden. Since they are used in relatively small quantities, gardeners can grow about every variety they can use or choose to experiment with without committing more than a few square yards of their garden space. As with the other things grown in the garden, if the grower is going to grow something at all, the grower might just as well grow the best variety there is, or at least that is available. Some herbs and savories come only in generic varieties, but with many, for the looking, preferred varieties or special-purpose varieties are available that are distinctly better.

Many gardeners grow a few peppers, but the many possibilities of size, flavor, and hardiness remain largely untapped. The garden pepper is another New World member of the prolific nightshade family, kin to eggplants, tomatoes, and potatoes. It probably originated in South America. Despite its name, the pepper is no relation to the plant that produces the peppercorns that are ground to make black pepper. This latter is a tropical vine native to the East Indies.

American peppers are of two main kinds—sweet or hot. The whole family prefers warm weather, and it is difficult to grow peppers where summers are short or cool—difficult, but not impossible. Most people begin with transplants from seeds they have started inside or purchased from a nursery. Cultivation for sweet and hot varieties is virtually identical. Set out the seedlings about 14 to 16 inches apart after danger of frost has passed. Peppers are cold-tender and will tolerate no frost at all. They need little care after transplanting other than making sure they never dry out. When hot weather stimulates them to rapid growth they appreciate a little side-dressing of fertilizer. Fertilizing should be accompanied by fairly heavy watering.

Green peppers will produce up to a dozen or so fruits per plant, which will mature over a reasonably long period of time; for me, usually four to six weeks. How many plants to grow will depend on the demand for peppers the gardener expects.

Green peppers should be picked when they are around 2 inches in diameter. If picked too young, they may have a somewhat bitter flavor. If allowed to remain on the plant, the peppers will begin to change color, eventually turning bright red or yellow, depending on the species. Some people prefer them in this ripened state.

Hot peppers such as Hungarian Wax and jalapeño can be grown

most anyplace green peppers are successful. Plant them at the same time and in the same way as green peppers. These hot varieties may be pickled or may be used fresh as seasoning in stews, chili, and Mexican and Italian dishes, where they add a piquant flavor. I make a chili sauce by boiling down tomatoes and peppers (Hungarian Wax or jalapeño), together with chopped onion, cumin, and salt. When canning, check your instruction books, because sauce made with peppers requires a longer processing time than plain tomato sauce.

Many of the hot peppers are little changed from varieties grown in the Americas before Columbus. Most of the green peppers are more recent, although the still popular Bull Nose, the first bell pepper developed, is over two hundred years old. The Aconcagua Giant is long rather than bell shaped—nearly a foot—light green, and sweet. It matures in 70 days. The Albo, an early sweet pepper, is white, and if left on the plant ultimately will turn red. A sweet pepper with a pungency and which is used chiefly for frying is the Cubanbelle. All three of these varieties are offered by *Gleckler's Seedsmen*. A pepper that ripens to a rich brown is the Sweet Chocolate *(Good Seeds)*. A cool weather sweet pepper is Staddon's Select *(Territorial Seed Company)*. There are also varieties of small sweet peppers that are earlier and more productive than the large varieties. They are good for most uses of the larger varieties, except for stuffing, and are regularly used for making sweet pickled peppers. The Italian Sweet produces green conical peppers up to 7 inches long. The Petite Sirah are yellow, and about 3 inches long. Both varieties are offered by *Territorial Seed Company*. The Italian Pepperoncini is from southern Italy and is said to be especially good raw, but is also recommended for pickles. For canned pimiento, the Pimiento Sweet is recommended. Both of these varieties are offered by *Nichols Garden Nursery*.

The varieties of hot peppers are almost endless. Every year I experiment with a few new varieties. However, I always grow some Hungarian wax and jalapeño peppers as a mainstay for chili sauce. The jalapeñoes are hot and the Hungarian Wax medium hot, and both have a full chili flavor and good body. I also usually grow one or more variety of cayenne. This pepper family is extremely hot and can cause skin irritation if you touch your face after having handled them. Cayennes are mostly used dried, but with caution can be used fresh as well, for example, to crank up the heat in salsa or chili. The Tepin is described by *Good Seeds* as "the hottest variety known on the planet." They are marble-sized and red, a domesticated cultivar of the wild Chilitepines from the Sonoran Desert, and require 90 days for maturity. A hot Japanese variety is the *Yatsafusa;* a medium hot is the Roumanian Hot Pepper (both offered by *Nichols Garden Nursery*). A cayenne pepper that does well in cooler weather is the Hot Portugal. It is used green, red, or dried. A pepper said to be only a fourth as hot as the regular jalapeño, while retaining the flavor of the pepper, is the Tom jalapeño. Both varieties are offered by *Territorial Seed Company*. An "ornamental pepper" is often grown indoors as a decorative container plant, sometimes set out pot and all in the summer. It produces many multicolored small peppers, which may be used for culinary purposes. They are hot, but do not have a particularly high quality flavor. Seeds are easily available, sometimes in the flower section of seed catalogues.

Hops are among the least likely of the herbs and savories most gardeners will grow. In the first place, a limited number of gardeners have the special interests that require their unique herbal flavor. By far the most common use is to provide the distinctive bitter flavoring in beer. Secondly, the plants grow what might charitably be called vigorous vines—otherwise they might be called rude and unmannerly.

The number of people who make homebrewed beer has been steadily on the increase, and the price of dried hops has been increasing outrageously, so a brewer who also has a little space might consider it practical to grow hops. Their size and ranginess might even provide just the thing to plant along a fence, or even to grow on a trellis around or over a patio for quick green summer shade.

Hops are a herbaceous perennial; every spring they put up shoots that rapidly develop into tough, upwardly mobile vines. If given climbing support, they easily grow 20 feet high, branching wildly into dense, junglelike plants. In midsummer the vines begin to put on curious green blossoms (more properly, strobiles), which as they develop look quite like soft green pine cones. Depending on variety, these blossoms will be at maturity from 1 to 3 inches in length, and up to an inch in diameter. These are the "fruits" of the vine, which are picked in late summer or early fall. These are the hops of commerce, which are dried at a controlled low heat (never above 140 degrees) and are stored protected from the air. The green resinous pollen inside is the essential flavoring ingredient and the source of the characteristic tanginess of beer.

Hops grow in two genders, and only the female blossoms provide usable hops. It is undesirable to have male plants, because female blossoms that have been fertilized are of lesser value. It is possible to grow hops from seeds, although they are more practically started from root cuttings. While these starts are not widely available, they can be located, and suppliers usually provide female cuttings exclusively.

Since hops are quite productive, it is unlikely anyone will want more than two or three vines, unless they are being grown for ornamental purposes, to provide a screen or overhead shade. Root cuttings should be planted in early spring. Place them in soil that has been enriched by the addition of compost or manure. Commercial growers set the individual plants up to 10 feet apart, but the home grower can space them considerably closer, 6 feet being adequate unless there just happens to be excess space that needs to be used up. Place the root cuttings in the ground on a slant, thicker end up, with the bottom about 8 inches below the surface, the top about 2 inches. If there is not a handy fence or natural trellis for them to climb, it will be necessary to provide something. A stout pole, ideally in the range of 20 feet tall, should be provided beside each hill when they are set in the ground. Hops will do well, although they will be less productive, climbing ordinary fences. In many places they have gone native and can be seen covering long sections of pasture fences with their heavy green foliage.

Shoots from the root cuttings will appear as soon as the soil begins to warm, and when they are a foot tall, all but one shoot should be pruned away; as soon as the shoot is 18 or 20 inches tall, fasten it loosely to the pole, or more effectively to a string attached to the top. This process is called, logically enough, "training" the hops. Pruning and additional training is usually done two or three more times, or until the vine is fully persuaded in the direction it should go and is climbing seriously. Commercial growers call their acreages "hop yards," and the fields are checkered with huge permanent trellises consisting of poles strung together at their tops with heavy wire. Every spring coarse, thick twine is strung from these wires and pegged to the ground, in a dizzying and endless study in the geometry of V's. The vines are trained up these strings, with one pair of shoots being allowed to grow from each parent.

Probably there will be no crop at all the first year after planting. In the fall the vines should be cut down and disposed of. The second year, blossoms should appear in midsummer and can be harvested in late August or early September. Cut and pull down the vines, and pick the blossoms before they have time to wilt. They should be dried immediately, and stored in air-tight containers.

The principal use of hops is in brewing, although in the past they have had a pharmaceutical reputation. Specifically, they were considered as calming to the nerves. An old-fashioned cure for sleeplessness was to use a pillow stuffed with dried hops instead of feathers. My grandmother made a cloth doll for me stuffed with hops when I was small to prevent me from keeping other people awake. People who work in hop kilns, as the places where commercial hops are cured are known, maintain that working among the dried and drying hops keeps them constantly drowsy.

These soporific qualities possibly account for the name "hop" being applied to drugs in general. Less likely, but also logically, the name could have originated because of a curious family connection hops have. They belong to a tiny but notorious family, which includes only themselves, a Japanese ornamental hop, and cannabis, or marijuana. During World War II the U.S. Government tried to make capital of this family relationship in developing an American hemp industry by grafting cannabis plants to hop roots. While this did not work out, the opposite graft did, hops on cannabis. This curiosity has not been widely publicized.

In England a bit of folklore has accumulated around hop cultivation. In years past the hop harvest with its heavy call for short-term unskilled labor brought cockney Londoners by the thousands to the hop yards in Kent. This was the only country outing most of these people ever had, and this self-supporting vacation became something of a carnival. Long after any financial inducement had faded these outings continued to be traditional, a sort of "busman's holiday." Although little used today, the countryside in southeastern England is dotted with a form of hop kiln they call "oasts," perfectly cone-shaped brick structures 40 or 50 feet tall. Even one nursery rhyme is associated with hop husbandry in this part of England.

> *Lady Bird! Lady Bird!*
> *Fly away home!*
> *Your house is on fire,*
> *Your children will burn!*

Children still recite this alarming little ditty while trying to persuade a lady bug (or "lady bird," short for "My Lady's [i.e., Mary's] bird") to fly from their fingers. Supposedly the rhyme refers to the practice of burning off the residue of the hop harvest in the early spring. Two varieties of hops, Cascade and Bullion, are offered by *Nichols Garden Nursery.*

However, when most gardeners think of herbs and savories, hops is not the first example to come to mind, even though it is likely the most spectacular herb cultivated in the temperate climates. The majority of herbs are modest-sized and usually undemanding in their requirements and attentions. Properly, every kitchen garden should have its little annex for seasonings and garnishes. Quite adequate plantings can be made using odd bits and corners of space. Since many herbs are perennials, an herb garden planted as a separate part of the garden arrangement can become an attractive garden highlight or accent point.

Planning an herb garden should take into account the habits and life spans of the individual plants. Although they may have their preferences, the majority of common herbs are adaptable to a considerable range of conditions. Mints, for example, characteristically take to a damp or even spongy soil, yet will do perfectly well in a normal garden situation when provided with adequate water. Mint's preference is for full sun, but it does nicely in partial shade as well. In fact, it grows so easily that it needs to be watched. If left unchecked, its "stoloniferous" roots would spread until it became difficult to eradicate. For this reason, mint is sometimes planted in large pots that are buried in the earth. Some solve the spreading problem by burying several cement blocks, forming a contained area from which the roots cannot escape. Sometimes metal "flashings" are driven into the ground in a circle, or whatever design is appropriate, to contain the planting.

Because of mint's fondness for water, many people plant a clump around outdoor water spigots. The occasional drippings keep the plants happy, and the gardener is always grateful for the refreshing smell as he connects and disconnects hoses, or digs a head in among the leaves for a drink of cool water.

Mint is most often started from clumps borrowed from a friend or bought in pots from a nursery. Mint also grows wild along streams and in marshy places over a large part of the country. This wild mint, if available, is a perfectly satisfactory source of starts. The wild strains, however, do not produce as much of the essential oil of mint as the "tame" varieties, and consequently would not be as satisfactory for use dried.

Less common in this country, but still usually available, is peppermint's near relative, spearmint. Although the two plants look much alike, spearmint has a narrower and more pointed leaf and is a lighter shade of green. The smell and flavor of the two plants is distinctly different, as anyone with a taste for chewing gum knows. The habits of spearmint are identical to the habits of peppermint. It prefers a moist soil but will not press the point. It also needs to be kept under control.

Another aromatic member of the mint family is Lemon Verbena. As with many plants that have been under cultivation or observation for centuries, there is confusion about names of several plants having a lush lemony aroma, but consisting of entirely different plants. Our common Lemon Verbena is probably of South American origin, but it frequently goes by the name of lemon balm, which properly is the name of a European herb noted and admired from antiquity, which is a quite distinct species. Lemon Verbena is sometimes called simply *verbena,* which is still another distinct European species. Whatever name our common herb goes by, it has square stems, light green opposing leaves (both of which features identify it as a member of the mint family), and grows to a height of 2 or 3 feet. Particularly in the spring and early summer when its growth is most lush it has the strong, mouth-watering odor of a freshly sliced lemon.

Occasionally advice about its culture will caution that Lemon Verbena is temperamental, but I suspect this information comes from confusing this plant with the other similarly named but quite distinct species (which I have never had occasion to see or grow). My experience has been that it is the easiest of the mints to grow, and they are all easy. In fact, it becomes difficult to control if allowed to get the slightest bit out of hand, because besides its persistent and aggressive roots, it seeds itself with wild abandon.

Lemon Verbena grows in sun or partial shade with equal zest. Like the other mints it is a perennial, and may be grown from pre-started nursery stock or roots obtained from another gardener. It also grows easily from seed. Set out the roots in early spring, and if at all possible plant in such a way as to contain the roots. Like peppermint and spearmint, it is pleasant to have growing under or surrounding a water faucet.

Once vigorous growth begins, sprigs may be removed at will for use as garnishes in iced tea, for example. For these purposes it is decidedly at its best before blossoming begins, although it can be used through the full summer. Lemon Verbena is dried to be used as a tea, which besides its pleasant flavor, is reputed to have calming effects and other beneficial properties. For drying, cut the branches when the plant begins to bloom, but before seeds begin to form, and dry it away from direct sunlight. Whether it is to be dried or not, it is certainly best to cut back and remove all blossoming stems to prevent it from going to seed, because it so easily becomes a troublesome pest. Besides these mints, there are more than two dozen available, including apple mint and pineapple mint.

Catnip is another herb easily recognizable as a member of the mint family because of its square stem and opposite leaves. It is a perennial, sometimes grown as an annual, that attains a height of about 2 feet. There is no question of the honesty of its name; cats find it so intoxicating that they make it difficult to get plants started. I have never been able to grow domestic catnip successfully because cats have grazed and wallowed the seedlings into oblivion the moment they appear. If sturdy nursery seedlings are used and provided some protection, they may get large enough to fend for themselves before cats can obliterate them. Once a good clump of it gets started, catnip can become an established member of an herb garden. Aside from its ability to drive cats absolutely goofy, its principal use is to make a tonic tea, although some people use it for other culinary purposes as well. Its importance as a cooking herb, especially as a seasoning for meat, was apparently more important in the past than at present. According to tradition, drinking catnip tea gave courage to the timid and strength to the weak. To dry for tea, cut the branches down to about 6 inches when the plant is in full bloom and cure away from direct sunlight.

A number of perennial herbs make such rapid growth that they are frequently grown as annuals, especially a few which are too tender to grow as perennials. One of these is marjoram, also called "sweet marjoram." In sufficiently mild climates, it will make an attractive shrub about 2 feet tall. However, its growth is so rapid from seeds or transplants that it may be satisfactorily cultivated as an annual. Because the seeds are somewhat slow to germinate, it is best started indoors or from pre-started plants obtained from a nursery rather than direct seeded. Once the plants are 6 or 8 inches tall sprigs may be picked as needed for use fresh. In late summer large branches may be cut and dried.

Oregano, although sometimes called "wild marjoram," has proven difficult to identify exactly according to its proper biological species. Like marjoram, it is a perennial often grown as an annual in colder climates. I have found that it does well sown directly into the ground where it is to be grown after the last frosts. When the seedlings are sufficiently strong that a good stand is assured, thin them to a distance of 8 to 12 inches. They may be used as needed all summer, or cut and dried when the stems are in bloom.

Rosemary is another perennial that can be grown as an annual, although during a single growing season most likely it will never bloom. In climates where the winters are not too rigorous, it will grow into a handsome evergreen shrub, eventually reaching a height of 4 or 5 feet. In Europe, where the climate permits, it is sometimes cultivated and trimmed as an ornamental shrub.

Grown as an annual, preferably seeds should be pre-started indoors, or purchase established plants from a nursery. Rosemary likes a full exposure to the sun, and unlike many of the herbs that actually prefer limited fertility, to make quick and savory growths it requires a fairly rich, or well fertilized, soil. The leaves resemble the needles of a fir tree, and they may be picked and used fresh as needed. Late in the summer the plant may be heavily cut back (completely cut back, if it is not expected to survive the winter), the branches dried, and the individual leaves then picked and stored. In the language of plants and flowers, rosemary traditionally has represented constancy in love. As Shakespeare expressed it in the words of the pathetic Ophelia, "Rosemary, that's for remembrance." It was also considered an effective preventative of bubonic plague if worn in bunches about the neck; in an outbreak in England in the late sixteenth century demand drove the price so high that only the wealthiest could afford it.

There are many varieties of thyme, mostly hardy perennials, and all are easy and undemanding to grow. Common thyme can be purchased in pots from nurseries, but is perfectly easy to start from seed in the place it is to grow. Plant the tiny seeds at about the time of the last frost, scattering them thinly in a shallow trench with loose earth lightly packed on top. When the seedlings are showing their second true leaves, thin the stand to about 12 inches between plants. Before the summer is out, they will make a little compact shrub from 10 to 16 inches tall consisting of many slender branches all attached to the crown. For seasonings, use the tender growing tips; they can be harvested as desired anytime after the plant is 6 inches or so tall. The plants are easily transplanted, as long as they are kept reasonably well watered for a few days. There are several varieties of culinary thyme available through herb catalogues, although I have grown nothing but the common "seed rack" variety.

Woolly thyme, or creeping thyme, is grown less often for a kitchen herb than for its own attractiveness. It is low growing, compact, and resilient, and consequently is commonly grown in rockeries and along pathways. One of the most charming uses is to plant it between or among flagstones in a garden pathway. The occasional errant branch that gets trodden underfoot fills the air with a most agreeable herbal smell. The plants thrive on this seeming abuse.

For many gardeners (and cooks) the queen of the herbs is basil. For me the smell of the fresh green leaves provides, next to vanilla, the most delicate and delicious treat a nose may have. It is a favorite herb in Italian cookery, and also plays a pretty role in an old tradition of Italian courtship. A young gallant would place a sprig of basil in his hat band or behind his ear, and, if he were lucky, a properly coquettish young lady he might meet would pronounce its common name in Italian—*baccia, Nicolo*—which translates as "Kiss me, Nicholas!" From this introduction they were free to write their own scripts.

Basil is an annual, and although it is frost-sensitive, it is easy to grow. There are several forms of basil—the common garden variety, a dwarf variety, and one with deep purple leaves, which is often grown as an ornamental. There are also at least twenty less common varieties, with apple smell, pineapple smell, and so forth. Although all prefer full sun, they will tolerate a little shade of filtered light. Plant basil in spring after danger of frost is past. The seeds are small, and should be sown sparingly in a shallow trench and covered with a thin sprinkling of soil. Standard varieties make a bushy growth of 12 to 16 inches, so the plants should be thinned when they are an inch or so tall to a stand no closer together than 6 inches. Wider spacing will promote bushier growth.

When the plants are 8 or 10 inches tall, if the very tips of the growing stems are pinched off the plants will be prompted to put out denser growth and more plentiful leaves. It is at its best as a cooking herb used green and fresh, and some Italian recipes—pesto, for example—call for it in copious quantities. For storage, the herb is harvested when the first flowers appear, cutting back the whole plant to about 6 inches above the ground. Most frequently it is dried, although purists insist it must be preserved by salting or freezing.

Besides common basil, I have grown fine-leaved basil—*Napoleano verde*—and lettuce-leaved basil—*Piccolo verde fino* (both from *Epicure Seeds*). The lettuce-leaved basil, as its name suggests, has enormous ruffled leaves. It is said to be high in essential oils, and is the superior variety for use in tomato sauce. Fine-leaved basil has a more slender, spearheaded leaf than common basil, and is especially pungent. Since it does not require cooking to release its flavor, it is considered the ultimate pesto basil. Also use it as a spaghetti seasoning, but use sparingly. When I grew these varieties germination was poor, but afterwards it flourished as luxuriantly as common basil.

Sage is easily grown as either an annual or as a perennial. From seed it makes a quick growth during a summer to a height of a foot or two. It is reasonably tolerant of cold, and in most climates overwinters easily. The seeds may be planted in the spring at about the time of the last frosts. Spread them thinly in a shallow trench, lightly covered. My experience has been after several plantings that they do not have an especially good rate of germination. When the plants are about an inch tall, thin to 10 or 12 inches apart. If they are to be grown as a perennial, allow at least 2 feet between plants. Young plants are easy to transplant, so surpluses may be given away or, for the sake of the color of their foliage, they may be transplanted as accent points in flower beds. Most nurseries stock sage plants in the spring pre-started in pots, which is also a highly satisfactory way to begin.

Sage plants are attractive enough, with their distinctive gray-green foliage, to be grown for their own right in border plantings. And their distinctive smell is treat enough to justify growing them even if their herbal qualities are not otherwise needed. For use as an herb, gardeners commonly pick the individual leaves for use fresh or for drying. Since the plants are so prolific (and the demand for its use not limitless) no gardener actually needs very many sage plants. On a camping trip when I was a boy, I mistook wild absinthe for wild sage, and in my youthful ignorance decided it would add variety to our camp fare. I dropped a handful into the pot simmering over the fire and ruined an otherwise perfectly fine hot dog and potato stew.

For some reason, although the plant grows easily and well in the United States, most commercial sage is imported from wild sage harvested from mountain slopes in the Balkan countries. During World War II, when many seasonings usually imported became unavailable, sage was successfully grown commercially in this country. It was grown as an annual field crop, mowed and raked and dried on the ground like hay, and shipped from the farms packed in burlap sacks. Even though it is easy to grow and harvest, after the war the practice seems to have returned to importing leaves from Europe.

A plant whose medicinal value may have been introduced to most people by Beatrix Potter is parsley. After having gorged on Mr. McGregor's bolted lettuce, Peter Rabbit bumped into that humorless gardener while in search of parsley to comfort his indigestion. This herb has a long but much faded reputation for treating digestive discomfort; whether it is a deserved reputation or not, I have never

heard an authoritative opinion. Some people like its strong and pungent flavor for its own sake, and some people eat the parsley garnishing
from around their Thanksgiving turkey to clear and revitalize surfeited
taste buds for the dessert course. As an actual food or health tonic, it
seems to have been more admired by our ancestors than by us, at least
if we can believe their accounts. For example, judging from what he
says in his letters, Sir Thomas Browne grew parsley in such prodigious
amounts he must have eaten it as something like a main vegetable.

Parsley is a compact biannual herb that does especially well
during cool weather. It is somewhat resentful of being transplanted;
in my experience transplants have a tendency to bolt to seed in their
first year, which much reduces the attractiveness and flavor of their
leaves. Nevertheless, because the seeds are notoriously slow to germinate, many people buy started nursery stock. For seeds planted in the
garden where they are to grow, sprouting will be considerably improved if the seeds are soaked in water twenty-four hours before
putting them in the ground. Plant seeds (or transplants) in early spring,
about the time of the last frost, in a trench half an inch deep, lightly
packed with loose soil. When the seedlings are an inch or two high,
thin to a spacing of about 18 inches. How many plants to grow depends
of course on how avid a given gardener is for the leaves. Most people
find three plants a gracious plenty.

Individual leaves may be picked as needed from the time the plant
attains a height of 8 or 10 inches. Some people who use dried parsley
extensively in cooking cut the plants back heavily when they are 15
or 16 inches tall, pick the individual leaves from the stems, and dry
them away from direct sunlight. The leaves of parsley left in the garden
will remain green all winter, and I have frequently dug them out of
the snow for Christmas garnishes. When growth begins again early in
the following spring the plants will each put up several tall stalks,
topped with green umbels full of seeds. It is possible to continue to
use the leaves, but most people prefer to use only first-year growth.
If allowed to mature seeds, parsley replants itself handily, annoying
gardeners by doing it accidentally so much easier than they did it
deliberately. Gophers love parsley roots and if unchecked will go
down a row and destroy an entire planting.

A savory that should be tried at least once is Florence fennel, or *finocchio*. Its closely grouped leaf stems resemble celery, although they are of a paler green and usually more slender. They are pretty enough to mix in a bed of ornamentals. Some Italian cooks make copious use of the stems in a variety of dishes, as well as raw on relish trays, usually with some of the leaves still attached. The stems have a crisp, refreshing flavor, with an unexpected spiciness reminiscent of licorice. They are nice, but I find that I don't remember to plant them too often.

Finocchio is a biannual, but is usually grown as an annual. The seeds should be planted in the spring at about the time of the last frost. Spread the seeds sparingly in a trench about half an inch deep, and cover lightly. When the plants are 2 inches tall, thin them to a spacing of 6 to 8 inches. *Finocchio* grows to a height of around 2 feet, but it may be used while much smaller. The leaves are used especially with various seafood recipes, and they may be clipped as needed any time after the plant is 8 to 10 inches tall. The stems are usually not large enough to bother with until the plant is at least a foot tall. They may be harvested from the plant individually as wanted. If the plant does not winter-kill (they are not especially hardy), during its second year it will send up seed stalks, setting seeds on tall umbels. The seeds have culinary uses as a distinctive flavoring in a variety of cakes and cookies.

The common name of dill, "dill weed," gives a clue to the ease of its culture. It is a tall annual, with attractive feathery green foliage. Depending on conditions, it grows from one to three feet and more, terminating in a spreading seed head. It has a distinctive mouth-watering aroma, reminiscent of generations of grandmothers' pickle crocks. The leaves are clipped while tender (before the seed umbel begins to form) and used as the principal seasoning accent of Scandinavian fish dishes, as well as numerous other, especially ethnic, recipes, breads, and so on. And it is, of course, the indispensable ingredient of dill pickles.

Dill is an annual that flourishes under a wide variety of conditions. It makes rapid growth, forming seed heads in about two months or slightly sooner. Many people try to time the planting of dill so that production of seed heads coincides with the maturing of cucumbers.

If planted too early the seeds may mature beyond optimum quality for use in pickle making. Because of its rapid growth, dill is sometimes interplanted with other crops, such as corn. Under such conditions the plants are apt to be dwarfed, which can be an actual advantage, since in their full height the plants are somewhat fragile and likely to be blown down by the wind.

The seeds may be planted around the time of the last spring frost, but if they are to be used in pickle making they should be planted later, from the first of May on, depending on when the pickling cucumbers are likely to be ready. Plant the seeds no deeper than a quarter of an inch, lightly covered. They will make a taller growth if thinned to 2 or 3 inches apart, but a fairly dense stand allows the stems to give each other mutual support. When it has been once grown in a garden, dill reseeds itself gladly from year to year, which no doubt partially accounts for it being called "dill weed." I have never heard of it becoming a problem to control; the roots are shallow, and the plants may easily be pulled at any stage of development. People most often grow seed rack dill, which is usually Long Island Mammoth. Actually this variety is best for seed. A superior variety for leaves is the Aroma LD (Denmark: *Territorial Seed Company*).

Even if there is no legitimate culinary need for dill in a given garden, its smell is so pleasant and evocative to justify cultivating at least a few plants, especially the casual volunteers that unexpectedly appear amid some other plants or vegetables. It is almost as if dill is fundamentally just a plain friendly plant that enjoys casual visiting about in the garden.

The most expensive savory is saffron. It consists of the dried pollen collected from the anthers of late-blooming crocuslike bulbs. These are planted in the late summer in soil prepared as for spring-blooming bulbs. Soon after planting, they should put up short blossoming stalks, very like crocus or colchicum. They are attractive and unusual enough to grow for ornamental reasons alone. Whether one could practically grow the plants and harvest saffron, I don't know. Those fond of Near Eastern dishes would surely like to experiment with it. To harvest, the entire anther is carefully picked (with tweezers or a similar tool) when it is freely ripening the reddish-yellow pollen. The anther is dried, out of the sun, and when cured stored in separate, one-recipe's—worth sizes in small, individual air-tight containers. Bulbs are offered in the *Van Bourgondien* catalogue.

One can always find room for an herb garden. I have known people with limited space who grew nothing but herbs and savories. I assume their theory was that if compelled to eat only what was available from produce markets, the inferior quality could be partially corrected by using flavorings that were at least genuine.

Cane Berries
and
Small Fruits

Tayberry

Some of the most satisfying long-range garden plantings are those generally lumped together as small fruits and berries. For some of them, once established there is the prospect of many years of harvest with relatively little maintenance and upkeep. Even some of the more unruly, such as raspberries and blackcaps, are not unreasonably demanding. Many of the small fruits and berries produce real delicacies, but they ship poorly, and varieties found in markets tend to be generic rather than selected quality. Even the poorest are often outrageously expensive. Most berries and small fruits are only modestly space greedy, at least in comparison with regular fruit trees. Although some require special care, most have no unacceptably fussy requirements. Many adapt well to otherwise hard-to-use space, such as fence rows, borders, and roadsides, and there are some that can double as ornamental plantings.

An attractive choice as an ornamental is the blueberry. Although it seems to be gaining in recognition regionally, it is nevertheless much neglected in garden plantings. It does have a reputation for being finicky, but its demands are not impossible. The first thing ever said when blueberry culture is mentioned is that it absolutely demands an acid soil. That it does, and some gardeners in locations with soil naturally high in acid have been complacently growing blueberries for years. However, preparing soil for conditions suitable for their culture is not especially difficult, certainly not as difficult as the task a great many beginning gardeners face in transforming marginal or sub-marginal soil into a productive growing medium before they can grow anything.

In my first attempt to grow blueberries, I decided to try them because I thought I had a spot they would like. It was a border area approaching a large blue spruce, where evergreen needles had been mulched in so long that the soil was a granular humus 6 inches deep, like a good ancient forest duff. This mulch I spaded and blended with the lower soil, and into this medium planted five bushes. They never flourished, and by the end of the second summer clearly were giving notice of their intent to die. I have since learned that especially resinous conifer needles such as spruce and pine are bad for blueberries, regardless of their acidifying character.

My second attempt, several years later, followed considerable reading about blueberry culture and was approached with a more clearly defined purpose. Much that has been written about their culture, I now conclude, is excessively cautionary, and makes it seem more complicated than need be. This time I located the blueberries along a fence row and used a sort of modified raised-bed system to maintain a separate soil system for them. Before planting, I dug the holes about 16 inches deep and 18 to 20 inches wide, mixing the planting soil about fifty-fifty with fine peat. About 18 inches from the fence I placed a line of 2 × 8's on edge, supported and kept upright by stakes driven into the ground. After setting the bushes in and watering them, I piled a couple of inches of coarsely composted vegetative material on the surface of the entire row. In early summer I spread a layer of peat about two inches on top of this, and during the summer made certain that the surface of the soil beneath it all never dried (which the layer of mulch made easy). In the fall I loosely mounded hardwood leaves (avoid walnut, buckeye, or others that might contain toxins or be especially difficult to break down) between the woven wire fence and the 2 × 8's, halfway covering the bushes. In the spring I added some more compost, plus about an inch of peat. The second summer I added a thin layer of composted manure, and leaves again in the fall.

This is the basic drill for growing blueberries, although it does not have to be in that strict order. In this way several inches of organic material can be built up, which closely approximates the growing habitat of wild blueberries. Blueberry bushes have both deep roots and shallow feeding roots, so the surface organic material needs to be readily available for them. Because of these shallow roots, cultivation should be limited to hand-pulling weeds. The deep organic mulch also helps here, keeping weed seed from germinating, and making those that do succeed easy to pull. And the mulch helps to conserve moisture. This also is a requirement of blueberries—the surface of the soil needs to be constantly moist, although not waterlogged, if the bushes are to flourish.

This description makes the process sound much more time-consuming than it actually was. It is no more care than is ordinarily devoted to a rose bed of similar size. The planting is hardly different from planting any other shrub, and the adding of the mulch is a matter requiring little time, made easier and more effective by the raised-bed configuration. Often instructions for blueberry culture suggest using chemical additives to increase the acidity. Aluminum sulfate at the rate of a half-pound per shrub at planting is a common recommendation. I suspect that even with aluminum sulfate, without some such mulching program as suggested the plants would never be thrifty, if for no other reason than uneven moisture retention.

Blueberries are especially well adapted to doubling as ornamentals. Their small, glossy, dense leaves are quite attractive. In the fall they assume rich shades of gold and maroon. In fact, wild huckleberry is collected for use by florists in floral arrangements. Blueberry blossoms are also attractive—white to slightly golden pendant bells in clusters looking like slightly oversized lily of the valley. And, of course, the beautiful berries. For planting as decorative shrubs raised beds similar to that described would be readily adaptable, especially if made of decorative material, such as brick.

Most blueberries are not self-fruitful. That is, for pollination, more than one variety must be planted. Many nurseries will not sell single varieties by themselves, only in multiples of two or more. There are quite a number of different varieties available, and I would be hard pressed to recommend specific kinds. I ordered, deliberately, varieties from three different nurseries in three different northern states. One variety, called simply "Michigan wild blueberry," I ordered for the sake of curiosity, because while described as small and not especially prolific, it was noted to retain the distinctive flavor of wild huckleberries, and that is a flavor I especially relish. Of all my berries, however, only this variety has failed to produce, and although growing well enough, has not kept pace with the commercial varieties.

In ignorance I made a fourth order from a southern nursery for a variety called a "rabbit-eye blueberry," because of the large size of its berry. It grows into a large bush, said to reach 10 feet or more in height, and requiring a proportionately wide spacing. Unfortunately it is not winter-hardy, as the catalogue I ordered from failed to indicate. Other catalogues, I have since noted, suggest that this variety should not be planted where winter temperatures regularly fall below 20 degrees. I planted three, two of which were killed the first winter; the second has held on to the present, having survived temperatures in excess of minus 10 degrees. I have no real hope for its long-range survival, although I continue to care for it as a sort of horticultural pensioner. The rabbit-eye varieties, by the way, for those with a climate that will sustain them are self-fruitful.

For many gardeners, space will dictate how many blueberries can be planted. If there is only room for two, so be it. However, if one can afford the space for six or more, the choice of varieties might well be influenced by ripening dates, since different varieties ripen across a relatively long period. As with most small fruits, actual production time for a given variety may not be long, so for fresh consumption it is nice to have them over as long a period as possible. Some of the earliest varieties are not of the choicest quality, so if you have only the option for a limited planting, probably it would better serve your interest to grow the highest quality, even if late. Lateness is of course relative, and no one is going to suffer because of a lack of early blueberries while strawberries and raspberries are ripening elsewhere in the garden.

Among the earliest blueberry varieties is the Weymouth. It is large, but for flavor the later varieties are superior. The Rubel is a mid-season variety, with medium-sized fruit that is sweet and flavorful. I planted two of this variety, and they produced a usable crop the first year (despite cautions to the contrary, I can never strip the blossoms). The Jersey is a late berry, very large—about the same as Rubel. The flavor is not as sweet or elegant as the Rubel, but they are beautiful. My bushes produced a handful each the second year. The Berkeley is early and likewise quite large, and light blue in color. I planted two, which have made exceptionally good growth, but have never had more than a couple of berries each. The Meader is a large berry developed in New Hampshire by Professor E. M. Meader and is said to be hardy to minus 25 degrees. Again, I planted two of this variety, which due to chance and accident not the fault of the bushes have not done well. The Concord is a mid-season variety, and said to be a heavy producer of large well-flavored berries. They grow to 6 feet, which might recommend them for certain situations where they are to double as ornamental shrubs. The Bluecrop is also mid-season, with large, light blue fruit. My two bushes produced lightly the second year, with a modest crop the third. The flavor is mild but good.

As with most garden things, when in doubt about varieties that might be locally adaptable, consult a county extension agent. Since in some regions blueberries are uncommon, advice may be hard to come by, and you may simply be told to forget it. In this case, be bold and do a little adventuring. Beware of ordering berries from splashy looking ads that say: "Imagine! Berries as big as quarters! Often in its first year!" I've fallen for most of the sucker deals, including a version of this one, and added what was sent to me through the mail to my dried twig collection. (Never order from an advertisement that uses bad grammar.)

While they are in no way as versatile as blueberries, currants deserve a larger play in small gardens than they get. Probably they are less frequently grown in America than in other countries because they are infrequently seen in our produce markets. Gardeners tend to grow what is familiar, as well as varieties of whatever it is that look like what they see in markets. Like gooseberries, currants are common in English markets, appear in varied English recipes, and seem to be afforded room in English gardens. Dried currants are called for in English recipes at least as often as raisins—currant buns, for example, instead of raisin buns. I often substitute dried currants in recipes where raisins are called for. For one thing, their smaller size makes them considerably more convenient—as in cinnamon rolls, where I can never seem to get raisins to adhere where they're supposed to.

Currants are quite effortless to grow, and like blueberries can make attractive shrubs in their own right, with numerous tall straight branches and large light green leaves shaped vaguely like maple leaves. They are also thornless, or at least the cultivated varieties with which I am familiar. Their blossoms are nothing special, but the ripe fruit is quite showy, hanging in long racemes, often conspicuously prolific.

Currants will do well in most any common garden soil. Plant them as any other shrub and, after setting, prevent the transplants from drying out. At the time of planting prune the top third from each. Although most stock will begin promptly to leaf out, if they fail to show life as soon as they should, do not give up. In my first serious attempt to grow them, six plants were delayed in shipment and arrived in very poor condition, in late April. While one began to grow immediately, a second did not show life until June. Two more put up shoots from underground in July. Two died. The second year all four survivors flourished, and quickly caught up with two others planted at the same time that I had obtained from a different supplier, and that had arrived in good condition.

Currants may set a few fruits the first year but the second year should make a good crop. Care is simple: keep down the weeds, and maintain moderate fertility with an annual light application of a general purpose fertilizer, or sustained fertilizing with organic material. Pruning should be light, primarily to sustain shape and size and to remove dead or damaged branches. Some instructions advise restraining the berry clump to five canes, pruning out the older canes when they are four or five years old. Probably nothing that formal is really necessary. When the clump matures, simply maintain it under control, remembering to retain two to four canes for best fruiting. When a bush comes into full production, the crop may be so heavy as to bend the canes and sometimes break off branches. Encircling the bush with a pair of old pantyhose to brace them together is a good preventative.

There are actually quite a few varieties of currants available if a gardener will care to look for them. The variety most commonly offered is called Red Lake. The berries are large and bright red, attractive, and are produced in long clusters. Another large red berry is the Cherry Currant, a recently developed berry released by the Washington State Department of Agriculture. One nursery rated it the hardiest and heaviest bearing currant they had tested. The Wilder is a long-season berry, ripening over nearly the entire month of July. The Perfection, also called New Perfection, is another heavy producer, although it is perhaps not the equal of the Red Lake or Cherry.

Among older varieties, Robert Nitchke of *South Meadow Fruit Gardens* rates a variety called Laxton's No. 1 as the best flavored of the red currants. This family of currants was developed in the nineteenth century by Thomas Laxton, who was a research assistant to Charles Darwin. Nitchke recommends the White Imperial, an ancient variety, as the best of the pale currants. The berries are not large and are not borne as lavishly as the Red Lake or Cherry Currant, but the flavor is full and sweet. Nitchke recommends blending its juice with raspberry juice for jellies; not given to hyperbole, he maintains "it makes one of the most delicious flavors known."

As little demanding as they are, and as attractive, currants deserve to be more widely planted than they are. Although currants are not a common ingredient in American recipes, they offer rare chances for innovation. Especially those people who take pride in the variety of things that they grow for themselves should find drying their own currants an attractive substitute for raisins, especially those who live in regions inhospitable to suitable raisin grape varieties. They are famous in currant jelly, but large quantities are needed for a few pints. More often I make currant jam, which is less demanding both on the berries and the cook.

Hardly more familiar to American cooks than currants are gooseberries, which are seldom or never found in the usual sorts of produce market, and if found are offered in limited variety. In England the fruiterers, or produce sellers, not only routinely exhibit them but display what is to an American's eye an astonishing variety. Most Americans visualize gooseberries as small bead- to small marble-sized fruit, with a pale to dark green skin and semitranslucent flesh. That describes only the barest minimum of the selection offered by an English merchant. Size ranges from that of a small marble to that of a medium plum, colored from green through shades of pink, red, orange, or tangerine. Characteristically their flavor is more sweet than sour, with a quality of richness in some that could be compared to a fig. One realizes why they are so popular in English dessert recipes.

For the most part, American nurseries offer only two or three green varieties. The commonest is the Pixwell, recommended because the berries hang in clusters below the thorny stems. More rarely offered is the Welcome, a nearly thornless variety developed by the University of Minnesota, the Red Jacket, and a new variety called the Colossal. A gardener will have to study an awful lot of general catalogues to find that many.

However, some of the European (and Canadian and antique American) varieties are being offered by nursery houses specializing in heritage varieties, notably *Southmeadow Fruit Gardens*. Nitchke recommends the Poorman as the best American variety: pear-shaped, dark red, sweet, and flavorful. Among the oldest of the English varieties is the Red Warrington, which is a bright but pale red and has traditionally been a favorite for preserves. A good "specimen" choice is the English variety Criterion, producing large yellowish-green fruit that are especially attractive hanging on the bushes. One of the most attractive, and some say the best flavored of all the European gooseberries, is Hoening's Earliest. It is a brilliant gold in color, with a sweet, plumlike flavor. Hinnomaki Yellow is a Finnish variety, medium-sized and rather pear-shaped. These varieties comprise only a representative sampling of a much larger list of varieties that may be discovered by examining other than mainstream sources.

To offer something of an index to the range of varieties of gooseberries that once existed, in the 1820s over 800 named varieties were registered in England. This treasure was the culmination of a fad of gooseberry breeding among fashionable young men of the period, who organized and belonged to a nationwide network of gooseberry clubs.

At least for the immediate future, the old European varieties are likely to remain in short supply in America. They are difficult to propagate and require particularly special handling by the nursery men. Nevertheless, gooseberries are not especially difficult for a gardener to grow. As often as not the standard American green gooseberries are allowed to remain year after year in a remote section of the garden, unattended, without even such minimum attention as maintenance and pruning.

Gooseberries will grow to a height of about 4 feet, more brushy than the generally erect currant bush. Plant them about 4 feet apart in ordinary garden soil, perhaps enriched with a little compost or composted manure. They are sensitive to potash deficiencies, which is correctable with a handful of ashes sprinkled over the surface of the soil. In an alkaline soil, supplement the potash with fertilizer rather than with ashes, which would contribute to further alkalinity.

Although I am not a gooseberry fanatic, I have two very old bushes of the green sour variety, which my daughters and their friends use in a game that rewards whoever can eat the most berries without making a face with a handful of jellybeans. I intend to use those berries as a point of reference in showing off my other varieties as they come into production.

The Kiwi fruit is an exotic that has become a familiar if somewhat expensive offering in produce markets. It originated in China, and for a while was called the Chinese gooseberry. In New Zealand it was popularized and became an export fruit under the name by which it is now familiar. It is now grown domestically, and its commercial acreage in America has increased vastly, mostly in southern areas of the country. Gardeners have been experimenting with the fruit in more northern ranges, finding it able to grow in much colder areas than expected. Further, varieties are being developed specifically with the purpose of improving its hardiness. Every year the estimates of the cold it can tolerate are being estimated downwards. Currently the vines are being successfully grown in many Zone 6 climates, occasionally in Zone 5.

The plant is usually propagated by root cuttings; it can be grown from seed, but the quality will be uncertain. The flowers are dioecious, so it is necessary to have both a female and a male plant. One male is sufficient for about five to eight females.

The vines are tall and fast growing, and require support or trellising. Fruit is borne the second or third year, and mature plants may produce up to a hundred pounds each. After blossoming in April or May, fruit ripens in September or October. Vines are said to have a life expectancy of fifty years plus. In marginal climate areas, Kiwis should be grown in a southern exposure and provided with winter protection. Although rarely seen a few years ago, Kiwi plants are now offered in general catalogues.

A related but distinct variety originating in northern China, generically called the hardy kiwi, is said to be hardy to minus 50 degrees. While the fruit is similar in flavor to that of the other kiwi family, the appearance is quite different, the fruit being about an inch in diameter and round. The vines are also long-lived and quite productive at maturity. It is a fast-growing vine, with attractive, shiny green leaves, and was first introduced to America as an ornamental. As with the other kiwi family, both a male and a female are required for pollination. Plants are available from *Raintree Nursery*.

For the berries sometimes collected together under the general classification of cane fruits and brambles, space may be a limiting factor to many gardeners, since these berries tend to be a bit space greedy as well as difficult to discipline in their growth habits. Space problems, especially with the brambles, may be at least partially solved by restricting them to fence rows, borders, and road edges. Most of these berries are not demanding about soil, and are easy to grow.

Raspberries are especially attractive to home gardeners, because growing them one's self is generally the only way to obtain them in sufficient quantity to use other than as a limited luxury. The ripe fruit is extremely perishable, and they do not stand up well to handling. When they are obtainable commercially, it is for only the briefest of periods, and at premium prices. Unlike strawberries, which are sold by the pint and quart, raspberries are merchandised by the half pint, and are very pricey at that.

There are three main classes of raspberries—red, purple, and black (also called "blackcaps"). The growth habits of each are slightly different, and they will require slightly different care, although all three are commonly grown as sort of hedge.

For the majority of gardeners, how many bushes to plant will be determined more by space availability than need. As Shakespeare pointed out, need is strictly relative, and "the basest beggar is in the poorest thing superfluous." On the other hand, as with strawberries, one can hardly have too many raspberries. I have five separate beds and plan to add another. I like my children to have all they can possibly eat, and to invite their friends to join them. For a gardener with more stringent space considerations, a half a dozen bushes is a decent start, but a mere clump in a fence corner is better than nothing.

Spacing is not crucial. Planting guides issued by three standard suppliers specializing in berries specify 4, 3, and 2 feet respectively as proper spacing between bushes. I plant with a spacing of about 3 feet, but if one requires a neat appearance in his garden, orderliness is easier to maintain with a wider spacing. If more than one row is planted, they should be spaced 3 or 4 feet apart, wider if mechanical cultivation is to be used. Raspberry bushes multiply rapidly, and would soon pack the rows as well as the space between if given a chance.

Depending on the climate, raspberries can be planted either in the fall or spring. In a Zone 5, spring planting is more successful. Raspberries will do well in any decent garden soil, and I have seen plants escaped from abandoned farm plantings marching up rocky hillsides, respectfully competing with wild roses. The best way to get starts is to borrow them from a friend. Unfortunately, in many cases even the best of friends often do not know the names of the varieties they are growing—not that it really matters if they are productive and good. Select starts in early spring, the earlier the better, although I have had transplants grow fine dug as late as June. The first harvest a year later was lighter than it could have been. If possible, select shoots growing a little distance from the main clump. Roots are shallow, and it is only necessary to get a main bud and fair-sized clump of roots, although the heartier the start, the better the yield will be on the first crop. Starts obtained from nurseries are most often rooted cuttings, and they should arrive either in individual peat pots or packed in sphagnum moss wrapped in plastic. They are quite perishable and should be planted promptly. If they cannot be set out immediately, put them in water and keep them in a cool, dark place.

To set out raspberry starts, dig a small opening into the prepared soil and insert the plant to the same depth it had been growing. Firm the soil around it, and water immediately. Do not let it dry out in the slightest until the temperature has warmed and the plant is growing vigorously. If growth does not appear for a while, do not give up. Keep it wet, and the chances are good that eventually a strong new shoot will appear from underground, and all will be well.

The only attention the first year is to keep the weeds down. Since the roots are shallow, cultivate lightly. Do no pruning at all during the first year. Fertilize in the fall after the canes have stopped growing and "hardened off," or turned woody. I like to build up and sustain an organic mulch, although people living in areas troubled by mice and certain insect pests may find anything but the most finely pulverized mulches too attractive as a habitation for such pests.

There are two different fruiting patterns for red raspberries—one crop and two crop. As the names indicate, with the former the year-old canes will set a crop in early to midsummer while growing new shoots for the following year's crop. With the latter, there is a crop on the old canes, and the new canes will blossom in the late summer and set a second crop in the autumn. Which to choose may depend more on one's climate than one's preference. In Zone 5 I find that the second crop seldom ripens. When I lived in a Zone 6 the second crop never failed to ripen and was sometimes larger than the first. It is recommended with a two-crop berry that the old canes be removed as soon as the first crop is over. This may be easier said than done because often, unless some rigid support system has been provided, the new canes are still depending on the old for support. The mechanical act of removing the old also sometimes messes up the new canes. The advantage in removing them is to encourage vigorous growth for the second crop and hasten ripening of the fall crop.

Raspberries are untidy in their growing habits and seem to resent attempts to force them to be orderly. One of the simplest methods of formal trellising is to string a single strand of heavy gauge wire between steel (or wooden) posts placed about 10 feet apart at a height of about 4 feet. In the spring three to five canes from each plant are loosely attached to the wire with a garden fastener (or lengths of old pantyhose), and any remaining canes removed at ground level. Another system is to use wooden posts spaced 7 or 8 feet apart with a crosspiece 3 feet long nailed to the top of each post 4 feet from the ground and parallel to the ground. A wire is stretched the length of the row on either side, attached to the ends of the crosspieces. The idea is that the canes will be loosely retained within the two wires, which makes pruning easier and allows more freedom in sustaining the size of the row.

It is also quite possible, and very usual, to maintain a plot as a hedge, without physical restraints of any sort. Such a planting is not neat, and is not as handy to pick as a trellised planting, but it works perfectly well; probably far more garden raspberries are grown in this way than in any other. I always do. I have tried both of the systems described above, as well as systems both cruder and more complicated, and have finally decided that for my purposes none of them are worth the effort. But please don't come to my bramble patch to take pictures.

The principle attention raspberries require is pruning. The shoots a two-crop plant grows one year produce the next year's crop, and after producing they wither away and die. Old canes may be pruned in the summer after the crop is finished, or they may be removed the following spring, at which time they will be dry and brittle. Whenever the old stalks are removed, in the spring thin each clump to three to five young shoots. Leave the strongest, and choose those not too close together. Let each individual plant cover an area about 16 inches in diameter if possible, and pruning season by pruning season try to maintain a distance between plants of about 3 feet from center to center. When the old canes have been removed and the young canes thinned, trim the top of each remaining cane to a height of about 4 feet. The exact height will depend somewhat on the strength of the canes as well as your experience in how that particular variety performs in your garden. For example, if the canes characteristically put out heavy side shoots, trimming them a bit lower will help them keep erect with a heavy crop. Those that are naturally short need only have the tip cut off.

To sustain heavy crops and good quality berries, the fertility of the ground must be maintained. Fertilize heavily only in the late summer, or in the fall if the berries are a two-crop variety. Fertilizing in the spring or summer tends to encourage rank vegetative growth and also tends to make the berries soft. In my estimation the flavor also suffers. I like to lay down a mulch of lawn clippings in the late summer, adding some leaves in the fall, plus a good balanced fertilizer. When available, I use manure instead. In some areas, heavy mulching provides a habitat for rodents and protection for insect pests, and under such conditions its use is discouraged.

There are many varieties of red raspberries to choose from, and there is hardly an area in the continental United States where there are not some varieties that will flourish. Many catalogues that offer extensive berry selections, such as *Dean Foster Nursery,* give enough real information—as opposed to hype—about berry varieties that an inexperienced gardener can pretty much make an intelligent choice on his own. Of course, consultation with an extension agent and other local gardeners would be wise.

One of the most widely grown varieties is the Latham, an old and dependable hardy variety. There are raspberry varieties that are more productive and that have more showy berries that also deserve consideration. Another old variety is the Fairview; like the Latham, it is hardy, but it is probably not as productive. Some, however, consider it the finest flavored raspberry grown. The Willamette is a general purpose berry, high in quality and an excellent producer. It is probably the berry most widely planted by commercial growers. Two varieties, which I have not seen, may be attractive to some potential growers because of their special attributes. People who wear dentures often cannot eat raspberries at all because of the seeds, and seeds trouble some people's digestion. Seeds can also be a problem in making raspberry jam. The Taylor variety is almost completely seedless. It has the disadvantage of not being as winter-hardy as other varieties, but with protection, it is said to be able to survive in a Zone 5. Some gardeners are put off from growing raspberries because of the thorns. The Mammoth Red Thornless grows extra large berries on extra large canes that are completely thorn free, and it is said to be an exceptionally winter-hardy variety.

In addition to these varieties, there are also several "red" raspberries that are golden colored. It is said that the paler color makes them less attractive to birds. One common variety is the Fall Gold. I have found it reasonably productive, although the canes are weak and need support. Their flavor is excellent, although slightly different than that of red raspberries.

There are also so-called everbearing varieties, which are in fact really a two-crop berry. After their initial production, the new growth will blossom and provide a second, smaller crop, for more or less continuous production.

Of the late one-crop berries, the Fall Red, or Fall Red Everbearing, or Fallred, a variety developed by the University of New Hampshire, is one of the earliest to ripen, two to three weeks before others. Another late berry, the August Red, produces exceptionally compact canes, only about 3 feet high, which might be an attractive feature to those with space problems.

Black raspberries, or blackcaps, are infrequently found in markets, and when they do appear are among the most expensive of fresh fruits. Their flavor is distinctive and pronounced, sometimes with a whiff of licorice. A few people don't care for the flavor; some react to it like a cat to catnip. With some varieties the berries are smaller, sometimes much smaller, than red raspberries, and they are much firmer. They make an elegant jelly, although it takes quite a bit more of them than red raspberries for an equal quantity because they are not as juicy. Many people combine them with red raspberries for jam and jelly, both to stretch their blackcaps and for the sake of the unique flavor of the blend and the pleasing color.

Blackcaps are cultivated essentially the same as red raspberries. Because of their tendency to grow long and rambling canes, they are most often grown with some system of support, such as the double- or single-wire trellis described before. However, like red raspberries, they can also be grown as a hedge, although an untidy one. To keep them under control, it helps if the growing tips of the shoots for next year's crop are pinched off twice each summer. This temporarily frustrates forward growth and encourages growth of lateral branches—which are much more restrained than those of red raspberries. As with red raspberries, old canes may be cut off as soon as the harvest is over, or they may be pruned back early the following spring.

Also in the early spring, the canes should be thinned to three to five per plant.

There are a number of varieties of blackcaps to choose from, and consultation with other gardeners or with an extension agent would be wise to determine what varieties do well in a particular region. The earliest of the blackcaps is probably a recently introduced variety called Jet. The Morrison, or New Morrison, is reputed to be the largest, with the additional advantage of having few seeds. The most popular variety, and the one most frequently grown commercially, is the Cumberland. It is also large and is particularly sweet. The Black Hawk, developed by Iowa State University, is quite large and nearly round. It is also quite firm, which enables it to stand up better than most varieties to packing and shipping. An older variety, the Bristol, has high marks for flavor, although it may not be quite as productive as some. It is a variety I have grown almost exclusively over the years because I like its flavor.

A good way to choose varieties, after taking local considerations into account, is the order of ripening. One may wish to synchronize blackcaps with raspberries in order to blend them for jelly. One may wish to expand the time over which berry crops may be available beyond a single variety, although I feel this aspect of planting is often overemphasized. So many things come available during the summer that what one can actually consume is limited. But if one really wants to extend the season during which they are available, this may be achieved by planting varieties chosen for their ripening sequence. If one is planning to grow six plants, for example, some such arrangement as two Jets, two Bristols, and two Black Hawks would provide a succession of berries over several weeks once the plants became established. With ample space to devote to their cultivation and sufficient appetite for berries, the selections and combinations expand. Some catalogues offer special combinations of varieties in small quantities precisely for the purpose of providing a continuous succession of ripening.

Developed in fairly recent times is a third category of raspberries, the purples. From my own experience and preference, if a person had limited space and would be able to grow only the barest number of cane berries, this would be the variety to choose. They are tall and erect, with heavy canes that need no support other than themselves, and they are absolutely profligate in their production. The berries are large—up to an inch in diameter—firmer than a raspberry, and fine flavored. They are somewhat late seasoned, for me beginning to ripen at the end of July, but they ripen over a period of two or three weeks. Two plants would supply a small family sufficiently, if not lavishly, for fresh consumption. Six might supply a large family with abundance.

Culture of the purples is about the same as for the reds, letting out the seams a little to accommodate their size. Plant them no closer than 4 feet apart, and maintain them at four to five canes per plant, spaced 6 or 8 inches apart, if that proves possible. In my experience they do not put up as many new shoots as the reds or blacks, so they tend to spread more slowly. The first year after I planted mine I promised starts for a friend but found in the spring I didn't have any to spare. I also prune them higher in the spring than other raspberries, to about 5 feet. Individual canes produce side shoots prolifically, which partially accounts for the abundance of their production. After pruning in the spring, I circle all the canes of each plant with an old pair of pantyhose, about 2½ feet above the ground, and again about 4½ feet up, pulling the canes together to form a more or less parallel mass into a cylinder 25 to 30 inches in diameter at the top. Later in the season, after very strong growth has been taking place, I add a third pantyhose to hold the top growth loosely together. This final circling to constrain the tops will take some effort, especially considering that purple raspberries are not thornless. Properly tied together, the canes are sufficiently strong to cross-brace each other. Without bracing or support of some sort, as strong as they are they will become so top heavy they will fall over. (I was sufficiently foresighted to have three daughters, so have exceptional resources in that versatile resource, used pantyhose. However, when I suggested that one of my daughters might add to my store by collecting for me in her college dorm, my wife fixed me with an unusually cold and negative stare. I quickly recognized how socially unacceptable the request might appear: "I'm collecting used pantyhose for my father.")

Although the purples are not yet widely planted, the commonest variety so far is the Brandywine. It is the largest of the purples, with a round conelike shape and a shallow core that pulls off easily when fully ripe. It is firmer than the red raspberry, but not quite as firm as the blackcap. The flavor is sweet-tart and full, and the berry has relatively few seeds. They are excellent for eating fresh and make fine jam.

The Sodus, or Sodus Purple, is a purple raspberry similar to the Brandywine, but considerably sweeter; the canes are weaker and require support. A third variety is the Clyde, which is similar to the Sodus, and is said to have an especially attractive color. For a gardener who has room for only one variety, perhaps the Sodus or Clyde would be a better choice than the Brandywine because of their sweetness. However, the tart—by no means sour—flavor of the Brandywine is admired by everyone who tastes it. In the best of all possible worlds we would all have sufficient space—and time—to grow specimens of everything there is!

Although a vine rather than a cane, another relative of the raspberry family introduced quite recently is the Tayberry, developed in Scotland and named after the River Tay, and said to be a cross of raspberries, blackberries, and Loganberries. It has been commercially available for only a short time and has gotten somewhat mixed reviews from gardeners. One complained that it is difficult to gauge its ripeness, since it did not always slip free like other berries when it was at the proper stage. He said it was as if the berry itself didn't know when it was ripe. Its flavor has also produced mixed reaction, some tasters objecting on the basis of excessive tartness. Its thorns also come in for comment; one critic said it didn't really seem any more thorny than a raspberry, but its thorns seemed somehow to be more obnoxious. There are those however, who praise its flavor. My daughter, whose judgment I respect, eats them with unbridled zeal. The Tayberry is said to freeze well and to be excellent in pies and jams. The berry itself is beautiful. It is impressively large; I have read of specimens described to be over 2 inches long, although I have never seen any nearly that big. Mine have produced berries as long as an inch. They are, like blackberries, rambling in their habits and, once established, prodigious producers of vines. The final word is not yet in on the Tayberry, but my guess is that it will probably not become a popular home garden berry without further development.

The ripe Tayberry resembles a ripe Loganberry, which like the Tayberry was developed from blackberries. Loganberry vines are quite attractive, particularly when loaded with their big red berries. Loganberries have a flavor as distinctively their own as a raspberry or a blackcap. They make a sumptuous pie and are widely used as a wine fruit. Although they are sometimes described as hardy, in a Zone 6 I grew them with modest success, but with no success at all in a Zone 5. They seem particularly happy in a marine climate, as do many other blackberry relatives.

The Juneberry is not common but is sometimes offered by nursery catalogues. The berry is odd, encased in a sort of a husk almost until ripening, and borne in fairly large, flat clusters. A ripe bunch resembles a clump of mountain ash berries. They are beautiful, but of poor quality. They are juicy, but the juice is thin and lacks sweetness. The vines are brambly and persistent. I am still trying to eradicate my first and only planting.

Regular blackberries are to me more trouble than they are worth. Unless tended constantly, they become unmanageable, and their thorniness makes caring for them particularly unpleasant. They are also difficult to restrain within bounds, putting out stout, fast-growing suckers far from the main plant again and again and again. No one will disagree, however, that blackberries are very, very good.

Fortunately thornless varieties have been developed, and although there are disadvantages associated with them, as far as I'm concerned it's the thornless varieties or none at all. If one has a back fence or a piece of terrain too irregular for normal cultivation, plant ordinary blackberries and let them do it on their own as semi-wildlings. In fact, given their sprawling, take-charge habits, they make an excellent wildlife habitation from which berries may be harvested, gingerly, as from any bramble patch. Remember Brer Rabbit. But since thornless varieties are available, that's all I grow in the regular confines of my garden.

There are, however, three particular disadvantages to the thornless varieties. The first is that the berries are not as full flavored as the regular varieties. If they are not quite as good, the difference is marginal weighed against the difficulties cultivation of the thorny varieties imposes. The second objection to the thornless varieties is that they are not thoroughly winter hardy. In my Zone 5 I have lost some to winter-kill, and have had others winter damaged, but by and large I am satisfied. The third objection is probably the most serious. There is an unpredictable tendency among some varieties to revert from slick skins to thorns. So far I have not had this problem, but other growers have. Breeders hope to overcome this problem.

Of the thornless blackberries, I have grown only one variety, the Black Satin. The first year I trained some of the new growth onto a fence, and all of these canes were winter-killed. It appeared they were killed by spring cold, after they had begun to break dormancy, rather than the minus-10 degree winter temperature, which it appeared they had survived. Canes that I had not trellised but left sprawling on the ground, seemed to suffer little or no damage.

Dewberries have always been a favorite of mine among the blackberries, partly because of their extravagant size and partly because of their mild blackberry flavor. Their thorny vines, however, are among the most disagreeable of the whole bramble family. It is their habit to grow very low to the ground, putting out long, twining and obnoxiously thorny runners. The backs of the leaves have long, re-curved thorns that are virtually inescapable. They quite refuse to be disciplined into any orderly system of cultivation. You meet them on their own terms or not at all. I let a few grow along a steep roadbank and harvest them with the same care I might harvest wild honey. They are slightly less hardy than blackberries, but although regularly I have some winter-kill, they nevertheless always manage an adequate crop for my purposes.

Varieties of dewberries have also been developed that are thorn-less. I have tried one variety, which was simply called Thornless Dewberry. In spite of the catalogue assurance that they are quite hardy, I have had severe winterkill among my plants. Nor did they grow as vigorously as the thornless blackberries next to which I planted them. The first winter two out of five plants died, and the other three suffered some degree of winter damage. The quality of the few berries which they have produced is fine. In a more genial climate, thornless dewberries might be an excellent choice.

Another garden variety bramble is the Boysenberry. They are midway between blackberries and dewberries in their growth habits and berry quality. They are viny and prostrate, and don't like to be told what to do. They bear over a longer period of time than blackberries and dewberries—a period of nearly two months—and the berries are larger than the fruits of either. Catalogues describe them as 2 inches and longer; I have actually seen them at an honest inch and a half. The flavor is mild, but quite sweet when fully ripe. There is available a thornless variety called Giant Thornless Boysenberry; these are considered moderately hardy, but I have not yet tried them.

Blackberries are an excellent fruit, with a flavor beyond comparison, but their thorniness and cantankerousness puts them beyond the reach of all but the devoted who have the space. The thornless varieties, however, make the difference. I will never again plant members of this family that have thorns, except to naturalize as wildlings. Having experienced the almost aggressive defenses of this family, it becomes a pleasure to weed tenderly and casually the thornless varieties. I feel something approximating a sensuous release when those smooth bare stems rub against my exposed arms as I weed among the very crowns themselves.

Strawberries are relatively easy to grow, and varieties have been developed that will do well in any of the lower 48 states. Strawberries are of two main kinds: June—or single-crop—berries, and everbearers. Depending on climate and variety, one-crop berries produce from early May through the end of June. Their advantage is that a lot of berries come off at once for ease in processing, and most varieties are bred for large size and good keeping and shipping qualities. Their disadvantage is that they all come off at once, and further, that they are not always of the best flavor. Some gardeners grow them especially for processing, but more grow two crop or everbearers.

Everbearing strawberries, as the name suggests (usually stretching the point) produce berries continuously from spring throughout the summer. Actually many of them begin with a strong first crop, which subsequently dwindles through the hot weather and then builds up again in late summer. By a large margin, the first crop is usually the most productive of the season. A few everbearers are called "day neutral," meaning that the length of day—which causes the sporadic production of many varieties—has practically no influence on determining the period of production, and they really do produce continually all season.

Gardeners differ in their preferences, although those with limited space usually choose everbearers over single-crop berries for the obvious reasons. Whatever pattern of production you choose, you should consult authorities about what does well locally. I grow only everbearers, usually several varieties at a time. Four varieties—two rather standard and two less common—do well over a wide range of climates. The Ogallala has a rather long season of production, and the berries have a fine flavor. Another adaptable berry, the Ozark Beauty, is especially large, but the flavor is not as fine as the Ogallala. Both varieties are widely offered. A recent introduction, the Quinault, is said to grow anywhere. It has a particularly sweet flavor and a long season, but the berry is somewhat soft and not good for freezing. The Tilicum is a new variety. The fruit is not especially large, but is extremely flavorful. It is day neutral, and for me produces evenly all summer and fall, until the weather turns cold. Although similar in type, the berry is more firm than that of the Quinault. If I could grow only one berry, it would be the Tilicum. Since both Quinault and Tilicum are recent developments, they are not always easy to locate. Both are offered by *Peaceful Valley Farm Supply,* and a few other Western nurseries.

A "wild" strawberry, usually under the name Alpine strawberry, is offered by a number of catalogues. It is commonly propagated by seeds; plants are sometimes offered, but they are outrageously expensive. They are advertised to produce berries the first year from seed, but they never have for me. The Alpine berry has been developed from European wild varieties and has some of the unique flavor of wild strawberries. The berry is small, sharply cone-shaped, and very seedy. Some people object both to their small size and their seediness, maintaining they aren't worth the trouble.

If beginning with seed, plant them indoors in mid-February and transplant to single peat pots when they have about three leaves. Set outside, pots and all, the time of the last frost. Set them about 12 inches apart. They form compact, somewhat upright plants, and never put out runners. The plants are attractive, and bloom over a long period of time. Some people use them as an ornamental border. *Yankee Peddler Herb and Health Farm* offers other varieties of wild strawberries.

Regular strawberries are always started from plants grown from runners. Usually they are set out in the spring but are sometimes planted in the fall. Plants are commonly sold in bundles of one or two dozen, bare rooted. If they cannot be planted immediately, keep them cool, and do not let them dry out. Set the plant in the row exactly as deep as it had been growing. If planted too deep, the crown will rot; if too shallow, the exposed roots will dry out, and if the plant does not die, it will never be properly healthy. Space the plants in the row about 16 inches apart, with 36 inches between rows. During the course of the summer the plants will put out runners that soon fill up between the hills, and across the rows if not pruned. Commercial growers often plant on hills a foot or more high, cultivating to train the runners to grow and cover either side of the hill.

Strawberries need plenty of moisture, but too much water can cause crown rot and other maladies, as well as causing the berries to mildew. By all means make sure that the area for a new planting is weed-free, especially free of noxious perennial weeds. Once a planting is established it is not easy to keep weeds under control. Plant the berries in enriched soil, but thereafter restrict fertilizing to autumn; otherwise the berries will likely be soft, and the plants will put on excess foliage at the expense of crops.

Frequently one reads instructions advising that during the first year all flowers should be picked off to direct the plant's energy to growth, to make it provide a higher yield the second year. Although this might sound like a good idea, I have never tried it. I am always anxious to see what a new variety of berries will be like and consider the small first-year's crop my due anyway. It has always seemed to me that the berries do fine the second year anyway, unless something more catastrophic hits them.

A strawberry patch usually peaks about its third year, and then gradually productivity falls off. After five years most likely it has seen its best. Many people plan a regular rotation of their strawberry patches, preparing a new planting a year before removing an old bed.

Oddments

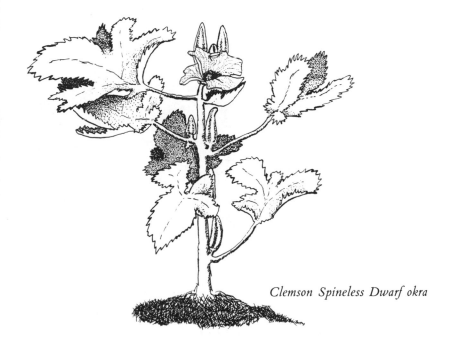

Clemson Spineless Dwarf okra

There is a wide assortment of crops that everyone, or nearly everyone, is at least nominally familiar with. There is another catchall category of things that are unfamiliar, or only regionally familiar, or familiar as a grocery store item but not as a garden item. It is always interesting to try crops normally considered beyond the possibilities of the local climate, or simply forgotten as a garden item. In any region, gardeners may be moved to try something because it is different and no one else seems to be interested in it.

Northern gardeners usually do not consider peanuts a possibility, even though they are grown more or less successfully as a garden crop in most of the northern climates. There are several varieties that are advertised as particularly hardy. The growing seasons required vary

189

from 125 to 150 days. If standard watermelons mature in your area you can likely mature peanuts as well.

There are two main varieties of peanuts, bushing and vining, although most of the cultivars suitable for growing in the northern areas seem to be the bushing varieties. They prefer a light soil, partially sandy even, and do not prosper or set nuts well in a heavy loam. Plant them about the same time as beans, in loosely tilled soil about 6 to 8 inches apart. They may be planted hulled or unhulled, but if they are hulled, take care not to break the brown husk protecting the individual kernels. In my experience they have been slow to germinate. They like warm weather and only begin vigorous growth when summer temperatures arrive.

The plant itself is especially attractive, very green and bushy, with a large leaf that resembles an oversized clover. Because they have shallow, spreading roots, cultivate them with care, treating them about the same way beans are treated. Like beans, peanut plants do not want to have their roots disturbed. The nuts form in a most curious fashion; they develop underground from blossoms pollinated in the air. The blossoms appear on stems on the lower portion of the plants, droop, and the fertilized ovary—"peg"—forces its way underground, where the nut develops and matures. In the fall, when the bushes begin to die down and the nuts are thoroughly formed, dig and dry them bush and all. Sometimes peanuts are dried on racks in the field. If allowed to remain on the ground they will mold or mildew, particularly if the weather is damp. A small crop can be dried indoors, or however the gardener finds it convenient.

Usually the nuts are roasted briefly in an oven before eating, although in the southern states they are often eaten raw. They are also dug green or immature in the South and eaten raw or cooked pods and all in soups or stews, or as a green vegetable.

Peanuts are familiar regionally as goobers or goober peas, which carries an interesting historical significance. Peanuts as a crop were popularized as a cheap and nutritious slave food in the early days of slavery in this country. Although peanuts originated in the New World, probably in the Caribbean, they were cultivated in Africa very early, then reintroduced to North America as a novelty. The word *goober* is African in origin, most likely from the Bantu or Swahili dialect.

Another crop introduced as a food for slaves is okra. This plant did originate in tropical Africa and was brought to the United States by slave traders. Its popular regional name—gumbo—is African in origin. The word is more often applied to cooked dishes containing okra than to the plant or its fruits. Because of the mucilaginous nature of the seed pods, gummy or sticky soil that is slow to dry is still called "gumbo," or "gumbo mud." Although okra is familiar as the essential ingredient of gumbo soup, many people in northern areas are not acquainted with it as a vegetable in its own right and may never have seen a pod of okra. The plant is of the mallow family, producing green pods that are filled with numerous round seeds about the size of BB shot. Depending on variety, the pods may develop to 6 or 7 inches, although in northern climates they do not usually reach more than 2 or 3 inches. The pods are cooked whole or, particularly when cooked in gumbo soup, cut into short pieces. They are added to green beans (traditionally, shelly beans cooked with ham) for a typical one-pot Southern dish. Sometimes they are coated with egg batter and rolled in flour and fried, usually sliced lengthwise. Although they are a useful ingredient in combination dishes, some people find that cooked alone their characteristic stickiness is unattractive and unpalatable.

While thought of primarily as a southern crop, okra does well enough in most northern gardens. There are several varieties, particularly dwarfs, that have been developed for colder climates that are offered by most seed catalogues. Plant okra about the same time as beans, after the weather gets settled and the soil warmed. Plant them thinly in rows, about half an inch deep, and firm the soil over them. When the plants are an inch high, thin them to 8 inches apart. Tall varieties should be spaced at least twice that distance. Like peanuts, okra will not begin to grow vigorously until the weather turns thoroughly warm. They are a plant that enjoys *hot* weather, provided they are supplied with sufficient moisture.

Depending on the variety planted and the climate, some cultivars of okra may grow as tall as 6 feet. Most of the varieties grown in the northern area are much more modest, making small bushes up to 2 or

3 feet high. The plants themselves are undistinguished in appearance. I always think they look like shabby weeds. The pods must be picked while still immature (the seeds inside well formed but pulpy soft); if allowed to become overmature the pods become fibrous and the seeds unpleasantly chewy. If the pods are kept picked, the plants will continue blooming and producing even in northern regions, up until frost.

Rhubarb is quite familiar, but since it fits no particular category and is sufficiently odd this seems a good place to discuss it. Its most appealing quality is its earliness, which is probably why it seems to have been more important to our ancestors than it is to us. When, along with asparagus and mustard, it was one of the earliest fresh crops to be had, it is easy to understand its popularity a few generations ago.

The plant itself is attractive, although somewhat greedy of the space it occupies. A single mature plant may overgrow a space 5 feet or more in diameter. Since it is a perennial, obviously a permanent location somewhat isolated from the mainstream of the garden must be provided. It likes full sun but will tolerate a little shade. A corner that is otherwise awkward to cultivate is ideal. My rhubarb is just inside the garden line next to a row of hazelnuts, a zone that gets too little sun for most garden crops, but plenty for weeds if they were not blocked by the rhubarb. Rhubarb is a good crop to be planted along fences, or even as an accent point in a flower bed.

It is possible but pointless to grow rhubarb from seed; the quality of seedlings is often erratic. Almost always rhubarb is propagated from a clump of roots purchased from a nursery or borrowed from an agreeable friend. Plant the root with the "eyes" about 2 inches below the surface. If more than one root is planted, space them about 4 feet apart. Remember that one well-established plant produces a lot of rhubarb, and a little goes a long way.

Rhubarb is principally harvested in the early spring. The heavy leaf stems develop quickly and reach a good size before the leaves themselves have much size. To harvest, twist the stem gently, and it will easily detach from the rootstock. If the stem is cut rather than pulled, the plant will be slow to replace it with fresh growth. The leaf itself is poisonous, but it is highly unlikely that anyone or anything would ever eat enough of one to be harmed. However, during World War I, an agency of the British government promoted cooking rhubarb leaves as a green to help conserve more critical food for the war effort. For obedience to this suggestion of their government a number of citizens died.

The stems are used for a variety of purposes. Their tart, pleasant flavor is attractive eaten raw (in small quantities). Children, for some reason, find rhubarb in the early spring almost irresistible. The two or three clumps I grow are principally for children to munch on. Probably the most popular preparation is to cut the stems into segments and cook and serve as a sauce. Rhubarb is also often made into pies, sometimes in mixtures of other fruits, such as strawberries. A common country name for rhubarb, in fact, is "pie plant."

For earliest production rhubarb is sometimes forced. For this purpose the roots are dug in late fall and for a couple of weeks allowed exposure to freezing temperature. Taken inside and deprived of light in a cool cellar or similar environment, the root will put out leaf stems in a month or so. These stems will be pale red, the leaves small and yellow, vestigial or even not there at all. Usually a second, and sometimes a third, crop of stems will be grown by the root before it gives up. The flavor of forced rhubarb is milder and less acid than field-grown rhubarb, and for those reasons is preferred by many people. Some early rhubarb of commerce is forced rather than field grown.

Our familiar garden rhubarb probably derives from an Asian species, or perhaps from a hybridization of Asian species. The rhubarb of medieval medicine was a similar but different species. Its acrid juice was used to purge rheum—that is, to open up the sinuses, clear the nasal passages, and induce the coughing up of phlegm. The dried root, or rhizome, was used for a laxative and as a stomach tonic. These European species were not, however, used for pies.

Salsify is a good plant to be enthusiastic about. Not to eat: to be enthusiastic about. It is frequently ebulliently described as a marvelous garden vegetable. The reason it is overlooked by many gardeners is that it has relatively little to recommend other than its ease of growth. It is an annual (sometimes perennial) that is cultivated for its root. The long, slim, white root, reaching the diameter of a slender carrot, is cooked in various ways—boiled, baked, fried, and in soups—and its flavor is said to resemble that of oysters, from which comes one of its common names, "oyster plant." But as was said of near beer, the man who named it was a very poor judge of distance. Frankly, salsify is not a very distinguished food plant, although avidly grown at least once or twice by some.

The seed is planted sparingly in mid-spring in a shallow trench, covered lightly and tamped. When the seedlings are showing their first true leaves, thin to about 3 inches apart. They may be harvested whenever the root is sufficiently developed to be worthwhile—at least the diameter of a pencil. If allowed to mature, they produce a single yellow blossom on the top of a 16-inch-long stem. The blossom matures into a seed head like a giant dandelion, with stiff little "parachutes" nearly 2 inches long attached to each seed. The appearance of the seed head gives rise to another popular name for the plant, "goat's beard." As with dandelions, these feathered seeds provide an unstoppable means of dispersal, and in some areas salsify is so widely distributed as to have become a serious weed pest.

An interesting plant to grow as a treat for children is sorghum, also called sorghum cane. This distant cousin of the corn family is usually associated with warm climates, but does well enough for casual purposes in cold areas. It is grown for its stems, which have a high sugar content, and is the raw material for molasses, also known as "treacle," "sorghum," or "larup." The seed head, if allowed to mature, produces a millet-sized kernel that makes good bird or poultry feed. The seeds grow attached to a brownish whisk at the top of each cane, where the tassel of corn would be found, if indeed it were corn.

Thinly plant the seeds in a row after the weather begins to settle, about the same time as corn is planted. When a couple of inches high, the plants should be thinned to no less than 4 inches. In their early growth the plants much resemble corn, having the same fibrous, jointed stalks, with long, flat leaves somewhat more slender than corn leaves. The stem itself may have a purplish to reddish cast.

In the few home gardens where sorghum is grown, individual canes are "harvested" as wanted, anytime after they are 2 or 3 feet tall, cut into segments, and chewed for their sweet, molasses-flavored juice. The stalks get sweeter as the summer progresses and they reach maturity. Indeed, growing sorghum helps stimulate interest in gardens and gardening in children. It is, of course, possible to crush the stalks for their juice, which when boiled down to a thick consistency makes molasses. The process is not at all difficult, if one can contrive an economical means of extraction. It is hardly likely to be worth it for most gardeners, but occasional small plantings are fun. Seed is fairly hard to find, but is available from *R. H. Shumway Seedsmen.*

Artichokes are an interesting plant to grow, but in areas other than the select climatic regions where they are grown commercially, the "fruits" are a disappointment. It is the base of the bud scales and succulent interior of the bud that is eaten and, except under choice conditions of soil, temperature, and humidity, these parts of the bud tend to be thin and of little succulence. Nevertheless, the artichoke is an attractive plant to grow, like sorghum, just for the fun of it. The buds, if not picked, and if frost does not come too soon, turn into a pretty purple flower, looking like gigantic thistle blossoms. They mature into a showy seed head with a dense cylinder of long white spikelets. These seed heads are frequently featured in dried winter arrangements, and the plant may be deemed worth growing for that purpose alone. Sometimes a single plant is cultivated as an accent point in a flower bed.

Artichokes may be planted from rootstocks or from seeds. Better plants are obtained from rootstocks, but these may be more difficult to find than seeds, which are offered by most mail-order houses. The plant is a tall perennial, with spreading habits. Therefore, a location that can be spared from cultivation for a couple of years at least (or until you get tired of the project) should be selected. Rootstocks are planted in early spring or fall, although in colder climates it is preferable to plant in spring. Set the stocks about 6 inches deep, and about 4 feet apart each way. Unless you have confidence that the heads grown in your area will be edible, one or two plants should satisfy your curiosity. I have started artichokes only from seeds, seeding an area about the size of a dinner plate with a dozen or fifteen seeds, lightly covered with soil and loosely packed. When the seedlings had developed their first true leaves I thinned the area to three, and then, when they were 6 or 8 inches across, to one per hill. If the crop does not turn out to be a feast, just enjoy the plants and let the buds turn into blossoms. Their heavy grayish-green foliage resembles that of an enormous thistle, although despite their appearance they are not especially thorny.

Where the climate is severe, a good heavy mulch after the foliage has frosted down will help protect the roots over the winter. Most likely the plants will not fruit until their second year. If a clump becomes too congested, it may be thinned and separated, with cuttings to spare to give to artichoke-less friends.

Eggplant, which the English call aubergine (it would probably be more popular with them if they used our common name), is a member of the nightshade family native to Asia. Its fruit is so outrageously large that it is downright preposterous; the eggplant seems counter to all known natural laws. From rather modest (1½- to 3-foot) bushes grow immense deep purple fruit, regularly 8 to 10 inches long, and often longer. When I see a small bush with several of these outsized fruits hanging from its middle (often resting their bases on the ground) I'm reminded of a bantam hen hovering over a clutch of goose eggs.

The eggplant is an annual that thrives on hot weather but is not especially difficult to grow in northern as well as southern climates. Usually seedlings are obtained from a nursery for transplanting, or started early by the gardener indoors. Since they are quite sensitive to cold, seedlings may not be set out until the weather becomes thoroughly settled. Plant them from 18 to 24 inches apart. Further care is similar to that of their cousins, the tomatoes. Eggplants make their best growth during hot weather, and during coolish periods seem sulky. A medium-sized purplish blossom resembling the bloom of the potato plant (another kin) is followed by the development of the large, bulb-shaped fruit. There are dwarf varieties that develop smaller fruit, typically more cylindrical than bulbous, and these varieties are sometimes preferred by northern gardeners for their relative earliness. Actually, since for me the size and elegance of the fruit is their main attraction, I plant the larger variety. An especially beautiful variety is the White Beauty *(Gleckler's Seedsmen),* which weighs up to four pounds, and has an especially mild flavor. The Pink Bride *(Gleckler's Seedsmen)* bears clusters of slender, small fruits, striped violet and white. For dependability of yield the Japanese eggplant is a better choice for cool climates. The Japanese Early Black Eggplant *(Territorial Seed Company),* about 6 inches long, is shaped like the popular American varieties, and matures in about 75 days. The *Ichiban,* a long slender Japanese variety, is commonly available.

The fruit is picked when it is from 6 inches or so long or when fully mature, as preferred. Egg-shaped varieties will be glossy when mature, while the Japanese varieties will be rather dull and lusterless. While the eggplant is not a fruit with a pronounced individual flavor, it adapts well in a variety of dishes in which it takes on the characteristic flavor of other ingredients. It is good sliced thin, dipped in an egg batter and fried, or casseroled, especially with various cheese combinations. It may be split or hollowed and stuffed with various meat mixtures. Eggplant also figures in a number of Mediterranean and Near East recipes. As interesting, and as good as the fruits are, most gardeners find their needs, gastronomic as well as aesthetic, are taken care of with no more than six plants, each of which will produce from one or two to five or six fruits in a good summer. Using a mean figure of three, six plants will provide an eggplant dish for eighteen meals. During the period of production, that gives eggplant every other day. And it is competing with the myriad of other good things of August and September. For practical purposes, six plants is plenty, but eggplant is pretty enough to grow more.

The popularity of eating mushrooms seems to increase almost as fast as this fungus grows, but still few people grow mushrooms themselves. Catalogues offer preplanted packages of spawn and growing medium, which is bought mostly as an oddity. Many catalogues also offer bricks of spawn, which must be planted in a growing medium the gardener must prepare. But for most gardeners, except for trying one of the novelty packages or taking a flier at trying to make spawn grow, growing mushrooms is a mystery—and too much trouble anyway. However, there is a recent introduction that really is a practical option. Called Garden Giant *(Stropharia rugosoannulata),* it may be grown in common garden mulch. There are many possibilities, but I planted the spawn in the heavily mulched raised bed of my blueberry row. All summer the bed produced—not profusely, but regularly— large purplish-red mushrooms, attractive and piquant. Use them like any supermarket mushroom, although some people may be put off by the color if eating them raw in a salad. If the level of mulch material is kept renewed, as they must be in a blueberry planting, the mushroom can be considered a garden perennial. The spawn comes in a large package of moist straw, which is planted in cud-sized wads under the surface of the mulch. Keep the medium moist. Spawn is offered by *Raintree Nursery.* This is the only easy and practical way to grow mushrooms that I know really works.

Celery is a vegetable nearly everyone uses but few gardeners plant. It has a deserved reputation for being a picky plant to grow. It likes rich soil that has good water-retaining qualities (but not a heavy clay). It is a cool weather plant that does especially well in a climate with coolish or dampish summers, but most varieties are frost sensitive. Seeds may be started indoors, or seedlings bought from a nursery. Transplant when they are about 2 inches high. Since celery is sensitive to heat, it is best to transplant the seedlings on a coolish or overcast day and protect them for a couple of days if the weather turns hot. Use lots of water and thoroughly "puddle in" the seedlings when transplanting, and take care in days to follow that they are never allowed to dry out. A good clue to celery's preferred growing medium is the common name given to it where celery is grown commercially, "celery muck." The plants should be kept well fertilized, giving them a side dressing of fertilizer every couple of weeks during the time of heavy and rapid growth. If not consistently fertilized, they will probably pout all summer and be next to worthless.

A pungent wild celery—smallage—was widely used in Europe before modern celery was developed. Seed for it is uncommon, but is offered by a few seed houses, including *Gleckler's Seedsmen.*

Some people prefer their celery blanched, that is, to make the main parts of the stems lighter in color by protecting it from direct sunlight. I have found that half-gallon milk cartons with the bottoms removed make a convenient blanching aid. Slip one over each plant after it is tall enough so that the leaves protrude several inches over the top of the carton.

Celery may be picked anytime if it is large enough. Cut the base of the plant free of its roots just below the surface of the soil. If kept in a cool place, the whole plant will remain crisp and good for some time. Celery may also be dug in the autumn, roots and all, and stored with the roots packed in damp soil (for example, in a tub or box) in a cool basement. The soil packing should never be allowed to dry out. Managed in this way the plants may remain good for many weeks. An unusual European variety offered by *Nichols Garden Nursery* is the

Golden Self-Blanching, early at 115 days. The same nursery offers French Celery Dinant, which has many thin stalks and an especially full flavor, which makes it particularly suitable for seasoning. It is also said to be good dried.

Occasionally gardeners, particularly those who are interested in subsistence gardening, but also those with a particular orientation toward natural foods, become interested in growing wheat or other small cereal grains. Here is a point at which I would inject a note of pessimism. Not that these grains cannot be grown—and with reasonable ease at that—but they are crops that are awkward and unsatisfactory on a small scale. As grown commercially, grains are sowed or drilled in rows 6 to 12 inches apart. The blades of the growing grain need each other's mutual support and protection to remain upright and healthy. For the small garden the volume just isn't worth it. These small cereal grains must present the exception to the rule—probably the grain is best and cheapest obtained from commercial sources.

Weeds: The Thieves of Time

Dandelion

Emerson's observation that a weed is a plant for which we have not yet discovered a use was a pungent and stimulating epigram until overquoted by those too conspicuously sensitive to nature. Taken literally, as too many do, there's enough saccharinity in that remark to candy a stalk of rhubarb. If you can't hate weeds, what can you hate? Practically, if a significant use were found for, say, wild morning glory, our experience as human beings as well as our experience as gardeners would cynically assure us that immediately a morning glory beetle, morning glory blight, Japanese morning glory smut, and western morning glory root nematodes would appear and make morning glory too temperamental to grow without a resident advisor from a state agricultural college. If discovered it could cure cancer, no doubt it would only be grown in petri dishes in a laboratory.

Desist from trying to think positively about wild morning glory. The wealth of common names this *weed* has earned affirm its detestability. In America it is commonly called wild morning glory or bind weed. The English call it, among other names, "devil's garter," "bearbind," "hell weed," "ropewind," and "devil's guts." There are numerous other names for it, here and abroad, confirming universal agreement that it is genuinely nasty.

The wild morning glory climbs if it can, creeps if it must, but flourishes under conditions adverse or advantageous. In heavy infestations it will cover the ground with a living carpet (almost visibly undulating) 6 or more inches thick, to the exclusion of all else. The roots of the plant are white or yellowish white, thicker than a match, many branched, and wide spreading. Experts say they go down as far as 15 to 20 feet and estimate that where it is growing unchecked, there will be several tons of the root per acre. An entire plant may be regenerated from the smallest segment; plowing or spading tends more to spread it than to control it, and I've never heard of a stand being wiped out or even harmed by plowing or cultivation of any form.

Furthermore, each plant produces 500 to 600 seeds annually, which may live ungerminated in the ground for years. Fortunately, a newly sprouted seedling, easily recognized by its heart-shaped first true leaves, *can* be wiped out simply by cultivation. When it establishes a root system, it cannot.

Eradicating wild morning glory has assumed among gardeners almost a mystique. It is possible to kill it by smothering, such as covering the ground for a season with sheets of black plastic. Lay the plastic in early spring, fastening it to the ground to keep it from blowing away with wire clips made from coat hangers, or any suitably heavy wire, or with mounds and ridges of earth (which tend to loosen with time and allow the plastic to blow away anyway). The following spring the plants should be dead, but watch for seedlings. Unfailingly they will keep popping up for years, perhaps unto the biblical seventh generation.

A dense covering of extra-heavy organic mulch, such as straw or rotted hay, will smother the roots if heavy enough and left on long enough. Apply it in the fall, to a depth of no less than 6 inches, and add more in the early spring. It is possible to grow a garden through this mulch as a standard no-till procedure, but if so, some morning glory will survive. If the land continues to be used as a garden probably several years will be required for complete destruction of the roots, although effective control should be attained after a couple of years. I have seen it killed where a haystack had stood on it for a year, but this is too impractical to be recognized as a procedure.

Hoeing morning glory will give the immediate satisfaction of doing physical violence to this arrogant weed, and the temporary satisfaction of seeing it gone for a couple of days, but even the most persistent hoeing is nothing but a delaying tactic. There is so much vitality stored into the massive root system that the plant can happily rejuvenate all summer, and with a moment's negligence burst into blossom, with plenty of energy left to do it all over again the follow-ing spring. Believing that if one continually hoes off morning glory eventually it has to be eradicated illustrates the same fallacy as believing that if one picks up a calf every day from the moment of its birth one will still be able to pick it up when it's a 2,200-pound bull. Hoe for revenge, or out of frustration, but don't hope for long-range control.

When the ground is spaded or roto-tilled in the spring, the thick white roots will be readily visible, turned up in the soil. They can be picked out, collected, and destroyed. I always feel compulsive about doing this, but it doesn't appreciably reduce an infestation. I have heard—and this is strictly in the realm of folklore and folk custom— that when the roots are dug during the season of a full moon they will wither and die. I have never experimented with this, and merely pass it on as an anecdote.

Most common herbicides are ineffective in combatting morning glory, inflicting only superficial damage. Although it may be an un-satisfactory solution for some gardeners, herbicides have been devel-oped recently that are effective in killing this weed and will sometimes do it with one spraying. These herbicides are nonpersistent, but do require careful handling. They may appear under a variety of trade names, so inquire for them at local nursery and supply stores, and if uneasy about their safety, make inquiry of agricultural extension agents. I have used them, and they work, and I have seen no undesirable side effects.

In all fairness to this despicable weed, I have heard, or rather read, a couple of good words about it, complete with pictures. One author extolled its virtues as a living mulch when left to its own devices in the garden. It was extremely effective, he claimed, in keeping down noxious weeds! A photograph showed a luxurious growth of at least 6 inches covering a garden, through which struggled unidentifiable—presumably vegetable—growths. Besides keeping down weeds, this article praised the value of morning glory as a mulch to keep in moisture. A different author in another article favorable to morning glory suggested that the immense and intricate root system was valuable in attaching and bringing to the surface nutrients deeply buried in the soil. To paraphrase the famous *New Yorker* cartoon: "I still say it's a weed, and I still say 'To hell with it!' "

An interested party will go far before he finds a good word said about quack grass. This curious name's etymology is a simple sound change from "couch grass." The root system of quack grass consists of an intertwining complex of stoloniferous roots. Segments of the roots are in effect similar to rhizomes, and each of the segments of the many branches may root and send up new plants if separated from the main plant. Or, as I once heard it expressed, "Before you can look twice, it's "stolon" over and rooted itself in half your field." The roots of established growths of quack grass are impossible to pull, unless growing in the loosest sort of mulch. The segments that break off in the ground will quickly send up blades and reestablish themselves. Like morning glory, it can be hoed off at the surface all summer without destroying the plant. If uncontrolled, quack grass will bed the soil of large areas in almost impenetrable masses of roots. It is especially persistent and debilitating to growth in such permanent plantings as berries. In a few years quack grass roots may become so densely matted that only with difficulty can a sharp shovel be forced into the ground. It has been suggested that the growing roots may produce a toxin that inhibits the growth of other plants.

Spading and turning the sod over is virtually futile, unless the roots are carefully removed, shaken out, and destroyed. Fortunately, unlike wild morning glory, the roots are relatively shallow—ten to

12 inches—and it is possible, although with a great deal of tedious labor, to remove them from small areas by hand. A spading fork is probably more efficient than a shovel. To succeed the operative word is *patience;* the soil must be sifted almost handful by handful to break loose and remove all the roots. Inevitably (unless the earth is actually screened) some stolons—the regenerative root stems—will be missed, but with careful attention they are not difficult to pull from the finely tilled earth when they begin to sprout.

Quack grass resists the effects of most conventional herbicides. Like morning glory, quack grass may be killed by smothering; the same techniques are used to kill both weeds. More practical and better, as far as I am concerned, are the same family of new herbicides that kill morning glory. When these herbicides are used against a heavy infestation of quack grass, the resulting dead roots in the soil deliver an actual benefit to the gardener. As they break down and decay, they form a superb organic layer in the top inches of the soil. In fact, killing a patch of quack grass makes an ideal beginning to a no-till garden. A friend who tried this said the results were so satisfactory it would almost seem an advantage to start by planting the field to quack grass. I think he was exaggerating a little, or he's no true friend of mine.

Chickweed is an astonishing plant. Unlike quack grass and wild morning glory, it has an unimpressive root system. It is actually much easier to pull than most weeds, although if the slightest bit of the top bud remains attached to the roots in the ground, it will regenerate. Unlike the conventional mental image of a weed, it is a moderately attractive plant. With its dense masses of small but lush green leaves and tiny flowers, and particularly its ability to flourish in chilly weather, it contributes a welcome touch of greenery to the garden as the snow melts back. It continues to grow in the winter except during the harshest weather. It is astonishingly prolific, capable of producing three generations of plants in a year. A plant may mature seeds five to seven weeks after it has itself first germinated, and in its life may mature up to 15,000 seeds. Theoretically, in a year's time, if all the seeds from one plant were to germinate and survive and mature seeds themselves, the total progeny could exceed 15,000 *million* plants. In two years, even Archimedes with his longest lever and firmest place to stand couldn't move the biomass. The seeds themselves are nearly indestructible, and chickweed's hardiness and versatility has spread the range of this weed from the arctics to the tropics.

Chickweed is something you can learn to live with because it can be kept within bounds by normal hand cultivation—hoeing and pulling. But apparently it will always be with us, waiting for a moment of neglect to take over a spot in the garden with its disarmingly lush greenness. Chickens, by the way, enjoy it, and in early spring I always fill wheel barrows with it, which I have shaved from the garden and waste spots to feed the greens-starved hens. A sprig or two during the winter months is a welcome treat to caged birds. And it is certainly cheaper than lettuce and celery to feed such small animals as guinea pigs. But don't forget that it is a weed and spiritually rotten to the core.

The plantain is another weed that was introduced from Europe which is occasionally troublesome. If we can trust undocumented traditions, American Indians called it a name that meant "white man's footprints," because its spread followed the westward incursions of white settlers in America, and because its large leaves, lying flat to the ground, with a little imagination do resemble footprints made by shod feet. It is a biennial, sometimes perennial, and is most likely to be troublesome in lawns. Its long taproots secure it in place, and its flat, tough leaves smother the grass and produce unsightly irregularities. In general, it is not terribly troublesome. Possibly here is an example of a case in which a weed's uses may be undiscovered, or perhaps only neglected. Traditionally, poultices made of the crushed leaves or their juice (the leaves are quite stiff and niggardly in yielding up their juice) are reputed to be effective in relieving the pain of insect bites and burns. It has been conjectured that the plantain was introduced deliberately by early settlers for such supposed therapeutic value.

Another weed whose time may be coming is the amaranth, otherwise more commonly known as pigweed, or red root (hence its name, amaranth, or deep purple). Unlike the other weeds mentioned, pigweeds are a New World plant, and their spread northward from their origin in South America was probably assisted by man. Before the coming of the Spanish, the weed was widely grown in Mexico and South America as a food seed. On ceremonial occasions figures made with dried human blood and amaranth flour were eaten by Aztec priests, which so offended Spanish sensibilities that they outlawed its cultivation. Recent research indicates the seeds contain a protein form especially valuable for people who live on a near-vegetarian diet, as did the Aztec. Suppressing this food possibly did severe dietary harm to those native inhabitants and, to an extent unrealized, assisted in the Spaniards' rapid subjugation of that noble civilization.

Recent investigation and experimentation hold promise for resuscitating the amaranth family. Giant strains of South American ancestry are being experimented with, producing favorable reports on the yield of seed and for the possible food uses of the seeds. Enthusiasts extol the value of the leaves of the common pigweed as well as the giant varieties of amaranth as a food, both cooked and raw. Be cautious, however: I have learned to mistrust the genuine edibility of plants for which cooking instructions include draining the liquid two or three times to reduce unpalatable flavors. As a garden pest, the half-pint cousin of amaranth, the common and ubiquitous pigweed, is not especially noisome. While the seedlings sprout prolifically, they are easily eradicated by hoeing or hand weeding. The inevitable few that are overlooked can be pulled, and there is nothing at all persistent about their root system.

The most visible of the Old World imports is the dandelion. If they know the etymology of no other word, or even what "etymology" means, all schoolchildren know that "dandelion" is an Anglicization of the French *dent de lion*—or "lion's tooth," in reference to the ragged outer fringe of the leaves. Less familiar and even surprising to Americans are some of the other names the weed goes by in its European homeland, most of which reflect its reputation as an herbal specific for the kidneys. Common names in England include "potty herb" and "pee-a-bed," translating the French *pissenlit*. Whether this is really its effect, or only its reputation, I have not been able to trace definitively.

With its deep-root system and particular botanical habits, a dandelion takes from the soil more iron than any other plant, as well as appreciable quantities of other trace minerals. Consequently, it has unusually high nutritional potential. It is among the top plants as a source of vitamins A and C as well. Unfortunately, many people do not find its flavor very appealing. For those who do, it is eaten both raw and cooked, especially the early spring growths. Roots may be dug in the fall and forced in bins of sand in a warm cellar or basement, and the forced leaves used as a salad ingredient. In fact, seed for improved varieties of dandelion are offered by some seed houses for culinary purposes.

Probably the dandelion was first introduced into this country deliberately, both as an herb and as a vegetable. As a weed, however, the dandelion poses a double threat. Not only does it take nutrients and moisture from the soil, as do other weeds, but the leaves exude ethylene gas, which literally snuffs the life from the grass it is competing with. This helps account for how tiny dandelion seedlings germinate and thrive in a dense lawn.

In comparison to the real terrors, dandelions are not difficult to control. In the garden they can be killed by deep and persistent hoeing, especially the young seedlings, before they are strongly established. They may be killed in a lawn by deeply cutting beneath the turf with a knife or other tool (the unsightly circle of dead grass that the ethylene gas has killed will grow back in good time). They are easily killed with a variety of herbicides. Infestations in a lawn can be easily controlled by applications of the so-called "weed and feed" lawn fertilizers. Of course when I say "easily controlled," the term is relative. Other perennials are so much more troublesome that, when speaking of dandelions, the word *easily* comes readily to the tongue.

There is some confusion about the names of the various thistles. The two chief weed varieties are the Canadian thistle and the bull thistle, and although their names are sometimes interchanged, they are quite different in habits and reproduction. Properly, the Canadian— which among other names is called locally "sow thistle," and which originated in Europe—is a perennial that reproduces both by wind-blown seeds and by creeping roots. A single seed may establish a colony that can quickly take over a large area of ground. Many states have passed laws establishing that this thistle is illegal, but somehow this information has not sifted down to the vegetative world where it thrives. The thistle is of medium height (about 3 to 4 feet), aggressive, difficult to handle because of its sharp spines, and difficult to eradicate because of its spreading roots. The roots may be dug up bodily and destroyed with dubious effectiveness, but the best control is by the application of appropriate herbicides.

The bull thistle (of Eurasian origin) is sometimes erroneously called a Canadian thistle. It is a larger and ranker plant, however, and is a biennial rather than a perennial. It reproduces only by seed, and does not have the proliferating root system of the Canadian thistle. While it can be a pest, if individual plants are cut off below the crown the plant usually dies, and no further plants from that root system need be contended with. If there is a heavy infestation, for example where the land has been little tended for some time, such as along fences, herbicides may be used efficiently. The seeds in the soil are long-lived, and seedlings will continue to sprout for a long time. Also seeds from thistles may be expected continuously to blow in on their highly efficient thistledown from long distances; the only means of control where they are a problem is vigilance.

The word *nightshade* has an ominous and foreboding connotation. Easily and almost automatically *deadly* creeps in front as a natural or bound part of the word. However, this large family produces some of our most familiar vegetables: tomatoes, potatoes, eggplants, and peppers are family members and the kinship is easily identifiable through the blossoms and fruits, and even the stems and foliage reveal family ties. The leaves and stems of all these cultivated vegetables, by the way, are unwholesome, if not downright poisonous, although there is little likelihood that any of them might be eaten in fatal quantity.

Several of the nightshades are common garden weeds. They are mostly annuals, and are not difficult to control, although their ominous reputations attach to them a sinister connotation other weeds are spared. They require no program of control more ambitious than pulling and hoeing. Since the seeds of the nightshades survive a long time in the soil, they will continue to germinate the full length of the summer, and this persistence will often pay off for them, resulting in a number of plants quietly maturing seeds, particularly under the concealment of their cousins, the tomatoes and the potatoes.

The nightshades are more troublesome to large-scale agriculture than to gardeners. Peas, for example, are about the same size (and color) as green nightshade berries. When harvested mechanically, the berries become mixed with the peas, and are difficult to separate. Since the berries are often poisonous when green, this presents a real problem to the commercial grower, but not one ever likely to trouble a gardener.

The renowned Luther Burbank in the beginning of this century tried to popularize what he claimed to be a newly developed annual berry to compete with blueberries, which he called a garden huckleberry. Apparently the great horticulturist was not above a little ballyhoo, if not outright charlatanism, because his claims were loudly attacked by a few horticulturists who challenged that this marvel was nothing but a variety of black nightshade that grew wild in a number of places. His counterblasts to the charges were none too convincing. What had started as a gardening sensation ended in a kind of horticultural scandal. Some editorial writers denounced the berry as a fraud. Maybe the writers were too hard on Burbank, because when considered botanically, other than the name nightshade there was nothing sinister about the berries. But then Burbank hadn't been exactly straight and level himself. He seems ultimately to have withdrawn from the controversy, but today a variety called "garden huckleberry" is still offered by seed catalogues. I have never grown it but have tasted the fruit; it is mildly sweet, bland in flavor, and not of much value as a blueberry or huckleberry surrogate. While it is closely related to black nightshade, this should no more concern a gardener than that tomatoes are also nightshades. The operative cautionary word is that they are not very good.

China lettuce, in spite of its name, is a weed of European import. A sometimes perennial, it is usually an annual. Its efficient system of spreading by windblown seeds makes it a persistent nuisance. It is a weed that continues to germinate all summer long, and if not diligently kept at bay will slyly mature a crop of seeds at a moment's negligence. It does have two curious characteristics that are worth noting. Unlike almost all plants, which are designed to present their leaves as flatly to the sun as possible, the leaves of China lettuce are aligned vertically to the sun. The leaves have a further peculiarity in that they tend to be arranged on the stalk so that they point north and south and east and west. These are most remarkable curiosities for such an unhandsome plant.

China lettuce is persevering and left unchecked can be a real nuisance, but with hoeing and pulling it can be kept under effective control. As the plants mature gloves should be worn when pulling them. While their thorns are not as tough and sharp as berry thorns, when the green thorns break off in the skin they are difficult to locate and remove. Since they don't fester, they may persist painfully for days. Livestock eats China lettuce with élan, but it is dangerous eaten in quantity; horses will quickly founder from eating it, and it can cause bloat and diarrhea in cattle.

A weed with a humble beginning and an arrogant and overbearing maturity is the common mallow. The white seeds clustered tightly together into a small wheel give the plant two of its common names—buttonweed and cheese weed, or cheeses. The seeds are reputed to be edible for anyone willing to take the trouble. They are able to survive in the soil and retain viability for a great length of time. As I heard one person express it, the time will never come when the supply of cheese weed seeds in the soil will be exhausted.

When the seedlings of cheese weed first appear, they are tiny and even insignificant and, except for being almost too small to get one's fingers on, are easy to get rid of. Soon, however, they put a white taproot deep into the soil, and are difficult to pull. They may be hoed off, but if any of the crown remains they will quickly rejuvenate. If neglected, by the end of the summer they reach monumental sizes never hinted at by their modest beginnings, and although the individual leaves are small, their sheer density will effectively smother most plants they compete with. I have seen individual plants more than 6 feet in diameter. Those plants not destroyed by them will be stunted and dwarfed into uselessness. Cheese weeds that are allowed to overwinter will spring to life at the first hint of spring, and will produce a crop of seeds before the first radishes mature. Hoeing and pulling will keep them under control. In one garden patch which had never been under cultivation until I planted it four years ago, tiny seedlings came up shoulder to shoulder and kept germinating at the same rate all summer. I am stunned that hoeing after hoeing, year after year, continues to be followed by a shoulder-to-shoulder resurgence of cheese weed seedlings. Every hoeing alerts a new generation of dormant seeds to trim their lamps, for the bridegroom cometh. And none have gone to seed in that area since I began planting it.

There are far too many weeds to consider all that flourish in the various parts of the United States. What may be a real pest in one part of the country may be an occasional stranger or real novelty in another. Perhaps strangest of all is the fact that most of the weeds we contend with in our gardens are imports from abroad—Europe, Asia, Eurasia, and points in between. Even cheat grass, which seems as Western as sagebrush, came in from Eurasia with seed of winter wheat. In the vegetable world as well as the moral and cultural, there appears to be truth to the traditional notion of the depraved Old World debauching the innocent New.

We might expect that a corresponding "courtesy" might have been extended from the New World to the Old, but surprisingly that is not the case. Weeds native to the New World are mostly quite rare in the Old. Whether a new species, from either the animal or the vegetable world, establishes itself in a new locale depends to a large extent on the competition at any given ecological level. We must assume, therefore, that the imported weeds from the Old World to the New found more unoccupied niches than in the reverse migration. It is perhaps something of an indication of the Old World pecking order in the plant kingdom that the New could not return something as aggressively possessive as devil's gut. We gave them corn, they repaid us with tares. And the fava bean.

Planning

Bean plant climbing cornstalk

Planning a garden is a good idea not because it won't grow well without, but planning makes everything more convenient and handy. Planning is a pleasant indoor winter occupation, and when spring comes it helps to make more efficient use of available space, especially if space is restricted. For those who in any regular way test new varieties or evaluate the performance of regular varieties, planning has to be an important part of record keeping. It is also essential to make an annual plan to practice any sort of crop rotation.

For me, planning the garden is more or less a mid-winter day-dreaming project. I begin with a sheet of paper and a ruler, and arrange the space I have at my disposal on a rough scale with the last year's plan. Expressing space to scale on a sheet of paper helps a great deal in being realistic about how much area there is to work with before beginning to order seeds. This is particularly true for someone preparing to grow a garden for the first time. When the seeds begin arriving you can quickly discover your eyes have been bigger than your real estate.

The first purpose in organizing a garden is to identify and determine areas for permanent plantings—perennial vegetables, herbs, berries—and areas for annuals. One hears of companion planting; that is, grouping together plants that seem to stimulate each other or separating plants that inhibit each other or including plants that are reputed to have value in discouraging bugs or disease. These ideas go back as far as Pliny, the encyclopedic and indomitable Roman naturalist who died investigating the eruption of Mt. Vesuvius. The scientific community has not given much support to these notions, but there are many gardeners who study works on the subject, follow their advice, and swear by the results.

The books and articles I have read have not inspired my confidence. For example, in one book the author advised interplanting asparagus and tomatoes. The author clearly had never done this himself, or even seriously thought about or visualized the practice. Asparagus spears are harvested during a brief period in the spring and early summer, and then the plants are allowed to do what they've been trying to do all along and grow into a mature "bush." A mature asparagus in no way resembles an asparagus spear—which is itself only a bud. Allowed to go its own way, it is fast growing, tall (3 or 4 feet), bushy, and completely and hoggishly occupies its growing space from mid-June on, even to the exclusion of all but the most persistent weeds. For anyone who actually gave the matter two thoughts, interplanting anything with asparagus is absurd. Therefore, my inclination is to be skeptical about anything that author had to say further on the subject of interplanting. If he had not thought about one combination, perhaps he equally did not know what he was talking about the rest of the time. I remain broad-minded on the possibility of there being combinations of plants that find each other's company agreeable, but am far from persuaded.

Planning is necessary for practicing crop rotation, although it definitely is not necessary to design a garden on paper formally to do so. There is nothing absolute or mandatory about crop rotation, but there are obvious advantages. For example, it simply makes good sense not to plant root crops in the same area two years in a row. Overplanting in the same spot encourages the buildup of underground insects and of certain kinds of diseases and funguses that affect the roots or tubers. If such root borers as wireworms are present, care should be taken to rotate. I have a gardening acquaintance who invariably plants potatoes year after year in the same spot. Year after year he has potato bugs. I always rotate, and am never troubled by them.

With some plants one plans rotation to take advantage of what they contribute to the soil. The legumes—principally peas and beans—fix nitrogen from the air that they store in nodes in their roots. Growing a crop of legumes is like giving a heavy shot of nitrogen fertilizer to the soil. Corn is a voracious feeder and takes a good bite out of the soil. Therefore, it is desirable to plant it in a different spot each year, especially planting it where legumes were grown the year before to take advantage of the nitrogen they added to the soil. Ultimately the basic rule for rotation is common sense. Each plant has its own nutritional requirements, and growing the same thing in the same place every year is going to sap those specific nutrients.

Planning the placement of perennials takes a little thought and foresight. While it is sometimes possible to transplant and move perennials that turn out to be in an awkward spot, transplanting mature plants usually results in a shock that will take them out of production for a year at least. They can't be moved around like switching light bulbs. Since many perennials are large, and some aggressive, these attributes must also figure in planning. Asparagus, again, is a perennial, and therefore a permanent planting. Also it grows rank and tall and bushy during the summer and remains in place through the fall. Not only does the space it requires needs to be thought on, but also the effect of its possible crowding on nearby plantings. During planning is a good time to consider how much of a given crop one really wants or can use; if space is restricted, the question may be how much can one *afford*. Because they are pretty and smell nice, I would like to have a dozen or more sage plants, but practically speaking I scarcely need one.

Some concern with the aesthetics of landscaping should also go along with the planning. Many herbs, for example (including sage), make perennial bushes that are attractive in their own right. A corner of the garden may be relegated to perennial herbs and made into a permanent planting that is both attractive and useful. While most of these herbs do not have especially showy blooms, taking their foliage, shape, and odor into account they can be combined within a small bed for a strikingly attractive effect.

Some permanent plantings are only relatively permanent. A row of leeks may continue in the same spot, reproducing themselves handily, for years. However, if different organization would improve the use of space, move them and they'll scarcely miss a stride in production. The same is true of a number of herbs. Although generally considered to be a permanent planting, it is as easy to move chives as leeks. Strawberries are best cultivated as being only semi-permanent. An established bed of strawberries has four or five good years of production at best and then rapidly begins to decline. The vines may also begin to get so matted and intertwined they are difficult to work. Therefore, a gardener should begin to plan where the next strawberry bed is going to be about the same time the first is planted.

A raspberry patch may be permanent, but after a few years the plants can get out of control. Even with careful pruning and cultivation to keep sprouts from coming up between the rows and between clumps, there will come a time when it is easier to move them to a new location than to continue to control an old planting, beat back perennial weeds, and maintain the soil. In England I have seen raspberries grown between rows of newly planted orchard trees. The farmer is able to harvest a cash crop from the berries during the long period it takes the trees to grow to maturity. By the time the trees are old enough to go into commercial production the raspberries are becoming too entangled and intergrown to be worked efficiently. The farmer then turns in sheep (having first protected the trunks of his trees with wire mesh) that eat the raspberries down to the ground and leave the orchard clean and clear for the fruit trees.

Relative height is an important thing to take into account when planning the arrangement of a garden. Tall perennials like raspberries should be located where they will not shade out smaller plants. Judging the effect of the height on other plants, take into account that usually afternoon light is more crucial than morning light, so tall plants on the west side of a garden will have more harmful effect than if planted on the east side. Depending partially on the latitude, the shade from plantings on the north and south side of the garden will have little if any influence. Tall annuals such as corn similarly must be situated to relieve the harm their shade may do to other plants in the garden. It is an advantage to the pollination of the corn if the rows can be planted running in the direction of the prevailing wind, but the advantage is not so great as to allow it to dictate the plan of the rest of the garden. My garden regularly gets strong westerly winds in the late summer, often with rain that regularly knocks down corn planted in rows broadside to the wind, so there is no question how I must plant corn.

Probably the major profit from planning the garden's arrangement ahead is the efficient use of space. Crops that are planted early and come off early may be replaced by later crops, making it possible to use the same space twice. Often this can be effected by interplanting, planting an early and a late crop side by side, so the first will be gone by the time the second will be needing to take over that space. Peas are an early and space-hungry crop; by spacing the rows about 36 inches apart, squash may be interplanted between them. By the time the squash vines are foraging for space, the peas have been harvested, the vines removed, and the squash will have all the space they need. Cucumbers can also be interplanted with peas in the same way, but since they are a little more timid than squash, will likely suffer a setback until the peas are gone. They will make a recovery, however, and except for being later, will produce almost as well as if they had all the space they wanted from the very beginning. Potatoes are planted early, but it is not until summer that their vines become rank and space greedy. A row of lettuce may easily be managed next to a row of potatoes and will have been harvested before the potatoes will have lapped over onto that space. If limited space is a severe problem, lettuce and certain other crops may be interplanted *between* potatoes.

Instead of interplanting between such early, sprawling crops as peas, the depleted vines may be removed and their space replanted with late crops, as soon as harvest is finished. By hoeing them off right at the surface, the nitrogen-rich roots are left in the soil as a fertilizer for whatever is planted next. Although carrots may and, for early results, should have been planted much earlier, this is a good time to replant the area with a main crop of late carrots. Late cabbage seedlings may be transplanted in this area from seed sown directly into the ground elsewhere in the garden, anticipating this space. The area may be replanted with late lettuce, particularly such varieties as Oak Leaf and Limestone. Rutabagas, turnips, and beets should mature easily if planted when the pea vines are removed. The range of possibility is large, but will vary with local climate and what an individual gardener really wants to grow.

Double use of space is particularly important with the large and ranging members of the cucurbit family. As mentioned earlier, an efficient double use of space is to interplant pumpkin or field (for example, hubbard or banana) squash with corn. From this traditional interplanting we get the familiar nostalgic autumn paintings of shocks of corn surrounded by heaps of golden pumpkins. However, in late summer when the pumpkins are climbing the corn it will become difficult for a person to move among the rows. Unless it is an early variety for which the harvest will soon be over, do not plant pumpkins with short varieties of sweet corn. The corn will virtually be flattened by the vines and swelling fruit. Pumpkins, which need horizontal space, can be interplanted with any crop that requires vertical space, such as pole beans or pole peas. Bush beans may be interplanted beside a row of lettuce, separating them from a row of potatoes. By the time the lettuce is gone, the spacing between the beans and the potatoes will be about right.

Onions are especially versatile for interplanting. Sets may be placed near a row of carrots (2 or 3 inches away), because by the time the carrot tops are large, the green onions will probably have been harvested. If the onions are to be allowed to mature, their long stiff leaves will not really be in competition with the lower frondlike leaves of the carrots. Sets for dried onions may be planted (early) near where late cabbage will be grown, since by the time leaves from the individual cabbages are sprawling and rank, the onion tops will be down and the bulbs curing. The light needs for the different crops are an important consideration when putting the garden together on paper. Tomatoes like full sunlight, but lettuce can tolerate some shade. Corn likes full sun, but climbing beans enjoy a filtered sun and can satisfactorily be planted within the corn rows and use the corn for support.

Obviously the do's and don'ts of planning become unmanageably complex, and a new gardener quickly comes to recognize that the dictums are really "maybe's" and "try it's." Some arrangements work better than others, but seldom is an arrangement disastrous. In planning, as in most other things pertaining to gardening, keep qualifying any dictum with "all other things being equal." They never are.

Tilling and the Goddess Runciana

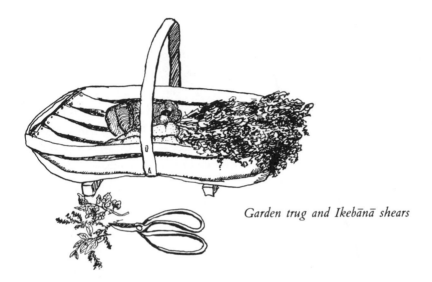

Garden trug and Ikebānā shears

Some would-be, or perhaps might-be, gardeners actually hesitate to become gardeners because preparing the ground for planting seems too laborious. It can be or not, as the individual chooses. Tradition pictures the gardener, spade in hand turning over the soil 10 square inches at a time. Soil may be manipulated mechanically, or it is within one's option to choose not to till at all.

This last option, aptly enough, is called "no-till" gardening; it is also sometimes called the Stout method, after the name of its most charming and articulate champion. Since the method and its advantages are so elegantly and entertainingly described by Ruth Stout herself in her readily available writings, it would cheat a gardener of the treat of reading her to present an extended treatise on the subject. However, it would seem appropriate to describe it sufficiently so that a gardener can decide whether it would suit his or her situation and inclinations to examine the proposition further.

The practice is based on the easy and logical premise that nature has been getting along very fine in the business of growing things for eons with no tillage whatsoever. Nature's way is to decompose vegetable matter on the soil surface, keeping the top layers of the soil itself in good tilth and suitable for seeds to germinate. There is more to the theory, but that describes its basic principle. The varieties and cultivars of modern crops grown at one place makes competition with more aggressively adapted plants difficult or impossible without a little help provided by the farmer. Tilling and subsequent weeding is one way; mulching is another.

Mulch is a general term meaning the piling up or accumulation of material on the surface of the ground. The material may be anything—vegetation, plastic, rocks, even dust. A mulch serves two purposes: it helps retard evaporation of moisture, and it closes off air and light to keep most weeds from growing. Mulching is the key element of no-till gardening.

To begin a no-till cycle—the cycle can be continued indefinitely—requires little work and little expense, but lots of leaves or other suitable organic material. It is best to begin a no-till cycle in the fall. Before the winter season sets in, strew the garden patch *thick* with leaves. Fallen leaves are a drag on the market in autumn, and most owners of shady yards give them away gladly, and have even been known to deliver them. City and park clean-up crews can usually be persuaded to part with all of the sacks of leaves you can possibly use. If leaves are not available, straw or hay is also suitable. It is surprisingly easy to come by spoiled hay for the taking. These are just the most common materials; locally a gardener might turn up amazing possibilities with a little ingenuity and instinct for scrounging (I read an article by a man who used seaweed exclusively, with spectacular results). Spread the leaves or hay to a depth of 6 or more inches. If the season is dry, sprinkle the area heavily, and keep the material soaked sufficiently to keep it from blowing as well as to assist the decomposition process.

During the winter, snow and rain will beat down and compact the material and begin a bonding, almost a melting, of the base of it with the surface of the soil. By spring the soil will be sufficiently "mellowed" that planting and mulching can begin on a permanent basis, with the soil never being further disturbed than setting plants in the spring and harvesting when crops mature. To plant, pull back the mulch only far enough to expose sufficient soil for seeding. Plant exactly as you would in tilled soil. When the seeds germinate and the young plants are well out of the ground, carefully re-cover the exposed soil, being certain to keep all of the young plant leaves above the mulch. Transplant seedlings in the same way: pull back the mulch, dig out about twice as much soil as the roots of the plant will occupy, and plant the seedling. Firm, do not pack, the remaining soil around it. Most seedlings should be watered as soon as they are placed in the soil. Finally, replace the mulch around the stem of the seedling.

A young friend when first trying no-till gardening had many doubts and reservations. She was convinced that long, heavy roots would not be able to penetrate into the unloosened soil. When she planted carrots, therefore, she poked a sharpened wooden dowel deep into the ground for the comfort and convenience of the root. I was amused, but my curiosity was sufficiently piqued that experimentally I planted short rows of several varieties of carrots, from the very long to the short and stubby in a new no-till section of my garden where the soil was dense and uncured. When they were mature, while there were indeed some forked-rooted carrots—but there always are a few—most of the very longest variety seemed to have no trouble at all penetrating up to a foot to produce smooth, straight carrots.

A well-mulched no-till garden requires considerably less irrigation than one with exposed soil. Other factors aside, this is an advantage to someone who must be away for periods of time, or who gardens a piece of ground some distance from home where rain or water from other sources is in short supply. It's refreshing during a hot, dry spell to pull aside the mulch and see the surface of the soil cool and moist.

Coolness of the soil does present a problem for early plantings in a no-till garden. When sowing seeds, be sure to expose enough soil for adequate absorption of warmth from the sun—a width of 2 or 3 inches for most seeds. When properly exposed, the soil gets the double benefit of the direct sun plus heat reflected from the mulch itself, but if the soil is not exposed, the resulting coolness may delay or inhibit germination.

Mulching has another advantage: the covering makes it difficult for weed seeds to germinate and make it to the light. Those weeds that do appear are usually much easier to pull than those in even finely tilled soil. Completely discounting the labor of tilling, time saved in weeding and time saved in watering constitute an impressive savings in labor.

The most common complaint about a garden cultivated by the no-till method is that it always looks untidy. There is something that loves a smooth blank patch of ground, broken only by orderly and geometric rows of produce. Ruth Stout's answer is perhaps the most direct and persuasive. After a few years of enjoying the appearance of a neatly tilled surface, she says, eventually fatigue and bodily decrepitude will teach a person to see the beauty of a field with no bare soil, but no weeds either.

There is no end to the length of time a field may be gardened without tilling the soil. One hears and reads of gardens managed in this way for thirty years and over, with the quality and fertility of the soil steadily increasing. It is only necessary that each year the thatch of mulch be renewed. After two or three years the surface of the soil will resemble a good rich forest duff; undecayed leaves on the top, a midsection of decaying and crumbling organic material, with a bottom surface of humus blending and imperceptibly melting into the soil. This bottom section should be densely populated by earthworms, whose digestive tract transforms the decaying vegetation into the super-fertile, pH-balanced organic material of their castings, or excrement. A gardener so unfortunate as to lack earthworms may buy a start from a worm farm, nursery, or seed catalogue. If the organic material for them to feed on is supplied, and if the supply of the material is maintained, planted worms will flourish and multiply.

Although fertility can be maintained over the years by the no-till method, some gardeners (including myself when practicing it) supplement the organic material with manure and, occasionally, commercial fertilizers. The decayed vegetation ultimately leaves plentiful nutrients in the soil, but the decaying process temporarily ties up nitrogen atoms, depriving plants of their immediate availability. Wood products, such as sawdust, shavings, bark, or paper require especially large amounts of nitrogen in decomposing, although the nitrogen eventually is returned to the soil. Therefore, while purists would sneer, I supplementally fertilize with a high-nitrogen commercial fertilizer. It helps break down the organic materials and helps feed the plants until further nitrogen is freed.

The practice of no-till cultivation is extending into commercial agriculture. For commercial growers, there are two additional positive considerations that do not necessarily concern the small gardener. On large farms, especially in hilly areas with heavy seasonal rainfall or snow runoff, the practice dramatically reduces water erosion. It is highly effective against wind erosion as well. In addition, since the number of times the soil needs mechanical attention is reduced by a factor of two or three, there is a significant savings in fuel cost to the farmer. Especially because of problems of controlling some kinds of weeds and voluntary reseeding of unwanted crops, as well as problems of fertilizer penetration, commercial farmers have a reduced yield but usually find the reduction more than offset by savings in fuel, equipment wear, and labor.

The modern concept of mechanical tillage originated in the eighteenth century. Previously the best kind of tillage was accomplished by a pie-shaped wooden plow, with a sharpened iron rod known as a "coulter" slotted in the apex of the front of the plow. Such a plow could not handle heavy or deep sod and could do little more than stir the surface of the soil that had long been under tillage. Otherwise, tilling was as it still is in some primitive agricultural societies, accomplished by a crude wooden plow usually fashioned to take advantage of the natural shape of a tree fork, or by a "foot plow," essentially a kind of spade, almost invariably made of wood. Other cultivation was done by hand, with wooden tools in the form of hoes, and so forth.

An Englishman in the eighteenth century by the name of Jethro

Tull, who had made a fortune building pipe organs, became interested in and was finally completely absorbed by farming. Since he had had absolutely no farming experience, he came to the business without any preconceptions, lacking the prejudices and traditions that can blind creative genius and invention. With unlimited leisure and capital and land to play with, plus the mechanical experience of building organs and the enthusiasm and dedication that only an eighteenth-century English eccentric could supply, he designed the prototypes of modern grain drills, iron plows, cultivators, and ditchers. His first and perhaps most ingenious contribution was the grain drill. He came up with his design based on the complicated configuration of the pipes in an organ. For the first time in history it became practical to plant grain in continuous parallel rows, controlling this spacing, improving the possibilities for cultivation, insuring uniformity of growth, with immense conservation of seed. Previously, all grain had been scattered from the hand of a sower walking methodically over the surface of the field. Tull's equipment, even with the limitations imposed by animal power, revolutionized agriculture and started it on the way to being a mass production industry.

Not that Tull's inventions were immediately accepted. Tradition resists change simply because it is change. It was argued, for example, that the intimate contact with the soil by so much iron would result in iron poisoning of the soil, which would in effect kill the land. Success, however, ultimately silenced the skeptics.

A more convincing argument against those changes might have been offered by modern theoreticians, although only history could have provided the evidence. Some of our contemporary ecologists have postulated that it was exactly the mechanization of farming introduced by Jethro Tull that initiated cycles of erosion and soil depletion that are an increasing worry to farmers on all levels. A farmer friend driving me across the rich fields homesteaded by his grandfather observed that they had yielded sixty crops. The question that concerned him was whether they would last to produce another sixty.

Nevertheless, we are the inheritors of Jethro Tull's legacy of innovation. With sense and awareness, particularly in the small scale of gardening, soil can be tilled mechanically from generation to generation, leaving it better every year. No tool from the generations descended from Tull's inventions would surprise the inventor more than the mechanical tiller, usually described by the generic name "roto-tiller." With a set of rotating tines affixed to a powered axle, the machine stirs and blends the earth down to a preselected depth. Although large, powerful machines may till the soil to a depth of 14 inches and more, commonly the soil is tilled shallower, 10 inches or less.

The advantages of the tiller are several. Most machines are small enough to be easily handled by most gardeners (but if you see one advertised as "effortless," or "nearly effortless," you know you are being lied to). They are relatively fast; a modest-sized garden can be tilled in an hour or so, and the machines are relatively economical in their use of fuel. They effectively turn under the surface organic materials, including the previous year's crop (although most machines balk at corn stalks). This mixing under of residue—homogenizing it with the soil, as it were—is valuable in bringing up nutrients roots have fixed into the lower levels of the soil, as well as from decayed roots themselves. Roto-tilling leaves the soil uniformly loosened and generally smooth on top (although some raking is usually necessary). A few designs do leave the surface smoothed like a table top and require no additional attention before planting.

Disadvantages are minimal. Only the largest and most powerful are capable of effectively turning under heavy sod or densely packed uncultivated soil. If a garden is to be made from a plot that has never been cultivated before, probably it is best to remove or kill the sod before tilling. Heavy machines may turn it under, but grass will continue to sprout even after being deeply buried, and the sod will continue to be a plague and nuisance during at least the first year under cultivation. The most disagreeable way to solve the problem is physically to remove the sod before cultivating. However, there are herbicides that will kill the sod without any harmful effects to the soil. For these check with local supply sources for brands that may be used with safety. Another way to destroy the sod is to spread sheets of thin, black plastic over the plot, preferably in the summer before it is to be tilled the first time. Even with the vegetation killed, the dead sod will be difficult to till. The easiest way to bring the new plot under cultivation is to have it tilled the first time by a hired professional who has access to heavy-duty equipment.

The major disadvantage of owning a mechanical tiller is that it is expensive. Some are designed to be attached to and used with riding mowers or garden tractors, and these are very expensive. Such a piece of equipment is pleasant to own, but except for large gardens or ebullient gardeners it is simpler and cheaper to rent the equipment. Easiest of all is to hire someone with a tiller to do your tilling for you. Such people are not hard to find; many gardeners who are trying to amortize their capital outlay in equipment eagerly take in custom tilling. And ambitious schoolboys hire out themselves and their fathers' equipment.

If a person chooses to possess his own tiller, the variety to select from is large. Before buying a machine, consumer publications and experienced people should be consulted. Some years ago I bought a tiller from a large retail catalogue chain store because it was on sale and seemed the right size for me. It never operated properly, and after numerous trips to the repair shop, I sold it to a tinkerer who finally made a usable machine of it by essentially redesigning and rebuilding the drive system. The moral is, consulting around may help keep you from being stuck with a bad design, as I was.

If you buy, don't buy too small a machine. The whole idea is to make the machine do the work; paradoxically, the smallest machine will work you to death doing and redoing in order to till deep enough, with the operator having to force and press the machine to keep it digging. However, moving up to the largest machine available gives you diminishing returns for the top power. They are so heavy that turning them in tight corners and generally bullying them around becomes a burden.

There are two main styles of designs of tillers. One has the tiller blades in the front, the other in the back. Most back tillers have powered wheels, which makes them easier (mistrust that advertising claim "effortless") to manipulate. Because of a smoothing plane on the back, these machines leave the soil beautifully smooth and flat behind them (providing the operator doesn't step there, which is sometimes not possible to avoid). Machines of this design are relatively expensive.

The other design of tiller has the tines in front, and as these tines rotate and till they provide the propelling power, clawing and dragging the whole machine forward. They require more physical effort steering, controlling, and in maintaining tilling depth than those powered by their own wheels. They also leave an uneven surface, although the surface is easily smoothed with a rake or other appropriate implement. These machines generally do a good job, however, and their defects are more inconveniences than real disadvantages. Perhaps most to the point, machines of this design are also usually a great deal cheaper than those of the other design.

The most familiar kind of tillage, although probably no longer the most common, is spading. It would seem unlikely that anyone would ever be so arrogant and superior as to dare give instructions on how to spade, but I have encountered such arrogance actually committed to print. Briefly, and without resurrecting inflammatory conflicting theories and opinions, those who have chosen to issue instructions recommend using the spade in three stages, making it possible to lower the top few inches of the soil to the absolute bottom, the bottom to the middle, and the middle to the top. This, or any other comparable scheme or system, entails double and triple handling of each spadeful of earth. I would guess that when the prototype of spades were first used by our ancestors they thrust them into the ground, worked the soil loose, and with a single movement involving the least possible lifting or exertion turned the spadeful upside down in the hole from which it had been removed, top to bottom, bottom to top. Even if a technical spader could convince me that his or her system really had superior merit I'd still do it my way. I have grown fine gardens for years; if they become any finer, I don't think I could stand it.

Among such technicians, there is controversy about what kind of spade is appropriate for spading. Since for practical purposes the length of the blade controls the depth of the spading, that is probably the first feature to take into consideration. And the longer the blade, the more work involved. Turning the earth to a depth of 8 to 10 inches is certainly sufficient. I always use an ancient heirloom shovel; it is so worn that I'm able to fudge an inch or so by forgetting that year by year the shovel gets shorter. There is also the tense question of whether the spade should have a blade that is squared on the cutting edge or rounded. A square bottom certainly gives a more uniform depth and evenness of tillage. A shovel with a rounded edge is certainly easier to use. Quite simply, the rounded surface presents a sliding, slicing edge to the soil and roots, while a square edge must force its way by main strength. Remember, when you use a knife you slice with it rather than press; that is the whole principle of the curved blade of a scimitar, the shape of which makes it slice rather than hack no matter what angle it hits its target. Ignoring the theoretical advantages of uniform tillage in favor of ease of penetration, I never use anything but a shovel with a rounded edge. And, as I've said, my gardens grow fine.

Some gardeners use a spading fork instead of a shovel. This tool is particularly useful if there is a quantity of sod or grass or surface roots of various kinds that the gardener is trying to remove as he goes. Ultimately what tool is used is a matter of preference and experience. I have always spaded (*when* I spade) with a shovel, and find a spading fork unnatural and even uncomfortable. To each his own.

When to till is not really a serious question. There are those who maintain that soil should be tilled in the fall (by whatever means are used) so that that the soil will "mellow" under the winter snow and rain. It may be given an additional cultivation in the spring, or merely smoothed and planted. Others say, by all means, till in the spring, as early as the ground may be worked.

These questions seem to be more matters of convenience than of genuine utility. It is handy to have at least some of one's garden ready for planting as soon as the snow is gone. Particularly in areas with long wet springs, often or even usually the ground will be too wet to till long after earliest possible planting for such things as carrots or lettuce. If the garden, or at least part of the garden, has been prepared in the fall, one may simply slog out in the mud, plant, and wiping one's shoes very carefully go back to the fireside until the weather improves. Of course, when practicing no-till gardening, planting can be done—and with considerably less injury to footwear—whenever desired. This consideration alone is sufficient argument to encourage one to keep at least a portion of the plot under no-till management.

For spring tilling, the only question of timing is relative to the condition of the soil. If it is so wet that it sticks to a shovel when attempting to turn it over, it's too wet to till, whatever means are used.

If it falls easily and cleanly from the shovel, it is tillable. Taking a mechanical tiller into a garden when the soil is too sodden is a messy thing indeed, and ultimately it won't work.

By "cultivation" cognate with the word *coulter* we mean, generically, all aspects of tending the soil. By a stretch of the imagination we almost mean "the civilization of the soil." Historically and socially we certainly mean something like that when the expression is metaphorically applied to humans and their interrelationships. A piece of tilled ground is "cultivated," but we "cultivate" a field or a garden of growing things by removing weeds and keeping the soil loose—in good tilth—among other things, maintaining a healthy dust mulch on the surface to help retard evaporation of soil moisture.

Plainly, there are some plants that like to have their roots scratched, some which do not. Peas, tomatoes, and beans like to have as little agitation in the area of their roots as possible. A little light hoeing, however, benefits most plants, especially if a sharp hoe is used that only shaves the surface, neatly cutting off weeds at their root level, and effecting a thin mulch of dust around the base of the vegetables. There is even a goddess of hoeing from the classical pantheon. She is named Runciana, after a Latin word for a kind of tilling tool, ancestor to the hoe.

Keeping in mind that some plants are chary of carelessly used hoes, it should become the most familiar and comfortable of garden implements. Always pick yours up (hoes become quite personal implements, and some gardeners would feel as uncomfortable using another's hoe as in using a stranger's toothbrush) and carry it with you when you feel like a reflective stroll through your estate. There will always be need for it, aside from its friendly companionship. In even the most carefully tended garden you will discover an explosion of primary leaves from a buried seed pod that has just germinated. Or a full grown weed will suddenly become visible at a spot passed by unnoticed dozens of times before. I attribute grudgingly a certain respect for the intelligence of weeds, for an ability to sustain until the last minute, just before maturing viable seeds, the appearance of a completely different plant that you are cultivating in that area. The most intelligent weed I know is the pigweed (or red root or amaranth). This versatile chameleon can masquerade as such diverse plants as potatoes and corn and fool you for weeks, until they see their moment and bolt into seed heads. The wise gardener always goes armed, carrying his sharp hoe against the contingency of encountering a mature weed as it makes its move. Consider that the hoe on the shoulder is a badge of identification, a symbol acknowledging and entreating support from the goddess of gardening, Runciana.

Fertilizer
and
Compost

Commercial composter

Much controversy among gardeners concerns how to sustain and improve soil fertility. The categorical imperative regarding fertilizing is that soil must be sustained if it is to grow good crops year after year. Not only must the fertility of the soil be maintained in terms of its nutrient content, it must also be maintained in terms of its physical condition, or *tilth*.

Gardeners argue about whether fertility must be maintained only with organic materials, or whether chemical components are acceptable. There is little disagreement that ideally the perfect way to maintain and improve soil is with the continued addition of organic stuffs— manure, rotted garden residue, or whatever is available or scrounged. Every garden and every household produces a wealth of organic material that can be added to or returned to the soil. If its physical form allows, material may be added to the garden in the form it is found, turning it under and allowing it to rot in place. Adding it directly to the soil as is has the disadvantage that there is a delay in availability of the nutrients to the plants. Some kinds of organic material, particularly of the coarse or woody varieties, not only take a long time to decay, but also may be physically awkward to have in the soil. And in the process of decay, especially of heavy materials such as sawdust or leaves, nitrogen will be tied up for a period of time, reducing the fertility of the soil. But organic material added directly to the soil certainly provides an effective way of improving the tilth of the soil and in attracting beneficial earthworms.

The handiest way to use organic materials is partially to decay it before adding it to the soil; that is, turn it into compost. To expedite the breakdown of organic materials, most gardeners employ one or another of the many varieties of the compost pile. At its simplest and most casual, this expedient is nothing but a heap of organic refuse piled in an unused corner of the garden, where discarded plant materials molder and disappear into a rich brown humus at the bottom. This simple "refuse heap" has served gardeners well for centuries.

The modern gardener's compost heap is more often dignified by being designated a "compost pile," or sometimes "compost pit." There are many ways of producing such a pile, and there are even entire books that lovingly lay out the laws that must be faithfully adhered to if good compost is to be produced. But keep in mind always the example of the compost heap of our ancestors, the heap at the back of the garden where compost was generated almost by accident. Like many other gardening maneuvers, maintaining a compost heap is a great deal simpler and easier and more foolproof than those who try to explain the practice would lead a person to believe. Basically, even if you call it a "compost pile," it's a collection of garden refuse and organic detritus stored in a handy spot, with a few refinements. Practically speaking, the only way to keep that stuff from rotting and turning into compost would be to freeze it or embalm it.

The simplest refinement on the concept of the basic heap is to go about the whole process with intention and purpose, rather than casually or accidentally as our ancestors mostly did. Reduce the sprawl of the pile, and keep all the materials in a roughly uniform base 4 or 5 feet across, and make it taller to increase the internal bulk. For each foot or so of organic material, add an inch or so of loose soil. If a small quantity of manure, especially chicken manure, is available, sprinkling it between layers will speed up the breakdown of the material. Some gardeners sprinkle a handful of general purpose fertilizer on every layer, some add complex formulas of ground limestone or gypsum. Water the pile occasionally. To break down properly it should never be allowed to dry out. In hot dry weather a plastic cover may be necessary to sustain the moisture. Compost piles may be maintained almost indefinitely. When the composted material is needed, lift off the top layer with a pitchfork and use it as the bottom layer of a new pile. It takes several months for a pile of this sort to produce humus, so it is a common practice to keep more than one going simultaneously.

There is a more complex, and to its practitioners much superior, way to produce compost. And it's faster. This method requires handling the pile as if it were a low-temperature kiln. It requires careful and selective layering of the composting material, careful and systematic watering, and temperature control. It has the advantage of being faster (weeks as opposed to months), of breaking down much heavier or bulkier organic material (woody limbs and even bones), and of killing weed seed, insects, and insect eggs because of the heat. But with all its recognizable advantages, it takes more time and care than I'm willing to devote; for me the advantages are simply not that great.

Another common composting technique requires the use of a container. Many varieties of composting containers are commercially available, but although they are neat in appearance and work well, they are not cheap. With little effort and probably no expense, an equally effective composter can be dummied up by the most un-handyman gardener. A common system is to take a length of woven wire—hog wire, chicken wire, cyclone fence, whatever—and form it into a cylinder of a workable diameter, something no less than 3 feet and probably no larger than 6 feet. Size is certainly not crucial. If the wire is stiff enough, the cylinder may be freestanding; otherwise a support post or pair of support posts can be driven into the ground to which the sides of the cylinder are attached. Wooden posts may be used, but it is easier to drive in one or two steel posts.

Accumulate the composting material in the cylinder just as if it were a freestanding heap, adding material as it becomes available, throwing in an occasional few shovelsful of dirt and, once in a while, a sprinkling of nitrogen fertilizer. The nitrogen in the fertilizer contributes to and hastens the decomposition of the organic matter, as well as contributing its own richness to the mixture. Water regularly. The development of the compost will soon be clearly visible through the mesh: raw vegetation on the top shading down into decaying material and, after a time, into rich earthy compost toward the bottom.

When a usable level of compost has developed at the bottom, cut a small square door at ground level, hinging upwards, and rake out the bottom level. Such a mesh-wire cylinder is handy both as a compost maker and as a compost dispenser. Someone who is so fortunate as to have more organic waste available than one composter can handle may easily make as many more as needed.

Other container composters provide exactly the same function, differing only in shape and the materials from which they are made. Some gardeners make little square turrets of concrete blocks, piled together rather than mortared together. In fact, it is advisable to space the freestanding blocks to allow a little air circulation. Other gardeners make a similar kind of structure of old planks. The design of such structures begins with four square posts of timbers planted in the ground so that their inner surfaces make a more or less perfect square or rectangle. Four planks, cut to fit, are arranged on the inside, without nailing, to form the first level of the wall. Add the compost material; its weight should hold the planks in position. As the level of the bin builds up, more planks are added. As with any other compost pile, throw in an occasional couple of shovelsful of soil and a sprinkling of fertilizer, and do not allow the material to dry out. At the proper time, slide one of the bottom planks aside to gain access to the lower layer of compost. One of the simplest forms of bin can be improvised from four pallet boards, if one can lay hands on them. Stand each on edge to form a square on the spot where the bin is to remain, and wire them together. This is quick, cheap, sturdy, and exemplifies the loveliness that comes of completely unadorned utility.

If there is a hillside available, gardeners often dig a compost pit against the hill, planking it on three sides. Sometimes a quantity of compost is collected into a pit dug into the ground—2 feet by 4 feet by 4 feet (or whatever). When the pit is heaping full, a new pit is dug beside it, and part of the dirt from the new pit piled on the first. And so on. After a few months the composting process will be completed, and the pit may be opened and the material used. This is indeed a simple method, but may require space a gardener does not have to spare. It also requires more digging and shoveling than any of the other methods, which is quite enough to dissuade me from ever using it.

The most ancient of all techniques for enriching the soil is the use of manure. In fact originally the Old French word *manouvrer* meant "to cultivate the land by manual labor," before it meant excrement in English. We can imagine the twelfth-century Norman landlord ordering his Saxon slave to *manouvrer* the land. To the landlord it meant everything associated with cultivation; to the slave it came to mean the one essential ingredient he was to spread on the land. So precious was animal dung in the Middle Ages that landlords required peasants who pastured their animals at a distance to drive them across his own fields for the manure they would deposit in passing. When livestock were grazed on cropped-over fields the fertilizer deposited was considered more important than the forage the animals obtained.

Any animal manure provides good fertilizer, and what a gardener will use most likely will be determined by availability less than choice. Often when it is available it is very available, and consequently cheap, most often for the hauling away. A serious inconvenience of raising any animals in quantity is getting rid of their accumulation of excrement. Volume statistics are alarming. A steer will produce about fifty *pounds* of manure per day, with a moisture content of about 80 percent. A dairy cow will produce about one hundred pounds per day, with moisture content of about 85 percent. By contrast, a human produces only about half a pound, with about 75 percent moisture. The real stunner is the chicken, each of which produces only a fraction of a pound less per day than a human, but with a lower moisture content.

What these figures suggest, other than a shocking breach of privacy by the researchers, is that any enterprise requiring large numbers of animals to be kept in anything like close quarters will accumulate staggering amounts of manure, and that is good news for gardeners. Because of the obvious distribution problems, only a small amount of the manure is composted for retail sale. The supply of raw material far exceeds practical demands. A gardener can buy composted manure, but probably it would prove too expensive to use on a large scale. If unprocessed manure is not available, other means must be sought to sustain the land.

While any manure enriches the soil, some kinds must be used cautiously. Used too lavishly, the immediate effect of an application of manure may be to "burn" the plants, so-called because the leaves or the entire plant may dry up and die as if they had been burned by intense sunlight.

An oversimplified explanation of how plants absorb nutrients may help understand why "burning" occurs and help avoid the problem. Liquids move through membranes (here the skin of the roots) by a mechanical process called osmosis. In this transfer, liquid moves from the lowest mineral concentration (which in this case normally is the soil) to the highest concentration (in this case normally the juice inside the root). However, if mineral concentration is reversed—more mineral salts in the earth than in the root—the flow of the moisture is also reversed. Thus, instead of absorbing moisture the root discharges moisture, and the plant quickly dries, with the characteristic burned appearance. Obviously lots of water, after fertilizing or overfertilizing, will in cases that are not too severe help dilute the salts so that this reverse flow does not occur. And obviously the soil should be kept reasonably moist in any case after fertilizing during the short period in which the concentration of salts may be abnormally high.

The safest to use is horse manure, which within limits will never harm the plants (although as with all manure it should not be applied while wet to growing plants, nor should fresh manure be allowed to touch growing plants). Cow manure that is completely fresh or undecayed can burn. Moderately composted, or merely cured, as it almost always is in a manure pile, it is safe to use in fairly large quantities. If applied in the fall, or applied in early spring and turned under, there should never be problems with burning. I once saw a garden plot with soil that had been badly run down spread with an 8-inch layer of cured but uncomposted cow manure in the spring and tilled under. I thought that was overdoing it and expected nothing would grow the first year, but the garden sprang into new life without a hint of ill effects.

The "hottest," that is the richest, manures available are rabbit, sheep, and poultry. All of these, particularly the latter, must be applied with caution. Apply them sparingly, and till them in well before planting time. Trickiest of all is chicken manure, perhaps the highest in nutrient content (especially nitrogen) of all barnyard manures. Ideally it should be composted before use, or at very least aged and cured. I once used a small amount that I considered sufficiently aged to be safe as "side dressing," applied to a few hills of potatoes that looked like they needed a little special treat. After about three days the vines all took on a very startled expression, then with an almost audible sigh withered and died. In other words, use chicken manure with care. It is best used as an ingredient added to the compost pile—and used only after being thoroughly composted.

Manure certainly has advantages over chemical fertilizers. For one thing, besides nourishing with its minerals, the organic material itself improves the water-holding capacity and tilth of the soil. For another, it is a moderately slow-release form of enrichment. Generally the nutrients of an application of manure will be only half assimilated the first year, and half of the remainder the second year. The soil consequently is improved on a long range rather than a short range, nutritionally as well as physically. If it would not be facetious we might say that manure has a half-life of one year.

If chemical fertilizers are used, as most gardeners do to a greater or lesser extent, it is wise to begin by consulting a local agricultural extension agent or a local nursery respecting soil problems or conditions of fertility. Soil conditions vary so much from region to region as well as within a region that it is impossible to make realistic or far-reaching generalizations. It is quite easy to test the soil of a garden plot and determine exactly what specific nutrients and what quantities a particular soil needs. Kits for testing are inexpensive and readily available from nurseries or mail order catalogues. The test is not difficult and requires no scientific training or experience. If even that sounds too difficult, most agricultural extension offices will test soil samples for gardeners, at either a very low cost or sometimes even gratis, and make specific recommendations for fertilizers. If available without too much hassle, I prefer to use manure, but when not, I use commercial chemical fertilizer without the slightest qualms; nitrogen is nitrogen, regardless of where it comes from.

A somewhat intimidating term used perhaps too casually for a beginning gardener's comfort is the soil's *pH*. Often expressed literally as "potential hydrogen," it is actually a mathematical symbol used to express the acidity or alkalinity of a soil in terms of a figure on a scale of 1 to 14. Halfway between—7—indicates a completely neutral soil. A soil-testing kit will indicate a soil's pH. A too acid soil can be corrected by adding such materials as lime, and a too alkaline soil by adding such minerals as sulfur. What is used is often determined by what is cheapest locally. Exclusively using quantities of organic material should ultimately balance the soil's pH, a little on the acid side.

A word of cautionary advice, however, is in order. There are some plants for which the pH is absolutely crucial—blueberries, for example, can only be grown in a very acid soil. The majority of garden plants, although they have their preferences, will do perfectly well within a rather large range from moderately acid to moderately alkaline, with the commonest preference on the acid side, about in the range of pH 6.

Too many gardening instructions express precisely a given plant's preference. From this it might seem that one must segregate a garden plot into distinct and exclusive pH districts. That, obviously, is silly, and can be a serious contributor to "gardener's paranoia." Asparagus, for example "likes" an alkaline soil. What that means is that a commercial farmer in an alkaline region in the West probably can grow good asparagus, but had better stay clear of blueberries. A farmer in Maine would come to a reverse conclusion. For practical purposes, a gardener can grow asparagus in most pH ranges likely to be encountered in garden soil. For a gardener, the pH asparagus "prefers" is a largely academic question.

If a significant number of local gardeners assure you that soil pH is a problem locally, then perhaps treatment is in order. With a little sly questioning one can probably determine easily enough if a given informant is a fanatic or is really worth taking seriously. But don't become earnest about the soil's pH. For the most part, consider it just another element of gardening that experienced gardeners seize on to show their own membership in the gardening fraternity and their superiority to the uninitiated. Who in life gets exactly what they prefer, so why should a humble garden plant expect better?

Appendix

D'Argenteuil Hative *asparagus*

The following list includes the addresses of all nurseries cited in the text. In addition, uncited nurseries are included that offer varieties that may be of interest to people seeking other than mainstream varieties of fruits and vegetables.

Aherens Strawberry Nursery. RR 1, Huntington, IN 47542.
This catalogue includes many varieties of berries besides strawberries and offers much information about berry culture.

Alston Seed Growers. Littleton, NC 27850.
This company offers many varieties of heirloom field corn.

Boston Mountain Nurseries. Rt. 2, Hwy. 71, Winslow, AR 72959.
Specializing in berries of all kinds, this nursery is an especially good
source for cane berries.

D. V. Burrell Seed Growers. Rocky Ford, CO 81067.
This company offers a number of peppers and is an especially good
source for melons.

Casa Yerba. Star Rt. 2, Box 21, Days Creek, OR 97429.
This company offers a broad range of herbs, plants as well as seeds.

Country Herbs. Box 357, Stockbridge, MA 01262.
This company offers herb plants rather than seeds, which many gardeners would consider an advantage.

The David Crocket Popcorn Company. P.O. Box 237, Metamora, OH
43540.
Their leaflet describes popcorn culture and offers ten different varieties
of seed.

De Giorgi Co. P.O. Box 413, Council Bluffs, IA 51501.
This company offers a large number of international varieties that few
American companies carry.

Dean Foster Nurseries. Hartford, MI 49057.
The number of varieties of raspberries offered by this company is
unusually large. They also offer varieties of berries not commonly
seen, such as June berries, young berries, and a broad selection of currants.

J. A. Demonchaux Co. 827 N. Kansas, Topeka, KS 66608.
This company offers a variety of seeds for French varieties.

Dr. Yu Farm. P.O. Box 290, College Park, MD 20740.
A good source for Oriental seeds, such rarities as bitter melon, edible
seed watermelon, and miniature corn are listed.

Epicure Seeds. Box 69, Avon, NY 14414.
This catalogue offers a wide variety of choice vegetable varieties.

Farmer Seed and Nursery. Faribault, MN 55021.
This is a fairly conventional catalogue, although for many plants it offers one or two unusual varieties.

Flint Ridge Herb Farm. Rt. 1, Box 187, Sister Bay, WI 54234.
This company specializes in herb and dye plants, both plants and seeds.

Fred's Plant Farm. Rt. 1, Dresden, TN 38225.
Offers a large selection of different varieties of sweet potatoes.

Gleckler's Seedsmen. Metamora, OH 43540.
Their catalogue is small, but consists almost entirely of rare and unusual plants, including some Oriental varieties.

Good Seed. P.O. Box 702, Tonasket, WA 98855.
This is a small company that lists only open pollinated varieties and appears to be the only firm currently offering tepary beans.

Gourmet Gardens. Dept. OGI, 923 N. Ivy St., Arlington, VA 22201.
This is an excellent herb catalogue that includes information about culture and uses of herbs.

Guney's. Yankton, SD 57079.
This is a large and splashy catalogue with many unusual and novelty varieties. There is a great deal of hype in their advertising.

Herst Brothers Seedsmen. 1000 N. Main St., Brewster, NY 10509.
This catalogue lists 35 different varieties of peppers.

Horticultural Enterprises. P.O. Box 34082, Dallas, TX 75221.
This company deals exclusively in peppers, listing some 30 varieties.

J. L. Hudson, Seedsmen. P.O. Box 1058, Redwood City, CA 94664. This company offers a wide range of unusual varieties, including Mexican and pre-Columbian varieties.

Johnny's Selected Seeds. P.O. Box 202, Albion, ME 04910. An extraordinary selection of heirloom and offbeat seeds.

Le Jardin du Gourmet. West Danville, VT 05873. This catalogue provides many gourmet and unusual varieties.

Illinois Foundation Seeds. Box 722, Champaign, IL 61820. Offers only hybrid sweet corn.

Kitazawa Seed Co. 356 W. Taylor St., San Jose, CA 95110. This is a small company, offering Oriental varieties exclusively.

Margrave Plant Co. Cleason, TN 38229. This company offers some ten varieties of sweet potatoes.

Nichols Garden Nursery. 1190 North Pacific Hwy., Albany, OR 97321. This is one of the most valuable sources for rare and unusual varieties of common plants, as well as of uncommon plants.

Nourse Farms, Inc. Box 485, Dept. OG12, So. Deerfield, MS 01343. This nursery specializes in berries. The varieties are mostly common, but the selection is good.

Olds Seed Company. Box 7790, Dept. N., Madison, WI 53707. This company offers a few unusual seeds, such as sugar beets, as well as an unusually large selection of varieties of potatoes.

Pony Creek Nursery. Tilleda, WI 54978. While the selection of varieties is relatively ordinary, the prices are unusually low. I have been well pleased with both their service and their seeds.

Otto Richter & Sons. Box 26, Goodwood, Ontario, LOC 1A0, Canada.
One of the top herb companies in the world.

R. H. Shumway Seedsmen, Inc. 628 Cedar St., P.O. Box 777, Rockford, IL 61101.
This company lists a number of items that are sometimes difficult to locate. It not only offers sorghum but more than one variety.

Southern Garden Co. P.O. Box 745, Norcross, GA 30091.
While northern gardeners will find this catalogue useful, it specializes in varieties suitable for southern planting. It offers a much larger selection of varieties of cowpeas than usually found, southern grape varieties, and fruit trees suitable for southern planting.

Southmeadow Fruit Gardens. Lakeside, MI 49116.
Probably the best selection of rare and unusual fruits and berries to be found in this country; not cheap, but the selection is hard to beat. The quality of plants provided is absolutely first rate.

Steele Plant Company. Gleason, TN 38229.
This company offers a large selection of sweet potatoes, as well as a few other plant varieties. It has one of the few catalogues listing Vidalia onions.

Sunrise Enterprises. P.O. Box 10058, Elmowood, CT 06110.
This company offers Oriental varieties, exclusively.

Taylor's Garden. 1535 Lone Oak Rod., Vista, CA 92083.
This is an herb company, listing about 200 varieties, which are sold as plants rather than seeds.

Territorial Seed Company. P.O. Box 27, Lorane, OR 97451.
Although they specialize in plants for the Pacific Northwest, many hard-to-locate varieties of general interest are listed.

Urban Farmers, Inc. P.O. Box 22198, Beachwood, OH, 44122.
This company specializes in European and Oriental varieties, and many of the things listed I have found nowhere else. Seeds are not cheap, and packages are very small.

Van Bourgondien Bros. Box A-OGI, Rt. 109., Babylon, NY 11702.
This company specializes in flowering bulbs of all kinds, and is one of the few places that offers saffron bulbs.

Vermont Bean Seed Co. Garden Lane, Bomossen, VT 05732.
The listing of varieties of bean seed is impressive indeed, but many conventional seeds are offered as well.

Yankee Peddler Herb and Health Farm. O. G., Burton, TX 77835.
This company specializes in herbs and health products but also lists some offbeat plant varieties like wild strawberries.